*A Study of Children's Thinking*

# A Study of
# Children's Thinking

MARGARET DONALDSON

*in collaboration with*

DONALD WITHRINGTON

*With an appendix by*

JOHN DUTHIE

TAVISTOCK PUBLICATIONS

*First published in 1963*
*by Tavistock Publications (1959) Limited*
*11 New Fetter Lane, London E.C.4*

*This book is set in 12 point Bembo*
*and was printed and bound in Great Britain*
*by Staples Printers Limited*
*at their Rochester, Kent, establishment*

# Contents

# *Preface*

THIS BOOK had its beginning in a thesis which I submitted to the University of Edinburgh in 1956. At the point when I began the task of turning the thesis into a book, I was joined in my research work by Donald Withrington and John Duthie; and all the studies which are reported here were conducted by one or other of us. It was at one time hoped that Mr. Duthie would be able to collaborate more fully in the work of preparing the account of the results than was in the end possible. But, in addition to contributing an appendix based on some inquiries of his own, he took part in the main researches by interviewing some of the children in Group O (ii) and in Group Y (i), and he made many important suggestions for the interpretation of the findings. Mr. Withrington interviewed all the children in Group S2, prepared the report on unquantified three-term series problems, and has been closely and continuously associated with the development of the work as a whole over the last five years.

The people who have at some time or another contributed to the production of this book are so numerous – and their contributions have been of so many different kinds – that exhaustive and detailed acknowledgement is hardly possible. But I owe special debts of gratitude to Professor John Pilley, Professor Ben Morris, and Mr. A. E. G. Pilliner for the help which they gave during discussions of the project in its early stages; and to Miss J. F. Reid for assistance that has ranged from searching criticism of the argument to help with the labours of proof-reading, and has, indeed, been so extensive and sustained that it is difficult to recognize in any adequate way.

Also, I must express thanks to the Education Committees of Edinburgh, Fife, East Lothian, and Midlothian for allowing us to work in their schools, and to all the headmasters, teachers, and pupils for their willing co-operation in the inquiries.

*16 March 1962*                                    MARGARET DONALDSON

# Acknowledgements

THE AUTHORS wish to record their thanks to the publishers for permission to quote the extract reproduced on pages 25-6 from the *Collected Papers* of C. S. Peirce, edited by C. Hartshorne and P. Weiss (The Belknap Press of Harvard University Press, copyright 1932, 1960 by The President and Fellows of Harvard College).

# CHAPTER 1

## The Prediction of Ability

WE ARE ALL constantly making predictions. We predict that there will soon be snow; or that we shall not reach home before we run out of petrol; or that the government will be defeated at the next election. Also, however, we make predictions of a slightly different kind. We say, for instance: 'Listen to that noise! There must be a mouse gnawing at the wood.' This last example is different from the others in that we are here not really foretelling the future, except in so far as we are predicting what we should find if we were to look to see; and it would be possible to argue that this should not be called prediction at all. But it is important to realize that many of the predictions of science are of this latter kind. The laws of science often do not tell us about sequences of events following one another in time, so that knowledge of earlier ones enables us to predict later ones, but rather about interrelated happenings, so that knowledge of one enables us to know about others that are occurring at the same moment.

An analogy may help to make this point clearer. In recent years people have begun to study seriously what is now called 'extra-sensory perception' – awareness, that is, of things which have not been directly perceived by the senses – and it is claimed that there are two cases to be distinguished. One of these is 'precognition' or knowledge of events which have not yet happened. This is the counterpart of what many people think of as the only type of scientific prediction. But there is also 'clairvoyance' which is claimed to consist in a knowledge of events or states of affairs that are contemporary with the having of the knowledge but inaccessible to the normal organs of sense-perception. And this has its scientific counterpart as well.

It may seem a little fanciful to speak of science as an instrument of extra-sensory perception – and yet this, in a way, is what it is. It enables us to know about things and events which we have not perceived directly. And it has its 'clairvoyant' as well as its 'precognitive' side. In the former case, what is predicted is that, if you look to see, you will observe that some specified event is occurring or has occurred or that some specified relationships hold. It is then only the looking to see which is in the future.

In the scientific study of human behaviour we are concerned, as in all science, with prediction. Here, as elsewhere, attention has tended to concentrate in the past on precognitive prediction. It may be, however, that in this study the clairvoyant type of prediction will prove to be of particular importance. Perhaps some of the greatest practical consequences will rest in the end on increases in our ability to make inferences about a present state of affairs from rather limited evidence.

Within the class of precognitive predictions, there is a distinction to be made that deserves attention. This is the distinction which Karl Popper (1957) has drawn between what he calls the 'prophetic' and the 'technological' or 'conditional' predictions. The prophetic predictions are the foretellings of things which it is beyond our power to prevent or control, such as the coming of a typhoon. The technological predictions, by contrast, tell us by what means a given event can be brought about: they tell us what we must do if we want to achieve something. Popper's own example of a conditional or technological prediction is the statement that if we want to build a shelter to withstand the force of a typhoon we must build it in a certain way.

When Popper makes this distinction he is discussing and criticizing notions of history as a process of inevitable unfolding about which only prophetic predictions can be made. However, not only the history of mankind but also the individual history of each one of us has been held by some people to be, in certain respects at least, an inevitable unfolding. And there is nothing of which this has been claimed more forcibly than the development of intelligence.

The great early advocate of this view was Francis Galton. In 1869 he published his book *Hereditary Genius*, the main argument of which was that intelligence is largely independent of environmental variation and that in each one of us its development is governed by hereditary constitution.

But, of course, if the *whole* of our intellectual development were inevitably determined from the start, much of education as we know it would be superfluous. If, then, a prophetic view of intelligence is to be reconciled with the retention of schools, a distinction has to be drawn between what can be prophesied and what cannot; and this has commonly been done by means of the distinction between intelligence and attainment. Galton himself did not make much of this distinction, and indeed he came near at times to expressing the opinion that education *was* superfluous, at least for the most able; but those who have come after him and who have agreed with him in his conception of intelligence have for the most part seen attainment as subject to a limited measure of conditional prediction, the limitation being imposed by intelligence. Intelligence is then regarded as the 'innate potential', that which makes attainment possible. Education has only to make it actual – and can, indeed, do no more.

This view is much less widely held than it used to be and many educationists and psychologists seriously mistrust it; but it still underlies much educational thinking in Britain and in the United States. It is a curious fact that the country which is at present most influenced by a conception of history as an inevitable unfolding – namely, the Soviet Union – is much less influenced than Western countries by a similar conception of the development of the individual.

We might ask, then: what is the evidence one way or the other? And this question has been asked repeatedly. It may be more illuminating, however, to begin by asking not what evidence we possess but what evidence we would be justified in accepting as

3

conclusive proof of inevitability; for the answer to this question may perhaps determine how efforts to get evidence ought to be directed.

For this purpose, let us suppose first of all that arguments about how to test intelligence were settled, so that no difficulties of measurement would be complicating the issue. What sort of evidence would we then require?

It turns out that this question is hard to answer. It would not be enough for our purpose to have evidence that one set of environmental variations had not affected the issue – not enough, for instance, to know that a pair of identical twins, reared in different environments from infancy and tested in adulthood, had proved in the end to be of very similar intelligence. It would not even be enough to know that a very considerable number of different sets of variations had not caused intelligence to vary.[1] For the claim we are considering is that *nothing* in the way of environmental variation (given, of course, an environment sufficiently favourable to sustain life) can cause intelligence to vary – and this is a very big claim. J. B. S. Haldane (1955) has remaaked that if we make a claim of this kind we are behaving rather like the physicists of a century ago who called certain gases 'permanent', meaning by this that they could not be liquefied. It turned out in the event that these gases were no more 'permanent' than any others: it was merely that the physicists who so described them did not know how to liquefy them. When they said the gases could not be liquefied they were describing their own incapacity.

Environmental variations that might conceivably affect intelligence are of so many different kinds that the task of testing their effects, even by very limited sampling, would present enormous problems and has certainly never been attempted. But even if it were done – and this is the point which most needs to be stressed – no evidence that development was unaffected by fortuitous environmental variation could ever establish the impossibility of

---

[1] This is not in any way intended as a summary of the results of actual inquiries of this kind. We are considering here not what evidence is available but what evidence would be necessary.

affecting it by deliberate action in the light of real understanding. The history of the physicists and the gases is again relevant. The discovery of impermanence did not come in the end through a random sampling of all the innumerable possible conditions that might affect gases: it came as all discoveries come (though sometimes chance helps them) through careful research and the gradual growth of knowledge. It is in the same way that we shall discover, if we ever do discover, how to affect the development of intelligence. But meantime, there is no justification at all, and it is hard to see how there ever could be justification, for a claim that its development is inevitably predetermined and entirely beyond our control.[1]

It is worth noting that this argument amounts to a rejection of any absolute and final distinction between things which can be conditionally predicted and those which can be prophesied, given that the criterion of a prophecy is our inability to affect the issue. This is because we can never be sure that our inability is final, and consequently anything which at one time admits only of prophetic prediction may come, with advance in our understanding, into some possibility of control. Popper would presumably accept this, because it is part of his own argument that the progress of our knowledge is itself something we can never predict. Thus it cannot be maintained that there is anything which we can never come to know – except for this one limit: that we cannot know what we shall know.

If the above arguments are sound, we must cease to claim that intelligence is innately determined – if by this we mean that environment cannot affect the issue.[2] In this case, though, what becomes of the distinction between intelligence and attainment? Clearly, the old basis for distinguishing the two has gone. On the view that intelligence was 'innate potential', its relation to attainment was that of 'rendering possible'. But if we are not prepared

[1] It should be emphasized that this is not at all the same as saying that heredity contributes nothing or only a little to the development.

[2] There are, of course, very few people who would want to make this extreme claim. Our concern is not so much to refute this claim, as to show what are the implications of accepting it as untenable.

to assert that the whole development of intelligence is innately determined, can we still hold to the view that intelligence is in some sense 'potential', or must we abandon that conception also? Can we give up trying to distinguish between what is 'innate' and what is 'acquired', yet still keep the distinction between 'intelligence' and 'attainment' and the notion that the one 'makes possible' the other?

There are two circumstances which would lead many people to give a negative answer to this question. In the first place, there is the old habitual association of the words 'innate' and 'potential'. These two have been used together so regularly and for so long now that their inseparability is liable to be taken for granted. When words come to be linked in this way, it grows easy after a while to slip into the unreflecting assumption that the one notion implies the other, so that the possibility of retaining one and rejecting the other is not even considered.

But there is a second reason why the idea of intelligence as potential is in danger of rejection. There is a current tendency to have misgivings about the whole concept of potential ability and its value for any scientific study. This appears to arise from the idea that whatever is potential is quite unobservable, an idea which is seriously, and curiously, mistaken. We are constantly observing potential. When we say of someone, 'He could be a strong swimmer, if he knew how', we are making a judgement of potential that is based on direct observation of physical characteristics such as well-developed muscles.

It is of more than incidental interest to notice that the distinction between potential and realized ability is more likely to be overlooked by an English speaker because of the fact that in his language the one word 'could' is used in both senses: 'He could be a strong swimmer, if he could swim', we might say, though we would tend to avoid this awkward juxtaposition wherever possible. In the French language, however, the distinction is very neatly provided for by the words *pouvoir* and *savoir*. The English 'he cannot swim' is quite ambiguous. But the French clearly distinguish *il ne peut pas nager* (because of lack of potential, a radical incapacity) from *il ne sait pas nager* (because he has never learned, never realized his perfectly adequate potential for the achievement of this skill).

Now the question of whether the strength of a man's muscles is innately determined raises just the same difficulties as does the similar question about the development of his intelligence, and these we have already considered. What must now be observed is that our inability to prove the complete innateness of his muscle strength in no way prevents us from regarding that strength as potential. And we can regard it in this way without necessarily being in a position to say exactly what influences have been exerted on this development by the food he has eaten or the ways in which he has exercised his body. Our ignorance on these matters does not alter the fact that, in relation to the specific attainment of swimming, his muscles represent a potential of unrealized ability.

In a similar way, the concept of intelligence as potential ability is not necessarily bound to the concept of intelligence as innate, and we can perfectly well give up the latter without having to deny the notion that intelligence makes attainment possible.

There is, however, a difficulty still to be considered. In so far as intelligence is not an inevitable unfolding, it may very justly be claimed that it is itself a form of attainment. And if intelligence is allowed to be attainment, what becomes then of the distinction between the two?

This difficulty is not so great as it at first seems. The fact that man is an animal does not mean that we cannot distinguish him from other animals or that we may not sometimes be justified in using the word 'animal' in a way which contrasts with, instead of including, 'man'. Similarly, then, there may be certain sorts of attainment which, because of some distinguishing features, can reasonably and usefully be given a special name: the name 'intelligence'. And it would be in keeping with traditional usage if this name were reserved for attainments which can be shown to be of special value for the clairvoyant and precognitive pre- diction of other attainments. But Ferguson (1954) expresses an important truth when he says: 'The concept of intelligence . . . is no longer a useful scientific concept except as subsuming some defined set of clearly distinguishable abilities.'

It has been argued in this chapter so far that we cannot prove that the development of intelligence is a process of inevitable unfolding. At the same time, it has been pointed out that this is by no means equivalent to an assertion that heredity does not affect the issue or affects it only a little. A sensible suggestion by Hebb (1949), which has been fairly widely adopted and has done a great deal to clear up confusion, is that we assume the existence of a certain genetic complement which is relevant to the development of intellectual power. This we call Intelligence A. We acknowledge, however, from the beginning, that we cannot directly test Intelligence A – that is, innate capacity in the strict sense. What we can hope to measure with some success is Intelligence B – the individual's effective developed intelligence.

Now the practical implications of giving up all claim to be able to test Intelligence A are worthy of consideration. So long as we speak or think as if we aim to find out about innate capacity we shall be tempted to try to use our test results for long-term prediction – to forecast, for instance, when a child is eleven or younger how he will perform in an examination that is five or six years away; or to forecast when a student enters a university how he will do in his final examinations. This is because innate capacity is something which lends itself to prophetic prediction, and prophetic predictions tend to be (though, as Popper points out, they need not be) long-term ones. Obviously enough, if we think we are dealing with an inevitable unfolding, we shall feel justified in making predictions about the fairly remote future. But if, on the other hand, we conceive ourselves to be dealing with a potential ability which develops and increases in the measure in which it is realized, we shall not be so likely to proceed in this way, for we shall understand that the child's abilities five years from now may depend not only on his present state but on what happens to him – and on what he does – in the interval.

Consequently, we shall realize that where there is any proposal to select a child for one kind of education rather than another our prediction will affect its own fulfilment, for what the child's abilities will be five years from now may depend in some measure on what education we decide he is to have.

This sort of circumstance is one which all students of human behaviour have to be prepared to encounter, as Karl Popper points out. In the social sciences, he says, a prediction 'may in an extreme case even *cause* the happening it predicts: the happening might not have occurred at all if it had not been predicted'.

How, then, would it be reasonable to make use of tests of intelligence if it is allowed that the development of ability may not be wholly predetermined, and unaffected by our decisions or actions? The implication would seem to be that they should be used not so much for long-term as for very immediate prediction. It would be reasonable to use them to tell us what a child is ready to go on to *now*, to indicate whether we can expect him, in his present stage of development, to start successfully on this or that new attempt at learning. The importance of the tests would not be reduced by this way of regarding them, because an unsuccessful learning attempt can be very damaging, and we want to see that children are not asked to tackle something for which they are not fit. But it is important to notice that this way of looking at the tests would have the effect of emphasizing the notion of 'readiness' and suggesting that, although the child is not ready now, this need not be final: perhaps he could be ready in a year – or less – and perhaps, if we understood more of his difficulties, we could even help him towards that readiness. However, before we can hope to help him as effectively as possible, we must understand better than we do at present, and in much greater detail, how his powers of thinking develop.

The rest of this book will be an attempt to add to this understanding.

# CHAPTER 2

## The Notion of General Intelligence and the Choice of Test Items

IT IS quite commonly argued nowadays that we are perfectly free to define words as we please (which is, of course, true) and that it does not matter how we decide to do this so long as we make explicit what we are doing. But there is a danger in this last idea, for it is possible to define a word in a way that fails to make some distinction which is persistently sensed, however dimly, by the users of the word; and when this occurs confusion of thought will generally ensue.

Something of the sort appears to have happened in the case of 'intelligence'. If anything is common to all conceptions of intelligence it is probably the notion of 'generality'. But what is it to say that intelligence is 'general'? By far the most common answer would be that intelligence is general in the sense that it manifests itself in a very wide variety of different kinds of behaviour.

Now the confusion arises from the fact that this answer makes no distinction between different kinds of behaviour with respect to their value as signs or indices of intelligence. While it does not necessarily conflict with the idea that some kinds of activity may be better indices than others, it certainly does nothing to suggest this and it might seem to be denying it. However, in practice we all of us act as if we believe that some distinctions of this sort are to be made. Anyone, then, who accepts this way of regarding the generality of intelligence has to reconcile it with his sense of distinctions between activities of different kinds – with the fact that though intelligence may manifest itself in the playing of table tennis he would not usually choose to judge intelligence by comparing people on their performance in this game. The need for this reconciliation is obviously particularly great for anyone who is setting out to devise a test of intelligence.

It seems evident, when one thinks, with as few preconceptions as possible, of the construction of intelligence tests, that the fundamental problem must be to decide what questions to put in them; and, consequently, that the main job for the theorist of the subject should be the provision of a basis on which this choice may be made. Intelligence may be general, but the test constructor has to include some tasks and exclude others. How is he to decide which should go in? How does he make his very first move in the selection of his material?

The critical nature of this decision, and especially of this initial step, goes strangely unrecognized in current practice and, with one or two notable exceptions,[1] in current theory as well. There are a number of procedures whereby the test constructor is helped to decide, at later points in the making of a test, what he will reject and what retain; but the starting-point is usually, quite simply, his 'hunch'. This 'hunch' is much influenced, no doubt, by the degree of his familiarity with the types of question which have been in fairly common use since Alfred Binet made up the first really important and influential tests around the turn of the century. There is now a tradition in the choice of intelligence test items; but as a rule no theoretical justification can be offered.

To support this, it is necessary to explain how 'theoretical justification' would compare with the sorts of justification that

[1] See, for instance, Loevinger (1957). Loevinger, however, is concerned chiefly with tests of personality. It may be remarked in general that, though recognition of the importance of 'construct validation' has been growing ever since the American Psychological Association published its technical recommendations for psychological tests (American Psychological Association, 1954), the work that has been done relates more often to personality than to intelligence testing. (See Clark, 1959, for a review of relevant studies.) Further, even those who urge the desirability of construct validation frequently say little that is relevant to decisions about initial choice of specific items.

are commonly offered. Let us take, for purposes of comparison, the three that are most often used at the present time. The first of these consists in the demonstration that a finished test 'works' with a certain measure of efficiency for a given predictive purpose: this is called 'validation by follow-up' or 'empirical validation'. The second consists in the demonstration that, when a finished test is given along with a number of other tests of various kinds, factor analysis[1] reveals that it has a high 'loading' in what is called the 'general factor'. The third rests on some measurement of 'internal consistency' and is used, before the test is complete, for the rejection of unsatisfactory questions, on the grounds that they are not sorting out the subjects in the same way as the test as a whole is doing at that stage in its preparation. That is, agreement with other items is here made the main justification for retention.

What do these three procedures have in common? The most obvious common characteristic is that they all begin to operate after the crucial event of initial choice, two of them after final choice also. This would not be a defect, however, if one condition were satisfied. It would not matter that they operated after the event if they could lead to an increased understanding which would guide the initial choice next time in such a way as to make progress possible. We could quite well begin with intuition if we did not have to continue with it. But it is not enough that we should come gradually to know that a type of item first chosen on someone's 'hunch' works reasonably well on the whole, and depend for progress on the chance of another good intuition on someone's part, to be subsequently slowly confirmed. Any satisfactory theory of item choice must make it possible to predict how well a new and untried type of test item will work. It must point the direction of fruitful change.

How are we to account for the failure to develop this kind of theory? The explanation (apart from the very real difficulties and

---

[1] This is a statistical technique whereby the intercorrelations of a group of tests are accounted for in terms of a number of 'factors' common to all or some of them. That factor which is in the highest degree common is called the 'general factor' and is frequently equated with 'general intelligence', although this was not done by Spearman, the originator of the technique.

perplexities of the undertaking) seems to be that test constructors have for the most part never really acknowledged the need; and this appears to be directly associated with the notion that they are testing something 'general', something which manifests itself in a very great variety of human activities. But to understand fully how the situation has arisen we must look briefly to the history of intelligence test construction.

Sir Francis Galton, the first of modern writers on the subject, did at least state the problem of choice of items directly – if he did not solve it – when he spoke of 'sinking shafts at critical points' and of the difficulty of how to ascertain the best points for the purpose (Galton, 1890). If this had been kept in the forefront of thought by those who subsequently exerted most influence on the study of intelligence and the development of intelligence testing, the difficulty might by now have been much nearer to solution than is in fact the case.

However, the man who has had the most decisive influence has been Alfred Binet and he, unfortunately, was very far from keeping this problem always in view. From time to time in his writings he acknowledged by implication that not all tasks serve to test intelligence equally well – that some sorts of question or problem may be better indices than others. For instance, he is inclined on occasion to be rather scornful of arithmetic, claiming that 'arithmetical ability depends on special aptitude and a child may be quite intelligent, though backward in arithmetic . . .' (Binet and Simon, 1914).

On the other hand, earlier in the book from which this quotation is taken, we find him saying: 'This [the procedure he has just been advocating] amounts to judging intelligence by the amount of instruction. Theoretically, such a method is open to plenty of meticulous objections of which the most important is that we are confounding intelligence and memory. To this we shall reply that the stage of instruction reached is not the result of memory alone. It presupposes also some degree of application, some facility of comprehension, quite a collection of diverse aptitudes.'

That is, in one and the same work we find Binet maintaining that we can best judge a child's intelligence by considering the whole sum of his scholastic attainments; and arguing that some of these attainments – specifically arithmetical ones – are invalid as indices of his intelligence.

It seems that Binet nowhere brings together the two parts of this dual recognition: that a very great many human activities manifest intelligence, in the sense that they may be performed more or less intelligently, and yet that certain sorts of activity are of central significance in the estimation of a person's intelligence. Unless these notions are reconciled, however, there is a very grave risk that the test constructor will be pulled to and fro between them. How can he make a case for the inclusion in his tests of some kinds of activity rather than others? If they all manifest intelligence the obvious course would seem to be to sample them quite randomly. And yet, in spite of this, he knows quite well that some kinds of task have a stronger claim than others to be represented, that a child may be quite intelligent though backward in this or that – in Galton's words, that there are critical points to be ascertained. Therefore, he never *acts* quite randomly. Yet so long as he fails to acknowledge explicitly that he *ought* not to act quite randomly, he cannot possibly develop any theory to guide the selection of questions.

It is certainly one of the strangest things about Binet's work that, in spite of his greatness as a psychological theorist, he does not support his practical test-constructing activities by any consistent theoretical justification of his choice of 'points'. Instead, he resorts to what Piaget (1950) has called *une sorte de probabilisme psychologique*: a sampling of tasks that is as wide as it can be in the time available for testing. His sampling, however, cannot properly be called random since it is continually guided by his own sense of fitness.[1] And it has proved remarkably successful: unfortunately so, perhaps, since its very success may have dis-

[1] He says that he chiefly aims to test 'judgement', but this is hardly more of a guide to item choice than the word 'intelligence' itself. Apart from this, he says that the tests should be 'simple, quick, convenient, exact, heterogeneous' (Binet and Simon, 1905).

couraged the sort of further inquiry that would have been most valuable.

It has, of course, to be remembered that Binet originally produced his tests to serve an immediate practical purpose – namely, the selection of children for admission to the special schools of Paris – and made for them very modest and cautious claims. The misfortune is that after his death a succession of immediate practical purposes occasioned the production of a whole series of tests based on a whole series of samplings that were not random and yet not guided by articulate theory. The question of how to choose the critical points and justify the choice was very frequently avoided, and this avoidance has even been encouraged and applauded, directly or indirectly, by a number of writers.

One example of incidental encouragement is to be found, perhaps rather surprisingly, in *The Concept of Mind* by Gilbert Ryle (1949), and is worth examining in some detail because consideration of it may help to make the issues plainer. The passage in question occurs at the point where Ryle is attacking the notion that 'theorizing' is the essential activity of the intelligent mind. He is objecting to the idea that intelligent action deserves the epithet only if it is prefaced by 'some anterior internal operation of planning what to do'. 'Intelligent practice', he says, 'is not a step-child of theory. On the contrary, theorizing is one practice amongst others and is itself intelligently or stupidly conducted.' Whether Ryle is right in rejecting the primacy of theorizing is irrelevant to our present concern.[1] What matters is the implication that no activity could properly be regarded as primary unless it were one which could only be performed intelligently. But there is no kind of activity that can only be performed intelligently. Whatever we think of, be it building bridges, or writing poems, or playing chess – or theorizing – if it can be performed intelligently then it can be performed stupidly as well. This being so, if we accept Ryle's argument, we shall find that it applies not only to theorizing but to any kind of activity whatsoever. If

---

[1] He allows later that 'intellectual work' has what he calls a 'cultural primacy'.

theorizing cannot be the essential activity of the intelligent mind (because it is possible to theorize unintelligently) then the same applies to any other activity.[1] The whole tenor of the chapter from which the above quotations are taken is such as to suggest that all the many kinds of activity in which intelligence manifests itself stand equal. And, though Ryle himself is not principally concerned with problems of assessment, his arguments appear to lend support to the view that there can be no grounds for assessing intelligence by performance on one kind of activity rather than another.

However, this conclusion is by no means inescapable. If there *were* kinds of activity which must be performed either intelligently or not at all, we might indeed call these 'essential' and judge intelligence by their mere presence or absence. The fact that there are not does not render the question of *kind* of activity irrelevant: it simply means we must take into account both the manner of performance and the kind of activity. The need to have regard to the former – that is, to whether the actual performance is more or less intelligent – in no way disposes of the question: what kind of task should we set?

The support which Ryle gives to the avoidance of this crucial question is, however, only incidental. A much more direct encouragement comes in Alice Heim's book *The Appraisal of Intelligence* (1954). It comes, too, strangely enough, in the course of Heim's consideration of how we are to validate or justify our test-construction procedures; and it comes as an expression of approval of Binet. Here is what Heim says: 'Binet was concerned to find some exact, external criterion with which to compare his test findings. As is well known, he observed and made use of the fact of mental development. Having noted that a normal child of six, for instance, can do things which a normal child of five cannot achieve, and that six-year-olds tend to fail on tasks which the normal seven-year-old can manage, he took "success at age X" as his criterion.'

[1] There are, of course, activities of kinds which cannot be performed either intelligently or stupidly, such as sneezing or digesting one's dinner, but they need not enter the discussion at all.

There can be no objection to emphasis on 'the fact of mental development'. But what Heim seems to imply by her approval of Binet's procedure is that 'development with age' is by itself an adequate criterion of suitability for inclusion in an intelligence test: that is, that every power which develops with age is equally important as an index of intelligence. And we have seen Binet himself deny this, in speaking of ability to do arithmetic.

What is more, Heim denies it herself also, for though she pays enthusiastic tribute to Binet's recognition that 'intelligence manifests itself in a multitude of ways' she goes on later in her book to imply that not even all 'cognitive matters' are to be regarded as 'matters of intelligence'. This occurs in the course of her discussion of test reliability (that is, the extent to which a test can be depended on to give consistent results) at the point where she is considering whether people may actually vary from day to day in their capacity for intelligent behaviour. She speaks also of variability in other respects, and says: 'The evidence . . . suggests that intrinsic variability is less in cognitive matters generally and least in matters of intelligence, specifically.'

But how are these 'matters of intelligence' to be distinguished? And especially, how are they to be distinguished from 'cognitive matters generally'? Both Heim and Binet slip, almost in spite of themselves, into speaking as if there *are* distinctions to be made. The question of how they are to be made must be faced.

To make discussion of this question easier and less confused two special terms will now be introduced. The suggestion is that when we consider a given action with respect to the estimation of the intelligence of the performer, we ought to make a distinction between the *status* of that action as an index of intelligence and the *mode* of its performance. Decisions about the status of an action would be relevant to the question of whether it was the sort of activity on which we would be well advised to base our assessment; and, given that the action was considered to have sufficiently high status, the mode of its performance would be the actual basis of our judgement. We would judge the person

17

intelligent in so far as he performed intelligently actions which were held to be of value as signs.

It is evident from this that the status of any kind of activity must be relative to the age of those who are to be judged by their performance in it. If it is to have high status as an index of intelligence, it must as a first requirement (but not as the only one) discriminate among people so that some can do it noticeably better than others. This is because when we judge a person intelligent we are necessarily considering him in relation to his fellows. But the fact of development with age, on which Heim lays so much emphasis, means that an activity which serves to discriminate at the four-year-old level is unlikely to do so effectively at fourteen. Consider, for instance, the 'Manikin' test in the Wechsler Intelligence Scale for Children. In this test a wooden figure of a child is presented, cut in five pieces which have to be re-assembled. If a four-year-old has solved this problem successfully, his behaviour in doing so may perhaps serve as a sign of good intelligence. If a fourteen-year-old has solved it, his success can tell us very little about his intelligence, for all fourteen-year-olds can do this, except perhaps the most gross defectives.

Status decisions, then – that is, decisions whereby some kinds of behaviour are judged to be more important than others in the estimation of intelligence – must always have regard for the age of the performer, and it must be recognized that what has high status at one age may have low status at another.

In contrast, if status decisions are relative to age, decisions about mode are absolute. The WISC 'Manikin' test will again serve as example. A feature of the test is that the legs are divided at unequal height, and three main ways of fitting them to the body can be observed. The one that would generally be judged the most intelligent is to notice the inequality and see at once that the shorter leg piece must be fitted to the longer leg stump; the next, to begin by trying the leg pieces at random and then to interchange them if an inequality of total length results; the least intelligent, to place them wrongly and be satisfied. These judgements of mode can be made quite independently of any knowledge of the person who is tackling the problem.

An item cannot have high status, then, unless it 'discriminates', and this narrows the field of choice considerably. Yet it still leaves a very wide range of tasks for possible inclusion in a test at any given age level. G. A. Ferguson (1954) suggests how we may make use of development with age beyond the point of simply achieving discrimination by having regard to it. He suggests that we choose for inclusion in intelligence tests those tasks which show the *steepest* decrease in difficulty with increasing age – and in saying this he is going well beyond anything which Heim proposes explicitly, or seems to imply. He is not leaving the test constructor with an enormous assortment of tasks which the six-year-old can do and the five-year-old cannot, and then slipping in later the implication that 'matters of intelligence' are distinct from 'cognitive matters generally' without indicating how the distinction is to be made: he is saying that the steeper the age-gradient the better the test as an index of intelligence, which is a very different thing.

Ferguson's arguments in support of this conclusion are roughly as follows. From a consideration of intelligence test scores of children in special cultural subgroups – gipsy children and canal-boat children, for instance – and the fact that the intelligence quotients of these children decline fairly sharply with increasing age, Ferguson concludes that 'for any particular test the change in performance with age may vary markedly from one cultural group to another. . . . This must be mainly due to the demands of the cultural environment, which dictate what shall be learned and at what age.' In other words, he sees the order of progress in development as culturally determined and goes on to draw the inference that 'those abilities that are of importance in a particular cultural environment, and that may be expected to correlate with performance in the important activities which the culture demands, are those which show a pronounced increment with age'.

From our point of view, what is particularly interesting is that Ferguson's whole emphasis is on finding tests that correlate with 'the important activities which the culture demands': he is recognizing the problem of status in a way that most writers on the subject singularly fail to do.[1] He is looking for abilities that may with some justification be regarded as central in a given cultural setting. Further, since he postulates that 'those more or less stable attributes of behaviour which we ordinarily speak of as abilities' are learned,[2] he is in fact advocating a search for central *attainments*. And the process of identifying the central attainments is, of course, the process of establishing status. The more central an attainment – that is, the more important because of what it leads on to by way of further attainment – then the higher its status: the more we can rely on it as an indication of what we want to know.

Whether status can in fact be judged by the criterion which Ferguson proposes is, of course, another matter. His suggestion depends, in the first place, on acceptance of 'what the culture demands' as an ultimate standard, and some might wish to maintain that what a given culture most highly values is not a sufficient guide: that 'intelligence' must somehow be judged on a less relativistic basis than this. But, in the second place, even if one were to accept Ferguson's final standard as sound in theory, one would have to decide in practice what 'the important activities' in a given culture were before one could put to experimental test his claim of relationship between these activities and tasks which show sharp decrease in difficulty over given age intervals. And it is very hard to get agreement on this issue of ultimate importance even within a given culture. However, Ferguson has at the very least rendered a service by explicitly acknowledging the problem.

It is plain that, whether one accepts a frankly culture-determined

---

[1] It is entirely in keeping with this that he is also one of the few people to recognize and deplore the absence of theory. Earlier in his paper, he laments the fact that: 'At present no systematic theory, capable of generating fruitful hypotheses about behaviour, lies behind the study of human ability.'

[2] Indeed, he postulates that their stability is the result of overlearning.

standard or not, the criteria of a 'high-status' intelligence test item are in the last resort necessarily predictive, since the high-status item is, by definition, one which will serve us well in the role of sign or index. A given type of item will be a good index if (a) it enables us to make successful prediction about certain other things which the person is at that moment capable of doing or learning to do (clairvoyant prediction); and (b) it enables us to predict certain things that he will be able to go on to learn to do (precognitive prediction).

Now the assertion that the 'goodness' of a test item must be judged in the last resort by predictive criteria would be almost universally accepted by test constructors. Indeed, the various 'item selection' methods which have been described in this chapter depend on precisely such criteria. However, these have already been criticized on the ground that they are very largely 'trial and error' procedures: they do nothing to help us to reach a better understanding than we have at present of why some tasks do better than others in predicting later intellectual development. An analogy may help to make clear what is lacking. For a long time, it has been known that certain moulds are useful in the treatment of infections: it is an old remedy to apply mouldy bread to a wound. But the people who found out that this could be beneficial knew nothing of penicillin and the related anti-biotics and so were in no position to understand what constitutes the difference between a mould which prevents infection and another apparently similar one which does not – for a great many different moulds can grow on bread and many of them are no use whatever against infection. Until the active component, penicillin, was identified, there could be no advance and no control.

What is needed for the development of intelligence testing is some comparable isolation of active components. We want to know not only *that* an item 'works' for a given predictive purpose but *how* it works: what there is about it which makes it success-ful, and what different successful items have in common. Now the distinction which any test makes is between those subjects who are defeated by the difficulties it presents and those who are not. So it seems reasonable to expect that the way to an increased understanding of why some tests predict later development better than others will lie in a study of the nature of these difficulties. But the difficulties which the test constructor envisages may not be those which the subjects encounter. So one must study actual attempts to solve the problems – attempts made by members of the groups for whom the test is intended – if one is to find out about the obstacles which stand in the way of successful solution and which are the basis of the test's discriminating power. Part of the reason why this has not been attempted more frequently in the past is the real difficulty of the enterprise.

# CHAPTER 3

## The Study of the Processes of Thought

BARTLETT (1958) says that thought is essentially a means of moving on. This is more true of certain sorts of thinking than of others. At one extreme, in the kind of thinking we might describe as contemplation, thought dwells on its object. But in studying the solving of problems, we are concerned with a process.

The great difficulty is how to observe and describe this process 'from outside'. Much of it is not normally overt at all. Because of this difficulty, much work on problem-solving has used as evidence and ground for inference only the final solution, and perhaps the time taken to arrive there. But a few writers have been critical of this,[1] one core of criticism being that identical final solutions may result from very different thought processes and that it is quite unsafe to make inferences from the former to the latter, at least until the possible variations have been studied directly. As soon as a direct study is contemplated, however, two questions arise:

Is the thinker himself aware of his thought processes?
And can an observer become aware of them?

The second question is much more important than the first, and not so dependent on the first as might appear, for it is not an evident logical necessity that only those of our mental processes of which we are ourselves aware should be detectable by others. A psycho-analyst, for instance, would certainly claim to know

---

[1] See, for instance, A. S. Luchins (1951).

of wishes and anxieties in his patient of which the patient had no knowledge at all.

The way in which the psycho-analyst would claim to come by this knowledge is important to consider. He would say that he does so by interpreting certain signs – signs which the patient himself can also observe but which he is unable to interpret: for instance, his dreams. Now this claim appears to carry an important implication: that, in some measure at least, we know ourselves not with immediacy but through a process of interpretation that has very much in common with the way we know other people; so that it is not impossible for others to know us better than we know ourselves if they are more skilled interpreters.

An important part of the psycho-analytic theory is, of course, the idea that when the patient cannot interpret the signs for himself it is because of certain emotional resistances. But this does not make it necessary to suppose that every failure to interpret one's own behaviour must be of this one kind, and does not affect the general implication of the psycho-analyst's claim, namely, that the gaining of self-knowledge is in some sense an interpretative process, and one which we can learn. Strong support for this general notion comes from a man who had no connection at all with psycho-analysis: namely, C. S. Peirce, the founder of pragmatism in its original form and one of the first symbolic logicians. Peirce argues that we have to learn to know ourselves by a gradual process of learning to interpret signs, and his arguments lead him to the conclusion that introspection is not so much an undesirable method of investigation as an impossible one. When someone claims to introspect he is in fact interpreting signs that are not essentially different in kind from those he would be interpreting in the course of studying another person.

To draw from this the conclusion that there is no fundamental difference between the methods of the 'introspectionists' and those of the behaviourists, since both proceed by way of the interpretation of observed events, is, however, to leave out of account the crucial consideration of the availability of these events for inspection by more than one observer. The critical question is whether the signs which are available to us when we observe and interpret ourselves are also available – or can be made available – as signs on which others may exercise their interpretative skill, so that there may take place the process of discussion and amendment that leads to the agreement in which, to quote Peirce (1931) himself, 'the community ultimately settles down'. This question, when directed more specifically to the study of thought processes, amounts to asking to what extent these processes can be rendered overt. Bruner, Goodnow, and Austin (1956) call this 'the great technical problem'. What we must do if we are to study thought is to render its processes available for inspection by more than one observer. Bruner, Goodnow, and Austin say that this can only be done by 'devising experiments that can get a lot of sequentially linked behaviour out of the organism where it can be observed'. In other words, we must contrive to avoid the state of affairs where all we know is what the subject arrives at as his final conclusion.

This still leaves us with the question of what kinds of behaviour we are prepared to accept as evidence: in particular, whether the reports that a person gives of his thinking may be accepted as dependable signs through the interpretation of which some knowledge of his thought may be obtained. At this point another passage from Peirce becomes relevant – so relevant that it deserves to be quoted at length:

'A man goes through a process of thought. Who shall say what the nature of that process was? He cannot; for during the process he was occupied with the object about which he was thinking, not with himself nor with his motions. Had he been thinking of those things his current of thought would have been broken up, and altogether modified; for he must then have alternated from one subject of thought to another. Shall he endeavour, after the course of thought is done, to recover it by repeating it, on this occasion interrupting it, and noting what he had last in mind? Then it will be extremely likely that he will be unable to interrupt it at times when the movement of thought is considerable; he will most likely be able to do so only at times when that movement was so slowed down that, in endeavoring to tell himself what he had in mind, he loses sight of that movement altogether; especially with language at hand to represent attitudes of thought, but not movements of thought. Practically, when a man endeavors to state what the process of his thought has been, after the process has come to an end, he first asks himself to what conclusion he has come. That result he formulates in an assertion, which, we will assume, has some sort of likeness – I am inclined to think only a conventionalized one – with the attitude of his thought at the cessation of the motion. That having been ascertained, he next asks himself how he is justified in being so confident of it; and he proceeds to cast about for a sentence expressed in words which shall strike him as resembling some previous attitude of his thought, and which at the same time shall be logically related to the sentence representing his conclusion, in such a way that if the premiss-proposition be true, the conclusion-proposition necessarily or naturally would be true' (1931, Vol. 2, §27).

This quotation from Peirce seems oddly at variance with some other things he says: for instance, that 'all thought whatsoever is a sign, and is mostly of the nature of language' (ibid., Vol. 5, §421). Perhaps the explanation is that Peirce uses the word 'thought' in two different senses: sometimes as process and sometimes as product. The above passage occurs in the course of an argument in which he is trying to show that the logician's task is not to study the actual movement of thought but rather to criticize the results of thought. Since he remarks in the same connection that for all he knows or cares there may be a hundred ways of thinking in passing from a given premiss to a given conclusion, one might perhaps object that in this case he, as a logician, is hardly qualified to comment on the nature of thought processes at all.

However, this cannot be said of another writer who comes to express views that curiously resemble those of Peirce. The writer is Binet, in one of the last articles that he contributed to *L'Année Psychologique* (1911) – a paper in which he reaches the conclusion that the error which above all must be avoided is that of seeing the mind as a succession of states and not actions. Thought is not a series of images; it is an act of understanding, of interpretation. The old theory of mental life was 'so rational' and supposed that 'all can be explained, all is co-ordinated, all can be justified . . . that reasoning is composed of premises and conclusions and that one deduces the conclusion from the premises and cannot arrive at the conclusion without having passed by way of the premises'. In contrast with this, the new theory is 'a theory of action, according to which mental life is not at all a rational life, but a chaos of shadow crossed by flashes, something strange and above all discontinuous, which has appeared continuous and rational only because after the event it has been described in a language which brings order and clarity everywhere; but it is a factitious order, a verbal illusion. . . .'

If we study the reports that a person gives of his thinking, are we then exposing ourselves to the full force of this 'verbal illusion'?[1]

It is relevant to notice that both Binet and Peirce are specifically concerned with the possibility of having someone *describe* the course of his thinking. There is, however, an alternative procedure which consists not in asking the subject to think and then describe, or even to try to describe as he goes along, but rather in asking him to make his thinking accessible to an observer by doing it 'aloud'. We must now ask whether this method is free of the disadvantages to which Peirce and Binet refer; and also whether, if it avoids these, it has any others in its turn.

In the first place, the change from asking the subject to 'describe' to asking him to 'think' seems to meet Peirce's objection – since frequently made by others – that if the subject has to describe what he is doing as he does it, his 'current of thought'

---

[1] Binet is not unaware of the irony of drawing his conclusion about the nature of thought from the results of introspective studies. His comment is: *Quel sujet de méditation pour ceux qui aiment philosopher!*

will be broken up and he will be unable to think uninterruptedly because of the need to watch himself thinking. Moreover, this same abandonment of the request for description has another advantage that may be at least equally important, for it at once removes any likelihood of resort to the complicated vocabulary of logical terms in which we are accustomed to describe thought, and which may be so misleading from the point of view of psychological, as opposed to logical, inquiry. If there is no call to 'describe' there will be no need to talk of 'such things as judging, abstracting, subsuming, deducing, inducing, predicating . . .' to quote Gilbert Ryle (1949): terms which he says are appropriate to descriptions of results reached but which we all too commonly use in efforts to describe the ways in which we reach them. He goes on to claim that it is because of this, and because we do not catch ourselves performing these acts which we 'describe' in this way, that we conclude that these acts must be 'very subterranean happenings'. And this might not be unjust as a comment on the conclusion of Binet's that has been quoted above.

So if we avoid this sort of terminology we may perhaps reduce a little the disparity between the word and the act of which Binet and Peirce were so aware; and we shall certainly make it possible to use the reports of a great many subjects who could never have told us that they had been inferring or subsuming.

There is one further advantage that may be of some importance – one that derives primarily from the fact that, when the subject 'does' instead of 'describing', his words are not retrospective. There is then not the same danger that they will misrepresent the course of thought because of the subject's forgetting what he did and being unable to retrace his steps with accuracy. On the other hand, however, it appears that in avoiding this risk we may incur another one. The finding of words may in itself affect thought, so that, though we no longer have the danger of in-accurate retrospection or of disruption caused by the effort to observe and describe, we may yet have altered the thought itself.

This would seem to be one of the two main objections that can be brought against the 'thinking aloud' procedure. The other is that much of the thought may be too quick for articulated speech or be for some other reason quite inaccessible to consciousness.

This brings us back to the point we made initially about the relation between a thinker's awareness of his own thought processes and an observer's awareness of them. It will be recalled that we took the view that the latter need not be dependent upon the former; and we went on to point out that this is true in the sense that an observer may be better able than the thinker to interpret signs which are available to the latter and can be made available to the former also. In this connection we spoke of the problem of 'rendering overt'; and after some discussion we have now reached the conclusion that if one is going to use verbal reports it is probably better to ask the subject to 'think' than to 'describe', better to have him speak as he goes along than comment afterwards on what he did. But suppose there is much of which he just has no awareness at all. Does this constitute an objection so great as to render any kind of verbalizing worthless?

The force of this objection depends on what one claims for the method. If one were to claim that by asking the subject to verbalize one could reveal the entire processes of thinking, then the force of the objection would be very great. But if one claims only that its use will enable one to discover more about the processes than would be possible from any study of the product, then the second objection is no longer valid; for even if, in Peirce's terminology, one can know only resting-places, it is an obvious advantage in mapping the route to have knowledge of the intermediate ones as well as of that which is finally reached when the journey is over.

However, it must be added that there is a second sense in which an observer may be said to be potentially capable of learning more about a person's thinking than that person knows himself: in the sense, namely, that he may be able to obtain evidence of what is going on of a kind that is not available to the thinker at all. We have in mind here the possibility of obtaining direct physiological evidence of the thinking processes. The extent to which this can at present be done is, of course, very strictly limited. But there is some recent Russian work on the structure of 'semantic systems' which holds out great promise. It has been shown by Luria and Vinogradova (1959) that the recording of vascular changes is a valuable means of exploring the networks of related meaning which we build up in the course of our experience with language. And it has further been shown by the same writers that these recorded changes do not keep step with verbal reports which the subjects can offer. Luria and Vinogradova conclude: 'Thus the system of links revealed by us is not of a clear conscious nature, and it is reflected much more fully in the system of vascular reactions than in the conscious account of the subject.'

Here, then, there are new possibilities of progress. Should we therefore, abandon all study that is based on verbal reports? Clearly this does not follow. In the first place, Luria and Vinogradova themselves believe that it is of great importance to discover how the unconscious links and the conscious systems are related to one another. For this purpose the conscious systems themselves must obviously be studied. In the second place, however, what we can do at present by physiological recording is severely restricted: there are many questions which we cannot yet tackle in this fashion. It would be foolish to refuse to study what the subject *can* report just because we have no grounds for supposing he can report everything. What we must do is try to develop also, and as rapidly as possible, means such as those used by Luria and Vinogradova to study thinking processes in so far as the latter defy all attempts at verbalization.

This leaves the first of the two objections that were mentioned earlier – and it is an objection which raises difficulties of a more serious kind. We can easily say: let us study verbal reports in the full awareness that they cannot tell us everything. But what if verbalizing actually changes the thought? We have to admit it may be true that when a subject thinks aloud he will think in a way that is different from that in which he otherwise would have thought. It may, therefore, be very unsafe to generalize the findings of studies conducted by this method, and claim that they would hold true in situations unlike those where they were obtained. Perhaps a person left to work out a problem on his own goes about it in a different way from that in which he proceeds when he is asked to verbalize his thinking.[1]

The objection is a grave one so long as the results of the 'thinking aloud' studies are accepted as conclusive. But there is an alternative to this. They may be regarded as providing not conclusions but hypotheses to be put to further test, and in this case the objection loses its force. If we take the subject's behaviour when he is thinking aloud as the basis of a hypothesis which we subsequently test in a quite different situation where he is not being asked to speak his thoughts, we are no longer in danger of drawing an unwarranted general conclusion – or, at least, the danger of our doing so will depend on our subsequent test, and not on our original clinical procedures.

There are also reasons, having nothing to do with this particular risk, why clinical studies ought normally to be used to provide hypotheses. These reasons are quite general, and concern the whole question of the relationship between clinical (or individual) and statistical methods of inquiry – procedures which are in fact most valuable when they are complementary to each other, but which are all too rarely used in this way.

In Britain and America, there has been a marked tendency for psychological and educational research workers to rely on large-scale statistical studies and to distrust clinical findings. On the continent of Europe a preference for clinical studies has always shown itself. The most important exponent of clinical methods in developmental psychology in recent years has been Jean Piaget. His work has aroused the greatest interest everywhere, but in Britain and America his ways of proceeding have been very much criticized.

Typically, he devises some sort of problem situation (often of a

[1] Some attempts have been made to discover whether this is so. For instance, A. J. Hafner (1957) reports that he gave a performance test to two matched groups of children, and instructed one group to verbalize as they worked. He found slight insignificant differences in favour of the 'verbalizers' in respect of time taken and number of correct solutions, and a difference, significant at the ·02 level, in their favour in respect of number of moves made. See also Cofer (1957) and Gagné and Smith (1962).

most ingenious kind) and then studies the behaviour of a number of children of different ages. Each child is observed individually and questioned closely about what he is doing. There is a plan of questioning, but the procedure is extremely flexible and the plan can be abandoned at any moment if something the child says or does suggests to the investigator a new and interesting line of inquiry. When a number of children have been studied in this way, the results are analysed and interpreted in relation to a vast theoretical system which Piaget has built up over the last thirty years, and which makes much use of notions deriving from mathematical logic. And that is all. There is no standardization of procedure (the flexible method explicitly precludes it) and there is no attempt at 'measurement' unless it be called measurement to define a number of distinct developmental stages.

It is understandable that Piaget should have been criticized for this. It is less understandable that so few of his critics seem to have asked themselves why he proceeds as he does, or to have reflected that the features to which they object can hardly be attributed to ignorance of scientific method or unawareness of its value. One of his recent books is a report of studies of the development of scientific thinking in children: development of understanding of the principle of holding variables constant, of considering all possible combinations in a system, of making use of exact measurement, and so on. If he does not use these methods in his own researches it is not because of ignorance of their significance as instruments of thought.

The reason would seem rather to be that when he began his work it was very largely a pioneer undertaking and this meant that he started with several large open questions: What are the child's ideas of causality? How does he conceive of space and time? How does he develop his concept of number? – and so on.

Now when an inquiry is directed by questions of this order, the position is very different from one in which research is aimed at providing evidence for or against a specific, definite, limited hypothesis. For these questions are not in themselves hypotheses at all, and the first step on the way to answering them must lie in the getting of hypotheses. But the adult who is trying to formulate hypotheses about the development of thinking in children is in some ways in a singularly difficult position. He is himself a thinking being, and he has a memory, which it would seem should help him. In fact, however, it may deceive him, because anything about his own earlier thought which he fails to remember he may find incredible. Now it seems to be the case – and we owe the evidence for this largely to Piaget's work – that in fact we forget completely, in some respects at any rate, how we used to think. When adults are told that children, at a certain stage, think that a substance like plasticine changes in amount as it changes in shape, they are frequently incredulous. So that if an adult bases hypotheses about children's thinking largely on his own thinking, he is unlikely to formulate the most significant ones. If, on the other hand, he adopts Piaget's clinical methods and observes individual children closely yet without the rigidity of a standardized procedure, he is likely soon to discover much that will shake his adult assumptions and preconceptions – and he will be in a much more advantageous position for the deriving of fruitful hypotheses for the very simple reason that he will know what it is he is trying to explain. Broadbent (1958) emphasizes this extremely obvious yet frequently overlooked point that we cannot produce satisfactory theories of behaviour till we establish as fully as possible what that behaviour is. He quotes Adrian (1954) in support: 'We must find out what human behaviour is like before we try to explain how it is produced.'

The great value of Piaget's work is that he has taken some very close looks at the behaviour of children and has then provided us with a wealth of hypotheses. It may be that he is to be criticized for speaking of his hypotheses, once he has them, with an undue measure of confidence, as if they had been tested more rigorously than in fact they have been. But this is a criticism of his failure to supplement clinical by statistical procedures, and it can be turned round and used with even more force against most of those who make it, since there can be no doubt that the exclusive reliance on statistical procedures is worse than the exclusive reliance on clinical ones. This is because clinical studies should come first and guide the statistical ones. The shortcomings of clinical procedures can at any point be made good by statistical test; but statistical inquiries which have not been preceded by appropriate clinical studies may be so misguided as to be useless or positively misleading.

It is as a means of getting fruitful hypotheses that the close and detailed study of individual children has its main value. Such a study will not yield hypotheses automatically, of course. The deriving of new and important hypotheses is generally acknowledged as the most difficult part of any scientist's task. All that clinical procedures can do is provide clues for an imaginative thinker to utilize.

The foregoing discussion of statistical and clinical methods arose from a consideration of the difficulties of observing the processes of thought; and the latter in turn arose from a discussion of the desirability of taking a close look at the manner in which test items function, and especially at the reasons why people fail to solve them.

The following chapters describe an attempt to start on the kind of inquiry which has been advocated. The aims of the enterprise are in one sense modest, in another, ambitious. The ultimate objective is the ambitious one of increasing understanding of the course of human intellectual development. The hope is that studies of this kind may make it possible in the future to assess this development more adequately, by means of tests constructed with greater insight and control – constructed, that is, with knowledge of what errors in thinking are particularly significant at a given age and with knowledge of how to devise items so as to invite a given error, once this has been judged desirable for a given predictive purpose. There is also the further and still more ambitious hope that a better understanding of the course of development, with particular reference to the difficulties that have to be overcome, may make it possible to further that development by teaching that is conducted in the light of the increased understanding. But this is a very long-term objective. The present aims are modest since we recognize that any increase in understanding that may be gained by the methods we employ is likely to come only slowly. In particular, since the studies reported do not involve attempts at prediction, they cannot, in themselves, contribute to the making of decisions about the status of test items. This is a matter for large-scale statistical inquiry. We are here at the hypothesis-finding stage and what emerges cannot be more than suggestive of further work to be done.

Since we shall be particularly concerned in what follows with obstacles to the successful solution of problems, it is important to make one terminological distinction. The word 'error' is commonly used of a wrong solution, as well as of wrong moves in the thought leading up to a solution. For our purposes here it will be essential not to confuse these two senses. 'Error' will therefore be used to refer to any flaw in the thinking process, and 'wrong solution' will refer to a mistaken end-result. Further, the term 'answer' will be used of the entire overt response to the problem. It should be noticed, then, that errors may occur even if the right solution is reached, but that a wrong solution cannot occur in the absence of error of some kind. Also, it is obvious that only those errors that manifest themselves in the answer will constitute our evidence – but there may occur other errors as well.

It is, of course, only in a restricted class of thinking situations that we are faced with problems the solutions to which can be classed as 'right' and 'wrong'. In everyday living, we very frequently encounter problems where the possible solutions have to be classed rather as 'better' or 'worse' by some process of weighing up the advantages and the disadvantages they offer. Yet those who have attempted to study thinking scientifically have tended on the whole to concentrate on the kind of problem to which a solution may be clearly right or wrong, and they have probably been wise to do this, so long as they have not overlooked the fact that other sorts of thought situation also exist. They have been wise because, where thinking is directed to the solving of a problem

35

which has one and only one correct solution, there is a structured and closed frame of reference which facilitates a little the enormously difficult task of observing and analysing the thought. But it would be quite misguided to assume or claim that intelligent thinking takes place only in structured situations of this kind. The writing of poetry and the building of bridges would undoubtedly have to be included in that large group of activities the mode of performance of which may reasonably be described as varying in intelligence; but there is no one exclusive right solution to the 'problem' of how to build a certain bridge, still less to that of how to write a certain poem.

Ultimately, any adequate account of intelligent thinking will have to include consideration of activities of this kind, but in the present state of our knowledge restriction to the more manageable structured situation seems very evidently the better policy. The studies to be reported here have been confined even more narrowly to a few types of problem of kinds that have been used in verbal group intelligence tests. These are already known to be reasonably useful as predictors. The aim is to find out more about the bases of their power.

CHAPTER 4

# Matching Problems

THE EXPERIMENTAL work which is now to be described was not planned as a whole. Rather, it grew stage by stage as one inquiry led to another. There are therefore two policies which might be adopted in presenting the results. It would be possible either to report the work largely in historical sequence, or alternatively to arrange it in an order which might appear more logical – for instance, by reporting first of all the results for the youngest subjects and going on then to the findings for the older ones. The plan adopted is in effect a compromise. In the various studies that have been conducted five main types of problem have been used. All the evidence relating to any one type will be drawn together for the purposes of this report – a procedure which will involve departure from historical sequence but will be necessary in order to avoid much repetition. The report on any one type of problem, however, will in the main follow the order in which the work was carried out, on the ground that this will make possible a clearer presentation of the issues and considerations which have guided the development of the inquiry.

*The Subjects of Group O*
The subjects in the first experimental group were twenty children whose ages were between eleven years nine months and twelve years three months at the time the inquiry began. Each child had previously taken two Moray House tests of verbal reasoning, at an interval of a year, as part of the normal procedure for secondary

37

school selection, the second test having been attempted approximately four months before the start of the investigation. The standardized score of each child fell within the limits $115 \pm 3$ on each test, so that in terms of group test total score the children were very nearly equal. By keeping narrow the age-range and the range of ability – so far as available evidence enabled us to judge the latter – we hoped to gain from this first study a better indication than would otherwise have been possible of the value of the method and of the further work that might most profitably be undertaken.

The children in this group were older than those in other groups to be described later. By calling them Group O, we hope to make this fact easier to recall in the discussions that follow.

*Procedure*

Each child was tested individually in the school which he normally attended. In some cases, a shorthand writer was present to take notes. When this was not possible, the record was kept by the experimenter. The child was told that the purpose of the inquiry was 'to find out more about the tests and what is hard or easy about them', and was asked to 'think out loud' as he solved the problems. He was assured that his performance would not affect his school career in any way. No time limit was imposed and the full session usually lasted about an hour. The children were given paper and pencil and were asked to record their solutions. They were also told that they might write down anything which they thought would help them.

In the type of matching problem used in this study,[1] the task is to utilize information in order to select one out of all the possible ways of associating a set of objects with another set of objects. We are here concerned only with the case where $n$ objects $(a, b, \ldots n)$ are to be matched one-to-one with $n$ other objects $(a', b', \ldots n')$.

[1] See Fiske (1961) for a discussion of matching problems.

In these problems there are five main variables, none of which can be assumed to be psychologically irrelevant:

(a) the content, that is to say, the nature of the objects to be associated;
(b) the number of the objects to be associated;
(c) whether the objects are physically present, are pictorially represented, or are only named;
(d) the manner in which the information is given, and whether any of it is superfluous;
(e) the way in which the task is described – for instance, whether the subject is simply told: 'match these with one another'; or whether he is asked: 'what does *a* go with?' etc.; and, if the latter, in what order the questions are presented.

We must now consider (d) more fully, for here a number of further possibilities arise. Of these the chief are:

(i) information may be conjunctive or disjunctive;
(ii) information may be positive or negative.

We shall not be concerned here with the use of disjunctive information (for instance, '*a* goes either with *a'* or with *b''*') and therefore no detailed analysis of possibilities in the use of disjunctive information will be offered, but it may be of interest to state formally the possible ways in which, when all the information is conjunctive, positive and negative statements may be combined. Suppose $n$ objects $(a, b, \ldots n)$ to be matched one-to-one with $n$ other objects $(a', b', \ldots n')$. Information may be given in one of the following ways:

(a) $n-1$ positive statements, associating $a$ with $a'$, $b$ with $b'$, and so on (information concerning the final association of $n$ with $n'$ being, of course, redundant, since $n$ and $n'$ will be the only objects remaining);
(b) $n-2$ positive statements, associating $a$ with $a'$, etc., and $1$ negative statement, dissociating $n-1$ from $n'$ or $n'-1$ from $n$;

39

(c) *n-3* positive statements and *3* [i.e. *2+1*] negative statements, which latter may be given in a variety of ways so long as two of them combine to rule out one pairing and the third rules out another. Thus the three negatives dissociating *n-1* from *n'*, *n-2* from *n'*, and *n-2* from *n'-1* would be adequate for this purpose but the three negatives dissociating *n-1* from *n'*, *n-2* from *n'-1*, and *n* from *n'-2* would not. (The three negatives which are adequate may be described as being in strong combination, the three which are not may be said to be in weak combination.)

(d) *n-4* positive statements and *6* [i.e. *3+2+1*] negative statements in strong combination. And so on until the limit is reached of

(e) *n-n* positive statements and $(n-1)+(n-2)+ \ldots +1$ negative statements in strong combination.

Thus one moves from a situation in which all the information is positive to one where it is given entirely in negative form.

In the first of these possibilities, where there are *n-1* positive statements, there is of course no 'problem' except in the deriving of the *n*th positive statement, since the information is in the same form as the required solution which is thus directly given. However, the deriving of the *n*th positive statement depends on a principle that is of fundamental importance in this sort of task: that of reaching a conclusion by 'elimination' or 'exhaustion' of all possibilities but one; and the application of this principle depends evidently on the ability to survey all the possibilities together, to have an overview of the situation in which nothing is neglected. Given understanding of the principle, then the surveying of possibilities will obviously become more difficult as the possibilities increase in number.

A grasp of the basic principle and ability to apply it with due regard to the complexities of the data would seem to be called for in whatever way the information is given. In all but the first of the possible ways, however, more is necessary. Positive information must be combined with negative information; and as soon as three or more negatives are introduced these must be grouped in strong combination so that positive conclusions can be drawn. This process of grouping negatives would seem to demand (increasingly as more and more of the information is given in negative form) that sort of understanding which Bartlett (1958) would call a sense of 'the directional properties of evidence': an awareness of where to begin and how to move which must derive from an appreciation, even if implicit and unarticulated, of the overall structure of the problem. It is worth remarking, however, that the order in which the statements are presented can probably affect the issue, at least for subjects who do not have this appreciation in very developed form, because a given order may or may not be one which leads directly and without re-arrangement to a solution.

It will be evident that the systematic variation of these conditions with subjects of different ages would be a task of very considerable magnitude. What we have to report is not even a beginning to that task. But we have presented the above analysis in the conviction that study of the effects of systematic variation in problems is the kind of task which psychologists must be prepared to tackle, however laborious it proves, if they are to advance in precise knowledge of the development of thinking and in their ability to construct tests that will adequately assess its progress in the individual person.

PROBLEM AI

The first problem was as follows:

Five boys, Jack, Dick, James, Bob, and Tom, go to five different schools in the same town. The schools are called North School, South School, East School, West School, and Central School.

Jack does not go to North, South, or Central School.
Dick goes to West School.
Bob does not go to North or Central School.
Tom has never been inside Central School.

1. What school does Jack go to?
2. What school does Bob go to?
3. What school does James go to?
4. What school does Tom go to?

If this problem is considered in terms of the formal description given (pages 38–41), it will be observed that:

(a) the content is 'boys' and 'schools', a very familiar one for the subjects;
(b) the number of pairs is five;
(c) the objects are only named;
(d) one positive and six negative statements are given, and these are arranged in a way that accords fairly closely with an order of treatment of the information[1] which leads directly to solution: the negative statements relating to any one boy are grouped together in one sentence, and the boy about whom three negative statements are made is the first named;
(e) separate questions are asked for each pairing except the one which is directly given in the positive statement, and the order in which these questions are asked accords fairly well with the order in which the information is presented, the exception being the intrusion of 'James' between 'Bob' and 'Tom'.

One further feature of this problem should be noted, namely, the wording of the negative statement about Tom – 'Tom has never been inside Central School'. This provides the information necessary for solution but it also provides some additional information which is quite unnecessary. The fact that superfluous information may be given in an infinite variety of ways greatly complicates the study of thinking.

---

[1] The other possible order of treatment would, of course, be to group by schools instead of boys, thus: 'Jack, Bob, and Tom do not go to Central School', etc.

*Results: Group O(i)*[1]

For the reasons which have been explained in the first few chapters of this book, attention has been concentrated on the study of errors. An analysis of the errors observed will therefore be presented for each problem.

In quotations of children's answers, round brackets contain words spoken to the child by the experimenter and square brackets contain comments and explanations to the reader.

As soon as we began the attempt to classify errors in the matching problems, we found that one distinction seemed inescapable. In solving these problems, the subject may in the first place fail to understand some principle that is necessary for solution: he may fail in some respect to appreciate the structure of the problem. In the second place, even if his comprehension of the structure is apparently flawless, he may fail to carry out accurately the manipulations which are involved.

This distinction obviously has application far beyond the bounds of the matching-problem situation. For instance, it is widely regarded as appropriate whenever the task is one which involves arithmetical computation. Accordingly, there is often, in a test of arithmetic attainment, a 'problem' section where computation is relatively simple and the difficulty lies in seeing what to do, and a 'mechanical' section where 'what to do' presents no problem to anyone who understands the symbols but where complicated calculation is required.

We shall find that we have to return again and again to this distinction. To make it, of course, is not to say that procedural understanding and executive skill can ever be completely divorced. The better the understanding of how to proceed, the less chance there is, other things being equal, of the occurrence of errors of execution, and we shall see later how in some cases an extremely good understanding of structure may almost rule out certain executive errors.

[1] These same children were seen again two years later. We shall refer from now on to Group O(i) and to Group O(ii) to distinguish the two sets of results.

If we turn now to the errors made by Group O(i) on Problem A1 we find that the large majority of them appear to be errors of execution. In the answers given by these children there was very little sign of failure to understand any of the basic principles involved in solution.[1] Yet in spite of this only four of the twenty made no errors at all in dealing with the problem, a further nine went wrong at some point but corrected their mistakes and eventually produced the right solutions, and the remaining seven each gave at least one wrong solution. So we have a problem which the children know how to do, apparently quite well, yet which they frequently get wrong. Of what order, then, are their mistakes?

One of the most common was to conclude that 'there is only one left' before this had in fact been established; in other words, to make an incomplete survey of the possibilities and thus apply the principle of elimination prematurely. Seven children made this error. For instance, here is Moira answering the question about Jack:

'He doesn't go to North, South, or Central, so he goes to West.' Moira, then, forgets or ignores the existence of the East School.

There are two things to notice particularly here. In the first place, when this error occurred it was usually, though not always, the East School which was neglected. Now the East School is the one which is not actually mentioned in the four statements which are the starting-points of deduction. So, if the subject is to avoid overlooking it, he either must have a very good appreciation of the whole structure of the problem or else at the least must constantly check his moves against the general introductory information that there are five boys and five schools. At one extreme, the person who had analysed the formal structure of matching problems, as we have done here, and who was articulately aware of the various possible patterns of information – who saw this

---

[1] Evidence is given later (pages 197 ff.) that children as young as five years can grasp the basic principle of the elimination of all possibilities but one, if the situation is sufficiently simple.

problem as an instance of the 'one positive, six negatives' type, let us say – such a person would be unlikely to make an error of this kind and would be free of the need for constant checking by virtue of his organized understanding of structural characteristics. He would know that the first step must be to combine the one positive with three negatives, and thus he could not make Moira's error. Here is the example, then, to which we referred (page 43), of understanding which rules out executive error. The person who does not have this organized understanding, on the other hand, must be constantly reviewing and checking if he is to be sure that all possibilities have been taken into account. There are, of course, two ways of doing this: one by constant explicit reference to the written statement of the problem, the other by attempting simply to 'hold in mind' what has been given. If the latter procedure is adopted, success would then seem to depend on what André Rey (1956) describes as the stability of the mental field: the extent to which one can 'hold on' to items of information while at the same time manipulating them mentally.

It becomes, then, a question of short-term or 'immediate' memory, and recent work on the subject is relevant. Most of this work, however, has been concerned with the situation in which the material that is to be 'held in mind' is presented to the subject and he is then asked to engage in some other activity so that the effects of this activity on retention may be assessed. Experimental findings[1] are consistent with our ordinary experience that the interference is serious and, further, that it is so because it prevents the continuous rehearsal of the material that is to be held in mind. We are all familiar with the experience of trying to hold on to a telephone number which we have heard only once and losing hold of it if we have to answer a question about something else. Broadbent believes that the experimental evidence suggests that short-term memory – as distinct from the long-term retention of something which we might say we have 'learned' – depends on some sort of circuit mechanism round which the information that is to be retained must be kept con-

[1] A review of relevant findings is given by D. E. Broadbent (1958).

tinuously passing – a mechanism, however, which has a strictly limited capacity, so that the arrival of more information calling for attention can cause the loss of earlier items.

Now the situation with which we are concerned is obviously similar to that in which there is interpolated activity, but it is not quite the same. We are dealing with a situation where information must be held in store, not while other information is attended to, but while it is itself attended to – while certain fairly complex operations are performed upon it. Of course, in effect, the results of these operations themselves constitute new information and may load the capacity of the mechanism beyond its limit, with consequences very similar to the effects produced by the presentation of some wholly new set of stimuli. But, naturally, it cannot be assumed that the effects will be the same. With this reservation, however, it may perhaps be reasonable to render Rey's 'stable mental field' in Broadbent's language as a situation in which the system for short-term retention is not loaded to capacity and in which consequently there is no loss, since this formulation seems theoretically the more suggestive and promising. From our present point of view, the interesting questions would then be those which concern individual differences in this capacity – differences between individuals and also differences in the same individual at different times. The latter, of course, may or may not show trend with increasing age – that is, there may exist, as well as developmental changes, fluctuations in performance of a more irregular variety. Rey, in describing a test which he has devised, gives norms from age four to age nine which indicate a marked increase in capacity over this period. Unfortunately, he offers no measure of test-retest reliability.

A second error which occurred in Problem A1 is in some ways closely akin to the first one. In 'incomplete elimination' one element in the problem is overlooked, apparently because immediate memory is at fault and the data are too complex to be held in mind while the work of solution goes on. The second error also seems to involve a failure of memory, but this time what is forgotten is the outcome of the operations that have been performed. Again, it is as if the load is too great, only this time it is the new information which suffers. What can be observed is that the subject, in the midst of his chain of reasoning, makes a statement and then promptly makes another one contradicting it, apparently because the first one has been immediately lost. We shall call this error 'loss of hold on reasoning' or, more briefly, 'loss of hold'. As an example, here is Stewart answering the third question, the one concerning James:

'Not West, nor East, nor South [here he is correctly using his own solutions to the two previous questions] so that leaves Central, North, and West – no, Dick goes to West. So Central, North – no, South, Central . . . oh, dear! It's getting more complicated.'

Here, then, the child does not simply overlook one element in the problem; rather, he confuses several of them because he 'loses hold' of what he has been doing, of his own reasoning. It will be evident that the resultant disorganization can be much more severe. Further, loss of hold on reasoning can occur at any point in any problem where a sequence of reasoning is involved.

It can sometimes happen that loss of hold leads to the neglecting of one or more possibilities and hence produces what is in effect incomplete elimination. When this can be seen to have occurred the error has been classified as loss of hold. It follows that when an error is described as one of incomplete elimination nothing which meets the description of loss of hold has been observed. It may, of course, happen that a subject makes both errors at different points in the course of an answer.

The third error does not seem to belong in either the structural or the executive class. The obvious name for it would be 'guessing'. We have preferred the term 'arbitrary allocation', not from any love of technical terminology for its own sake, but for two reasons: first, because this term will be a convenient means of relating this error to, and distinguishing it from, errors to be discussed later (see pages 50 and 67); and second, because the term 'guessing' tends to carry implications that might mislead.

The whole question of what it is psychologically to 'guess' is an interesting one. Let us first of all define 'guessing' as the making of a choice in the absence of any justification, conscious or otherwise, for preferring the alternative chosen. Randomness is then implied. But how often do people act truly randomly? Bartlett says that, when his subjects declare themselves to be guessing the solutions to one of his problems (the problem in question is actually a kind of matching problem), they are not in fact working randomly; rather, their choices appear to be determined by considerations of which they are not themselves fully aware. Bartlett goes as far as to assert that 'at this level[1] "guessing" *never* is random'. Again, there is evidence from work on subliminal perception that subjects may believe themselves to be acting randomly when in fact they are being influenced in the direction of correct decisions by stimuli of which they are not conscious. For instance, Baker (1937) finds that, when subjects are asked to report on subliminal stimuli, the errors are significantly fewer than chance expectation at points within a certain distance below the conscious threshold, but approach chance levels as the intensities of the stimuli are progressively diminished. Thus when the subjects think they are guessing they are not in fact always doing so, if our definition of 'guessing' is accepted. On the other hand, as we shall see, it is possible for subjects to make an apparently unjustified choice and seem not to have noticed the absence of justification.

It is better, then, not to imply that choices are random simply because they lack explicit justification. They may perhaps more reasonably be described as 'arbitrary'; and, accordingly, the term 'arbitrary allocation' will be used whenever a subject seems to decide among different possibilities in a way which involves the ignoring of part of the given of the problem and which includes no attempt to justify the choice. It is interesting that there was no instance where an entire problem was 'solved' in this way. Rather, a subject would proceed by explicit reasoning for some part of the way towards a solution and then suddenly appear to

[1] The implications of the phrase 'at this level' are not completely clear from the context in which it occurs. See Bartlett (1958, page 62).

give up reasoning entirely. Moreover, this abandonment invariably occurred when a point had been reached at which only
two alternatives remained open. Thus Morag (answering question
4 – 'What school does Tom go to?'): 'Tom has never been to
Central so he must have been to North or South. It'll be South.
(How do you know?) I don't know really.'

Morag had proceeded up to this stage by careful, though not
flawless, deduction. The earlier part of her answer was as follows:

*Question 1*: 'East – because Dick goes to the West, Bob goes
to the . . . Jack doesn't go to North, South, or
Central.'

*Question 2*: 'Not to North or Central . . . Dick goes to West –
so Bob must go to the West School.' [Loss of hold.]

*Question 3*: 'James isn't there . . . [pause] Jack goes to East, Bob
to West. . . . [Long pause. Finally, the experimenter
suggested that she try question 4 and the answer
quoted above was obtained.]

From this it may be seen that when Morag was perplexed
by question 3 she did not allocate arbitrarily. At that stage three
possibilities remained open according to her argument: James
might go to North, South, or Central. Of course, if this were an
isolated case no significance whatever could be attached to the
fact that Morag 'guessed' only when the possibilities were reduced
to two. It might simply have happened that at this point she tired
of effort. But it is not isolated: there were only two instances in
this group and on this problem, but others occurred elsewhere and
always when two and only two alternatives remained. We have
at the moment no very satisfactory explanation to offer of why
this should be so. Sometimes it seemed as though it might be
associated with some judgement of the odds in favour of success.
We have no evidence to suggest that this judgement is conscious
if it is operative at all, but it may be more likely to be operative
when, as in Morag's answer, there is evidence of awareness of
inadequacy in reasoning in the admission that: 'I don't know
really'. This awareness is not always present, however. Some-

times in cases of this kind it is as if the child has no sense of 'either A or B' as a statement of uncertainty that must be resolved but is regarding the 'or' as implying that unjustified choice is appropriate – that he has powers of allocation. If this is a correct interpretation, then the question still remains of why his powers should be limited to the case when only two possibilities are open.

Arbitrary allocation proved to be only one of a number of errors having as their common feature a failure to adhere rigorously to the given of the problem. To the categories of structural and executive errors it therefore became necessary to add a third category of arbitrary errors defined by this characteristic.

So far, then, two executive errors and one arbitrary error have been described. The remaining errors, unlike the first three, have features which make it reasonable to classify them as errors of structure.

Progress in these problems depends on the use, in subsequent reasoning, of the solutions which the subject has already arrived at: the conclusion that Jack goes to the East School is itself part of the basis for concluding that Bob goes to the South School. This is another way of saying that the information must be treated in a certain order – actually one of two alternative orders, according as one groups by boys or by schools – if complete solution is to be possible. Now it has already been pointed out that the manner of presentation of Problem A1 accords rather closely with the order in which the information must be taken. Thus the child's awareness of structure is not, in this respect, put very sharply to the test, and if he works straight through the questions he will have available to him, except at one point,[1] all the information he needs. Of course, this is no guarantee that he will use it, and we found two instances of a child's failing to use his own solutions in answering further questions.[2] This might appear, then, to be a failure to understand a principle that relates to the ordering and

---

[1] The one exception is the question about James. Unless the child changes at this point from grouping by boys to grouping by schools, he must treat the question about Tom first.

[2] It will be recalled that the children wrote down their solutions as they arrived at them.

combining of information and is essential to solution. We did not, however, find any child in Group O(i) who consistently failed in this respect: in each of the two cases observed, the failure occurred only once in the course of solution of the whole problem and held up solution for only a short period of time.

Another way in which failure to order and combine can show itself is in the introducing of some part of the given at a point in the reasoning where it is irrelevant. Two children, while they were working out or explaining their answers, made reference to given pieces of information which were at that moment of no help to their argument. Here is an example:

*Pam* (answering question 2 – 'What school does Bob go to?'): 'If Dick goes to West, that's one out. If Jack goes to East, that's North and Central left – no, North, South, and Central. And Tom can't go to Central because he's never been inside.'

It might be argued that this last statement has relevance in the sense that if Tom did go to Central then Central would be eliminated for Bob. If one allowed this, one would have to allow that any piece of information that formed part of the given would have relevance at any point in solution. But clearly, what is relevant for Pam, when she is left with North, South, and Central as possibilities for Bob, is either negative information about Bob or positive information about someone other than Bob: negative information about Tom is not really of much value to her. The fact that she introduces it at this point suggests that she is groping for the next step (which in fact she finds shortly afterwards), and this in turn implies that her grasp of structure is not perfect. However, as was the case with failure to use one's own previous solutions, this kind of error in Group O(i) appeared only as a momentary obstacle and seemed like the remnant of a difficulty almost overcome.

The final error concerns the statement: 'Tom has never been inside Central School', which seemed to be much more trouble-some to some children than the other negative statements in the form 'X does not go to Y School'. For instance, Mary reaches a point where she is left with Tom and James on the one hand and the Central and North Schools on the other. She then says: 'If Tom has never been to Central, there is only one left. So James goes to North.' Betty uses almost identical wording in reaching the same conclusion: she too calls North School 'the only one left'. Both these girls later corrected this error, but two others made the same mistake and left it uncorrected. The question then arises whether the difficulty is due to the wording or to the nature of the problem situation itself. Probably both contribute, for although no similar difficulty arose in the handling of the statements 'Jack does not go to . . .' and 'Bob does not go to . . .', they had to be used differently. They were direct starting-points for inquiries concerning their own subjects, Jack and Bob. But here we have an inquiry concerning James, who does not himself appear in the statements, and so the starting-point is a negative statement about Tom. Yet if that statement had been quite straightforward – 'does not go . . .' – there might have been less likelihood of error.

We consider that this, too, must be described as an error of structure, although a very limited one.

*Results: Group O(ii)*

It was unfortunate that, by the time the subjects of Group O were tested again, approximately two years and three months later, one of them had left the district. The number of subjects on the second occasion was therefore nineteen; and their ages were between fourteen years and fourteen years six months.

The purpose of the retest was, of course, to see what changes had taken place, and the same problem was used. An analysis of the errors revealed no new types: the categories which had been set up on the basis of the Group O(i) results seemed very adequate for the sorting of the second-occasion errors. However, some of these categories were superfluous, no instances being observed.

*Table 1* shows the frequencies of error in the different categories on occasions (i) and (ii). Thus there is an overall diminution in frequency, but one error, loss of hold, stands out for its failure to decrease at all.

TABLE 1   GROUP O—PROBLEM A1

| Error | Number of children making the error on occasion | |
|---|---|---|
| | (i) | (ii) |
| (a) Incomplete elimination | 7 | 3 |
| (b) Loss of hold | 9 | 9 |
| (c) Arbitrary allocation | 2 | 0 |
| (d) Failure to use solutions | 2 | 0 |
| (e) Irrelevance | 2 | 0 |
| (f) Difficulty with negative statement | 4 | 2 |

*Table 1*, however, does not present the whole picture and fails to reveal what is in some ways the most interesting feature of the comparison between the two occasions. As well as asking whether aggregate frequencies decrease, one can ask how the totals are composed: whether, in so far as errors continue to be made, it is the same children who are making them. There are then four possibilities: error on both occasions, error on the first but not the second occasion, error on the second but not the first, error on neither. Of these possibilities, all but the third are perfectly compatible with smooth developmental progress. The third, however, would be expected to be relatively infrequent if any general progress were occurring over the period studied.

*Table 2* gives the numbers in these four groups for the different types of error. If the entry in column A is added to the entry in B, one obtains, for any error, the number of children who made it on the first occasion; and, similarly, if the entry in A is added to the entry in C, one obtains the number making the error on the second occasion (cf. *Table 1*).

It is evident from *Table 2* that, as might be expected, there are more instances where children stop making errors, as between occasions (i) and (ii), than where they start making them. However, column C is not entirely empty: we find a certain number

TABLE 2     GROUP O—PROBLEM A1

| Error | A | B | C | D |
|---|---|---|---|---|
| | Number of children making the error on occasions | | | |
| | (i) and (ii) | (i) not (ii) | (ii) not (i) | not (i) nor (ii) |
| (a) Incomplete elimination | 1 | 6 | 2 | 10 |
| (b) Loss of hold | 5 | 4 | 4 | 6 |
| (c) Arbitrary allocation | 0 | 2 | 0 | 17 |
| (d) Failure to use solutions | 0 | 2 | 0 | 17 |
| (e) Irrelevance | 0 | 2 | 0 | 17 |
| (f) Difficulty with negative statement | 0 | 4 | 2 | 13 |

of children who, at age fourteen, make an error which they did not make at age twelve.

Here, then, we have the first evidence bearing on the questions raised in considering the nature of the error of 'incomplete elimination': questions of fluctuations in performance and of irregular variations as opposed to developmental trends. The numbers, of course, are very small. However, if, when the same errors recur in a variety of problems, the same tendencies show themselves, the evidence will be strengthened. The critical issue, though, however extensive the data available, would seem to be not so much the absolute frequencies in column C as the comparison of C with B, for it is this which bears on the question of whether or not we are dealing with some developmental progression. Take the extreme cases by way of illustration. Suppose the pattern:

| A | B | C | D |
|---|---|---|---|
| 10 | 0 | 0 | 10 |

Then there is obviously no evidence of progress, since there is no change between the first and second occasions: ten children made the error both times, ten made it neither time. On the other hand, suppose the pattern:

| A | B | C | D |
|---|---|---|---|
| 0 | 10 | 10 | 0 |

Then we have total change, but whereas ten children 'progress', another ten, on the face of this evidence considered in isolation, would seem to 'regress': that is, they make the error the second time not having made it the first time.

There are at least two possible explanations of this latter state of affairs. One is that we are dealing with an irregular fluctuation of such a sort that a given child may 'happen' to make the error on one occasion and 'happen' not to make it on the next or vice versa. Now, of course, fluctuation in the occurrence of error is not entirely incompatible with developmental advance: it could occur, for instance, and most probably does occur, at points of transition from one mode of responding to another. But we are dealing in the present studies with a time-gap of as much as two years. So if we find types of error where fresh instances are almost as numerous as disappearances, we can hardly explain this by postulating a transition point.

Let us return now to the distinction which was made earlier between understanding 'how to do' something and skill in carrying out the manipulations involved, and try to relate this distinction to the question of regularity or fluctuation in the occurrence of errors. It seems, on the level of imprecise, everyday observation, to be true that there is more irregular fluctuation in the case of ability to execute than in the case of 'knowing how' – in those types of activity, at any rate, where the distinction is fairly easy to draw. If one understands how to do a problem in arithmetic, then one understands it with a certain finality. One may through time forget just how to go about it and have to search around again for the exact method, but one is not likely to make a gross error of principle if once one has understood well. The same cannot be said for ability to execute. Most of us never reach a point where it is inconceivable that we should make computational errors in arithmetic. We advance to a certain stage of accuracy and there, over long periods of time, we stay. During these long periods it could very well happen that, doing the same problem twice over, we might make a computational error on the second occasion which we did not make on the first. Indeed, this would be just as likely as the reverse occurrence and it would not mean we were regressing in our ability to count. It would simply mean that this ability is not an all-or-none affair and that our level of proficiency has to be assessed somewhat probabilistically. Of course, this is not to say that the occurrence of computational error on one occasion and not on the other must be dismissed as inexplicable. We might try to explain it in terms of some such concept as 'alertness' or 'vigilance' – some notion that would have regard to the general state of the organism at the time. This is a concept which is already accepted as useful in many fields of psychological inquiry. What would have to be shown, however, if it were to serve our present purpose – namely, to offer some account of different patterns in the occurrence of error on two occasions – is that raised or lowered vigilance in the subject could decrease or increase certain errors while not affecting others (or at least affecting them to a very much smaller extent). Of course, for this purpose vigilance would have to be assessed by some measure independent of any of the errors the frequency of which one was proposing to observe and compare.

It may be as well at this point to mention one set of experimental findings that may at first sight appear to have more relevance to this issue than they in fact possess. In a recent monograph, Charles C. Anderson (1958) discusses what, following Thouless (1936), he calls 'function fluctuation'; and in the course of this work he reports a finding to the effect that, on a comparison of the 'mechanical' and 'problems' subtests of Moray House arithmetic tests, 'the Problems items show significantly more fluctuation than the Mechanical items'. This appears, then, to be experimental evidence that is directly in conflict with what we have been suggesting. However, the sense in which Anderson

uses the term 'fluctuation' is different from the one in which it is
used here. Anderson's procedure is to give two parallel tests on
one occasion, repeat the same two tests on a second occasion with
the same subjects, and see whether the differences between
occasions are significantly correlated. The argument is that in this
way 'test error' – that is, errors of measurement due to the unreliability of the instrument – can be distinguished from errors
due to the unreliability of the person, on the assumption that the
latter will be correlated while the former will not. So when he
reports more 'fluctuation' in problems items than in mechanical
items, this means that the two sets of problems items have shown
a greater tendency to vary *in the same direction* when any two
occasions are compared. And this is quite consistent with the
suggestion that there may be more irregularity (less sign of trend)
in the occurrence of executive than of structural errors.

It is important to appreciate that, while Anderson says that he
means by function fluctuation a type of variation that is distinct
from the variation in scoring 'which is the product of test error,
differential practice effect or functional maturation' (1958, p. 1),
nevertheless, the index of function fluctuation which he uses is,
as he himself allows, one in which a high value 'could be the
product of differential practice effect' (p. 14). Thus the distinction
between variations in response which show trend and those which
do not cannot be clearly made by means of this measure.

Anderson's mode of thinking is wholly based on the idea that
there are 'functions' of the mind and that tests measure them,
any test being composed of items which sample 'the hypothetical
item-universe of the function'. This position, which is the classical
one, leads to the idea that a test may sample a 'universe' more or
less successfully and thus measure more or less adequately whatever it purports to measure. But room is left for the possibility that
the 'functions' may operate more or less efficiently from occasion
to occasion. Thus 'crude variability' of total score has to be regarded as possibly composed not only of 'test error' but also of
variation attributable to these 'function fluctuations'.

It is possible to regard the whole question from a position

closer to the actual events. We have a set of stimuli – objects, words, marks on paper – which constitute 'problems', that is, specify conditions and call for certain manipulations. We offer this 'same' set of stimuli twice. Now there are two respects in which it may be claimed that it is impossible to offer the same stimuli twice. In the first place, the very fact that they have been presented before will of itself make them different on the second occasion: they will no longer be new. Unless one has access to the waters of Lethe, this must be accepted as a limiting circumstance in all study of the behaviour of living things. In this sense, then, it is impossible to give a subject the same problem twice. In a less profound sense it is difficult to do so. Mode of presentation will never be precisely the same; there may be interruptions and distractions on one occasion which do not occur on the next; in the interval the test paper may have become dirty, less legible, and so on. In so far as changes of this latter kind occur, we may unhesitatingly speak of the unreliability of the test – or of the person who administers it. But for the rest, the unreliability is of the person who tackles it;[1] and what we are concerned with at the moment is the nature of the changes in a person's response from occasion to occasion. In particular, we are concerned with the distinction between those changes which have direction or trend and those which fluctuate in an irregular way.

It is of great importance for the development of this discussion to realize that, when one is deciding about the presence or absence of trend, the length of time involved is critical. Measures which show trend over a short period of time may cease to do so if they are continued over a longer period. Thus, if we suppose there to be variations attributable to alterations in vigilance (thinking for the moment of the performance of one given subject), these may have marked trend in the course of a day but may have none over a period of weeks, months, or years. However, if the period is lengthened still further, so that an appreciable part of the life-span of the individual is in question, then some

---

[1] This argument does not apply to 'parallel test reliability', of course. Here, some such notion as that of 'sampling a universe' does seem to be necessarily involved.

general pattern may be discernible in spite of the variations which, over the shorter term, are quite properly to be regarded as random. A further similar point is that one must be clear whether one is speaking of trend in an individual or trend in a group of subjects (thinking for the moment of any one given period of time). If individual trends are for the most part of the same order, then obviously they will show themselves as group trends. But trends in the individuals who compose a group are quite compatible with absence of group trend if the individual trends are such as to cancel one another out.

Both of these points have bearing on Spearman's attitude to the distinction between variations which show trend and those which do not – an attitude which calls for comment in view of the ways in which it differs from the one adopted here. Spearman (1910) draws a distinction between 'variations of a *regular*, generally a continuously progressive character' which 'admit of investigation, explanation, and, in large degree, control' and 'others of such a discontinuously shifting sort that investigation, explanation, and control are almost baffled'. Variations of the former sort he conceives as attributable to practice, fatigue, and so on. Variations of the latter sort he can only attribute to 'accident', and he goes on: 'Now, it is the superposed accident that the present paper attempts to eliminate, herein following the custom of all sciences, one that appears to be an indispensable preliminary to getting at nature's laws.'

It is at this juncture that our point of view may most readily be seen to be at variance with that of Spearman and of the very numerous psychometrists who have been profoundly influenced by his conceptions. The difference can perhaps best be made clear with the help of a metaphor which we have used already in the same connection. Spearman stands well back from his subject-matter – he deals in total scores for groups of subjects, tries to discern the general sweep of the pattern, and is prone to resort to statistical 'corrections' when the pattern is blurred. Thus he regards as 'accidental errors' those irregularities which, at his distance from the events, spoil the pattern. And he can even call them 'accidental errors *of measurement*', although he allows them to be variations in the subject of study rather than in the testing instrument or in the tester. We, on the other hand, although we are entirely prepared to accept that for some purposes it may be desirable to discount these irregularities,[1] do not accept that this should be the end of the matter. We propose rather to take a much closer look at them – to try to estimate their extent and to see in what circumstances they chiefly arise. There would seem to be no reason why the two observational procedures should not complement one another.

There is, then, the possibility, when the number of subjects who begin to make an error almost balances the number who stop, that, over the interval between the two testings, there really is no trend in the responses of these subjects, but only an irregular fluctuation.

However, there remains a second possibility. Suppose that the cases of disappearance of a given error, X, occur because the subject has moved on to produce a correct answer, but that the *new* cases of error X occur because the subject has advanced to X from some more primitive error. One would then have a situation where absence of group trend arose because of overlapping individual trends – and therefore in no way indicated a lack of developmental progress over the period in question.

It follows that the evidence concerning changes in the occurrence of any one error cannot be considered in isolation from evidence concerning changes in the occurrence of other errors: the whole pattern has to be held in mind.

This may be easier to do if the raw data of *Table 2*, and later similar tables, are expressed as indices, and we propose to use three indices for this purpose. The first provides a measure of

[1] Sir Cyril Burt agrees that one's purpose must determine what one discounts. He says: 'The word "error" tends to suggest an antithesis between a "true" measurement and a measurement that includes a superadded "error-factor". It seems . . . that the real antithesis is between what is *relevant* to your purpose at the time and what is irrelevant. Thus my own definition of an error of measurement would be "that part of the measurement that is attributable to factors irrelevant to the quality or quantity I want to estimate".' (This is quoted by Clarke, Clarke, and Brown (1959) from a personal communication from Sir Cyril Burt.)

the amount of error which has occurred on both occasions combined; the second, a measure of the magnitude of change from one occasion to the other; and the third, a measure of the extent of preponderance of one direction of change over the other.

It will be recalled that column A in *Table 2* (page 54) records the number of subjects who made a given error on both occasions; B, the number who made it on the first but not the second occasion; C, the number who made it on the second but not the first; and D, the number who avoided the error both times. If, then, we put the sum of the entries in columns A, B, and C upon the sum of all four columns, we obtain the ratio of subjects who actually made the error to those who might possibly have done so. This gives the 'index of magnitude of error', or IME, with a range of from $+1$ to $0$.

Next, it is possible to ask: of those who did make the error, how many made it consistently (that is, on both occasions) and how many changed from one occasion to the next? We may answer this question by putting the sum of the entries in B and C upon the sum of the entries in A, B, and C, thus obtaining an 'index of magnitude of change' or IMC which, like the IME, ranges in value between $+1$ and $0$.

The third question concerns the direction of change and here we are interested only in the comparison of column B with column C. If we attach the minus sign to the entry in B and the plus sign to the entry in C, then add these algebraically and divide by their arithmetic sum, we obtain an index (the IDC) ranging in value from $+1$ to $-1$. Both extremes then represent a situation in which all the change there is occurs in one direction – that is, either column B or column C has a zero entry. Midway between the extremes, an index of direction of change of zero magnitude represents the position in which the entries in B and C are exactly equal – that is to say, where there has been as much change in one direction as in the other.

If we now carry out these three operations on the entries in *Table 2* we obtain the following results:

TABLE 3     GROUP O—PROBLEM A1

| Error | IME | IMC | IDC |
|---|---|---|---|
| (a) Incomplete elimination | ·47 | ·89 | −·50 |
| (b) Loss of hold | ·68 | ·62 | ·00 |
| (c) Arbitrary allocation | ·11 | 1·00 | −1·00 |
| (d) Failure to use solutions | ·11 | 1·00 | −1·00 |
| (e) Irrelevance | ·11 | 1·00 | −1·00 |
| (f) Difficulty with negative statement | ·32 | 1·00 | −·33 |

The IME is highest for loss of hold: 68 per cent of the children make this error at some point or another. On the other hand, only 11 per cent make errors (c), (d), and (e). The IMC is fairly high in all cases – that is, there is not a great deal of consistency from one occasion to the next. The IDC ranges between zero for loss of hold – which is to say that increase and decrease are exactly balanced – to the negative maximum for errors (c), (d), and (e), which is to say that in these errors there were no fresh instances on the second occasion.[1]

## The Subjects of Group Y

We have seen that the children in Group O, at the age of twelve and again at the age of fourteen, seemed to have a good general grasp of how they should proceed with this problem, though in the course of trying to put the procedure into effect they were liable to make errors of the kinds we have been describing. However, it is evident that if one goes down the age-scale one must sooner or later reach a point at which errors of a different sort begin to appear, for one can be confident that very young children will not have an understanding of the principles involved. We decided, therefore, to study next a group of ten-year-olds and see how their errors compared with those of the children of Group O.

---

[1] No significance tests have been carried out (see footnote to page 217).

Our aim was to choose, for inclusion in this second group, children who would be comparable in general level of ability to our first subjects. We had no group test results to help us in making the choice because the procedure for secondary school selection had not yet begun for children of the age we wanted to study; and we could not administer full intelligence tests to them in case there would be a practice effect which would give them an unfair advantage when, in a relatively short time, they did come to take the selection tests. We therefore decided to ask teachers in the four schools from which Group O had been drawn to pick for us children who, in their opinion, would have a reasonable chance of being admitted to academic courses in secondary schools but who would be unlikely to distinguish themselves academically. Since the 'borderline' intelligence quotient in Edinburgh is around 110, we thought this might give us a group rather like the first one. When we came to test Group Y, however, the range of ability seemed considerably wider than that in Group O; and when later we obtained group test intelligence quotients for the children from the local education authority, this impression was confirmed, the range being from 96 to 133 with a mean of 118.

There were twenty subjects in Group Y and their ages, when testing began, were between nine years nine months and ten years three months.

*Results: Group Y(i)*

All the errors which had been observed in Group O appeared again, and with frequencies quite similar to those obtained from the members of Group O on the first occasion, that is, when they were twelve years old (see *Table 5*, page 71). However, there were signs of new errors; also, some of the already familiar ones were more gross of their kind.

In particular, there were several cases of loss of hold of a more severe and persistent order than anything that occurred in the answers of the older children. And the error of one child, shown in *Table 4* (page 69) as failing to use his own solutions, seemed this time to be part of a more general difficulty in understanding how different pieces of information were to be combined.

This child's answer is of considerable interest because of the conflicting modes of procedure involved. He begins in what seems to be a very promising manner by offering spontaneously a statement of the principle of elimination.

*Robin:* 'Well, you look at the name of the boy and then you look at all the schools and then you look at all the schools again and then you look at all the names of the boys who are going to schools and the one who [which?] is left out is the one the boy will be going to.'

He then proceeds by elimination of North, South, and Central to deduce that Jack must go either to the East or to the West School. But at this point he hesitates and seems to be uncertain how to continue: he does not see, apparently, how to combine the positive statement about Dick with the negative information about Jack and so eliminate all but one possibility. After a pause the experimenter asks: 'How can you tell which one it is?' And Robin replies: 'You would have to find out the district he was in.' So quite suddenly he substitutes for consideration of the stated problem consideration of circumstances which he knows to operate in his own experience of living: he imports into the problem, as a basis for decision, his knowledge that in general children are sent to schools in districts near their own homes.

Here, then, we have something which did not occur in Group O – at least not in this problem. Compare with it now the following two answers, both from Group Y:

*Isabel:* 'Jack goes to North School. (Why?) Jack's name is the first on the list and North School is the first school. So Bob goes to West School, James goes to East School, and Tom goes to Central School.'

*Frank:* 'Is it Jack goes to number 1, Dick goes to number 2? (Well, no. Read the whole question.)' In spite of this advice, however, Frank proceeded to match boys and schools in the order in which the names were originally mentioned.

So here we have two children who act on the basis of an assumption which receives no support from anything that is stated in the problem and, indeed, involves the complete neglect of a large part of what is stated. Their basis of solution is different from that of Robin, but they have in common with him a failure to have scrupulous regard for the conditions of the task as set, and a readiness to introduce, quite arbitrarily, new conditions of their own devising, additional premisses to serve as grounds for their reasoning.

Why is this done? One answer which immediately suggests itself is that the child imports new bases for solution when he cannot handle those which are offered him. However, the evidence does not entirely support this explanation. One of the three children quoted, Isabel, proves to be quite well able to solve the problem in accordance with the information provided. After matching boys and schools by order of presentation, she suddenly exclaims: 'Oh! I've made a mistake – I wasn't bothering about that bit there.' She then proceeds in the correct manner, though making the error of incomplete elimination. Frank, on the other hand, apparently cannot envisage any other possible mode of solution. The experimenter asks him to try to find another way but he can see none. Between these two comes Robin with his partial understanding. It is true that Robin does seem to introduce extraneous considerations only at the point where he gets into difficulties. And, as we shall see later, there can be little doubt that difficulty in seeing how to deal with a problem increases the likelihood that the child will draw quite freely on his general experience or introduce some completely arbitrary assumption on which to act. On the other hand, this way of dealing with difficulty is not universally adopted. One might call it true by definition that the mature, intelligent thinker does not resort to this mode of disposing of his intellectual problems. So we have, at the one extreme, cases where a problem is not beyond the subject's power or even very hard for him (as proved to be true in Isabel's case) yet where extraneous considerations are introduced; and, at the other extreme, cases where they are never introduced even if all attempts at rigorous solution fail. It is possible that in the beginning the child introduces extraneous considerations because of a total failure to see them as extraneous, because of some radical lack of appreciation of the need for loyalty to the given; then avoids them except when he gets into difficulties; and then, if he ever reaches a sufficiently advanced stage, excludes them entirely.

The first draft of this last sentence contained the word 'finally' as a qualification of 'excludes them entirely'. The omission of the suggestion that change ceases when this point is reached is a consequence of certain studies of problem-solving in ageing subjects and notably of work done by members of the Nuffield Unit for Research into Problems of Ageing. Welford (1958) reports a study by Allan which is of the greatest interest in this connection. The subjects were presented with sets of statements and were requested in some instances to discuss the compatibility of the statements with one another, in others simply to draw whatever conclusions were justified. The subjects were allowed to take the statements away and return their answers several days later. Welford reports: 'The clearest finding that emerged from the results was that, although the older subjects seemed as capable as the younger of giving answers *of some sort* [his italics] to the problems, they did so in a different way. In particular, they tended not to draw logical deductions based strictly on the statements as given, but to introduce supplementary premises or to confine themselves to comments upon the statements.'

In trying to explain this finding, Welford considers two possibilities: that, as subjects age, their general experience becomes better organized and more firmly entrenched, and consequently they have well-established opinions which are liable to obtrude themselves to the point of interfering with the operations of logic; or, on the other hand, that there is some real decrease with advancing age in the ability to organize complex material. After reviewing some experimental attempts to control the effects of past experience, Welford tends to favour the second possibility. The evidence that the same kind of phenomenon is observable

66

in young children makes it clear at any rate that the first explanation is inadequate – unless one supposes the same behavioural manifestation to have different causes in the young and in the old. But the evidence that some children who prove quite 'able' to solve a problem logically still nevertheless fail to confine themselves to the given makes the second explanation seem a little unsatisfactory in its turn.

It was necessary to mention the studies of ageing at this point in our discussion. It will, however, be appropriate to defer further consideration of these issues until we report on our work with syllogisms and sorites and can present evidence more closely comparable to that which Allan obtained.

Meanwhile, it should be noted that, when a subject introduces some extraneous basis for solution, he may be said to be failing to adhere rigorously to the given, quite as much as when the lack of rigour involves simply leaving something out. Errors which consist in adding to the premises fall, then, into the arbitrary class.

It will be recalled that we said (page 48), '. . . the term "arbitrary allocation" will be used whenever a subject seems to decide among different possibilities in a way which involves the ignoring of part of the given of the problem and *which includes no attempt to justify the choice*'. The novel feature of the error exemplified in the answers of Isabel, Frank, and Robin is that an attempt at justification is made: some rule or principle is introduced. We shall therefore call this the error of 'arbitrary rule' to distinguish it from the type of arbitrariness which invokes no principle at all. It is not certain that this distinction is significant, especially since a subject who offers no justification may still possibly have some in mind. However, errors must be classified on the basic of what can be observed. If it later appears that we are here trying to draw a distinction where there is no important difference, it will be easy enough for the categories to be combined.

There remains for comment one further feature of the ten-year-olds' answers. Two cases of arbitrary allocation are listed in *Table 4*. There was a third case which might have been so

67

classified, but it seemed sufficiently different to have to be recorded separately. Here is the relevant quotation:

*Philip* (answering the question about Tom): 'Is it the South School? It's a guess because I can't quite work it out. (Why not?) There's a choice of North and South, and there's five boys and only four questions. So I'll have to make a guess.'

Now this is different from the other cases of arbitrary allocation which we have encountered, in that the child gives up deductive reasoning because he thinks the structure of the problem gives him no option. To be puzzled because there are five boys and only four questions is to fail to realize that one pairing is already directly given in the positive statement assigning Dick to the West School. (In fact Philip got himself into the position of being left with North and South as possibilities for Tom because he had earlier wrongly assigned Bob to the West School.) To believe, moreover, that the absence of a fifth question makes guessing necessary is apparently to confuse the functions of questions and premises. So the error may clearly be described as structural. One other child in the group also commented in some perplexity on the fact that there were five schools and only four questions, though he did not conclude that guessing was the only course open to him in such a situation.

*Results: Group Y(ii)*

When two years had passed from the time of their first testing, the subjects of Group Y were given the problem again. At the time of the second interview, then, they were twelve years old, that is, the same age as the subjects of Group O had been on the first occasion. So we have two groups, one seen at age ten and age twelve, another seen at age twelve and age fourteen.

*Table 4* gives the results obtained when the errors made by Group Y on the first and second occasions are analysed in the way that has been described (pages 53 ff.). When this table is considered in conjunction with *Tables 2* and *3* (pages 54 and 62) it is evident that the patterns are fairly consistent.

TABLE 4    GROUP Y—PROBLEM A1

| Error | A | B | C | D | IME | IMC | IDC |
|---|---|---|---|---|---|---|---|
| | (i) and (ii) | (i) not (ii) | (ii) not (i) | not (i) nor (ii) | | | |
| (a) Incomplete elimination | 2 | 8 | 3 | 7 | ·65 | ·85 | −·45 |
| (b) Loss of hold | 5 | 5 | 4 | 6 | ·70 | ·64 | −·11 |
| (c) Arbitrary allocation | 0 | 2 | 0 | 18 | ·10 | 1·00 | −1·00 |
| (d) Arbitrary rule | 0 | 3 | 1 | 16 | ·20 | 1·00 | −·50 |
| (e) Failure to use solutions | 0 | 1 | 1 | 18 | ·10 | 1·00 | ·00 |
| (f) Irrelevance | 1 | 3 | 0 | 16 | ·20 | ·75 | −1·00 |
| (g) Difficulty with negative statement | 1 | 1 | 3 | 15 | ·25 | ·80 | +·50 |
| (h) Expectation of five questions | 0 | 2 | 2 | 16 | ·20 | 1·00 | ·00 |

Column headers B, C, D span "Number of children making the error on occasions".

For loss of hold, all three indices are closely comparable in the two groups. IME is ·68 for Group O and ·70 for Group Y; IMC is ·62 for O and ·64 for Y; IDC is ·00 for O and −·11 for Y. In other words, over the whole range from age ten to age fourteen this error is very common, and, though there is considerable change from one occasion to the next, there is no sign of any trend in the direction of diminution. On the other hand, incomplete elimination, which shows still more variation in individual performance (IMC of ·89 for O and ·85 for Y), becomes less common in both groups on the second occasion as compared with the first (IDC of −·50 for O and −·45 for Y), and is, overall, less common among the older children (IME of ·47 for O and ·65 for Y).

For Group Y, as for Group O, the absolute frequencies of

occurrence of all the other errors are low, and we shall therefore defer further comment until we can observe the patterns of their occurrence in different problems. But the error of difficulty with the negative statement should perhaps receive some mention now, since it produces the only positive IDC that we have yet found. As will be seen from *Table 4*, three children in Group Y made this error at the age of twelve, not having done so when they were ten, as against a movement by one child in the opposite direction. The probability that this is significant is increased by the fact that, in other problems also, difficulty with negative statements has sometimes been observed to become more and not less common with rising age. The interpretation of this will be discussed fully later, in a context where more illustrative material is available (see pages 173 ff.). It seems to be an instance of the general principle that the occurrence of one type of flaw in reasoning may inhibit the manifestation of another, so that when the former is overcome, the latter for the first time appears. Two of the children who produced the fresh instances of difficulty with the negative statement had made arbitrary errors on the first occasion and thus had not then grappled with the full complexity of the given.

It is quite possible, although no other case of actual increase in error frequency was observed in Problem A1, that some of the falls would be steeper but for this same type of situation.[1] Thus incomplete elimination, for instance, is a possible error only when the problem is tackled in a way that is in principle correct. If the child acts entirely on some quite arbitrary hypothesis, such as that the order of naming is critical, then he will not attempt to eliminate at all and thus cannot make the error of doing it inadequately. Likewise, he cannot be guilty of irrelevance in the sense in which we have used the term here. The fact that one error can make the appearance of another less likely, or even logically impossible, considerably complicates the study of patterns of error with changing age. We shall call this phenomenon 'error replacement'.

Earlier in this chapter, before breaking down the error fre-

---

[1] See page 60 where this is discussed as a theoretical possibility.

quencies into the four columns used for calculating the indices, we gave the straightforward first- and second-occasion totals for Group O (*Table 1*, page 53). The corresponding figures for Group Y can easily be arrived at from *Table 4*; however, we now print them here, along with the figures from *Table 1*, so that a general indication of change in total frequency over the whole age-range is provided.

TABLE 5    P<small>ROBLEM</small> A1

| Error | Frequency of error among children in Groups | | | |
|---|---|---|---|---|
| | Y (i) (age 10) | Y (ii) (age 12) | O (i) (age 12) | O (ii) (age 14) |
| (a) Incomplete elimination | 10 | 5 | 7 | 3 |
| (b) Loss of hold | 10 | 9 | 9 | 9 |
| (c) Arbitrary allocation | 2 | 0 | 2 | 0 |
| (d) Arbitrary rule | 3 | 1 | 0 | 0 |
| (e) Failure to use solutions | 1 | 1 | 2 | 0 |
| (f) Irrelevance | 4 | 1 | 2 | 0 |
| (g) Difficulty with negative statement | 2 | 4 | 4 | 2 |
| (h) Expectation of five questions | 2 | 2 | 0 | 0 |

PROBLEM A2

We have seen that Problem A1, when given to ten-year-olds, produces a certain number of errors that clearly indicate failure to comprehend the structure of the problem, but still does not produce very many. Consequently, at this stage in the inquiry we decided to construct a new problem of the matching type, with the special intention of making a further study of errors of structure among younger children. For this purpose we made changes in two main directions: we reduced the number of pairs from five to three; and we altered the manner of giving information and asking questions in such a way as we believed would increase the difficulties of solution for any subject whose grasp of structure was imperfect. Thus we were deliberately trying to reduce the occurrence of errors of execution – for loss of hold and the like would seem to be rather evidently connected with the size of the 'mental field' to be dealt with (cf. pages 45 to 46) – and to increase the occurrence of errors of structure, the nature of which we hoped in this way to perceive more clearly.

Problem A2 was as follows:

Here are three boys:

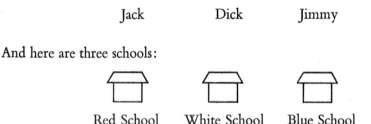

Jack          Dick          Jimmy

And here are three schools:

Red School    White School    Blue School

Each of the three boys goes to one of the three schools.

Dick does not go to Red School.
Jimmy does not go to White School.
Dick does not go to White School.

What school does Jack go to?    ——————
What school does Dick go to?    ——————
What school does Jimmy go to? ——————

It will be observed that this time the subject is told only that 'each boy goes to one of the three schools', not that each goes to a different one. So, strictly, the possibility that all three boys go to the same school is not excluded. This was done to see whether the children assumed a one-to-one matching situation, and it seemed to be the case that they did, even when their allocation of boy to school was quite arbitrary.[1] However, this feature of the problem gave rise to one instance of difficulty in interpretation of a kind not foreseen (see page 79).

When Problem A2 is compared with A1 in respect of the categories listed at the beginning of this chapter, it appears that:

(a) the content is the same, except that the names used have been changed;

(b) the number of pairs is reduced from five to three;

(c) the objects are represented diagrammatically instead of being merely named;

(d) all the information is negative, and it is not grouped helpfully as in A1 – the two negative statements concerning the same child are separated by the negative statement concerning the other child;

(e) the order in which the questions are asked does not accord with the order in which information is presented nor with the order in which information must be handled – indeed, the child about whom no information is directly given is the one about whom the first question is asked.

Each change was made with a particular effect in mind. The fact that all the information was negative would mean that the child had no comfortably safe starting-point in the shape of one pairing directly given, but must at once face the need to combine negatives; the fact that the information was not grouped for him would make this a harder task; and the fact that the order of questions did not correspond to the order in which solution must proceed would mean that he must actively organize the problem before he could begin at all. The reason for the reduction of pairs from five to three has already been mentioned. The change

---

[1] It is a question of some interest whether, in general, children assume that a problem is so 'tight' as to have only one solution. We have some other evidence, as yet unpublished, which suggests that they may find it very hard to admit the possibility of two equally correct alternatives. This attitude, curiously enough, can apparently coexist with arbitrariness of the kind already described. For present purposes, the assumption of one-to-one correspondence is not counted erroneous, though it is, strictly speaking, unwarranted.

of the school names was intended to serve the same purpose, namely, to render errors of execution less likely, for red, white, and blue are an easy trio to remember and manipulate. The diagrammatic representation was meant to contribute to this same end, but it also had a purpose different from that of any of the other changes. It was intended to place before the child a specific and rather powerful temptation: that of simply matching according to spatial proximity. It will be recalled that, using Problem A1 with Group Y, we noted a tendency to introduce bases of solution that had, strictly, nothing to do with the problem; and that one such basis offered was order of presentation while another was the nearness of the boy's home to the school. To add a diagram of the kind used in A2 was, in effect, to make matching on either of these grounds, or on both of them combined, very easy and tempting indeed. Thus A2 was designed not only to be structurally difficult, but also to invite a certain type of arbitrary error.

It might be argued that the introduction of the diagram is 'unfair' – a charge which raises an important general issue. To what extent in testing is one justified in setting deliberate traps?

There is first of all an obvious distinction to be made between the setting of traps in experimental studies and the setting of traps in finished tests which are actually to be used as instruments of assessment. In the former case there would seem to be no reason why one should not set traps if one thinks one can gain any information by so doing. In the case of a finished test there would obviously be need for more caution, and the following criterion (which is, indeed, only a special statement of the general criterion we would suggest for all test items) is perhaps reasonable: there should be evidence that walking into any particular trap is a significant error – or, in other words, that the question as set with the trap in it has higher status as an index than the question without the trap. That is to say, there should be grounds for claiming that falling into the trap is a relatively immature response and that the making of this response is importantly indicative of developmental level. The kind of thing which might 'catch out' an intelligent adult if he was 'off his guard' is what one would want at all costs to avoid.

In experimental work, then, one must set traps precisely in order to gain the kind of evidence which will enable one to judge how important they can be as indicators of development. It was mainly for this reason that the schematic drawings of boys and schools were included in Problem A2.

*Results: Groups S1 and S2*

Problem A2 was given to two supplementary groups: ten children aged between nine years ten months and ten years ten months (Group S1); and forty children aged between nine years eleven months and ten years ten months (Group S2). Unfortunately, these children were seen on only one occasion, so no evidence of change in error patterns is yet available for this problem.

The familiar errors appeared again but, as had been expected, there were also new ones. Here is an example of the kind of protocol which was obtained.

Michael reads the first question, which concerns Jack, looks puzzled and says, 'It's only about Jimmy and Dick', meaning apparently that only Jimmy and Dick are mentioned in the statements relating boys to schools. The experimenter asks: 'Can you not say which one Jack goes to?' Michael replies: 'He goes to Blue School. Dick goes to Red, I think, and Jimmy to White [that is, he is treating the negative statements as positives, though he read them aloud correctly] and that's the only one that's left – and [with scarcely a pause] there's another Dick – that's Dick and that's Dick. (Two boys called Dick?) Yes. (Which Dick is it asking about, then?) This one down here [the second statement about Dick]. (How do you know?) Because Jimmy doesn't go to White School, Dick doesn't go to White School. . . . I think I done it wrong. [At this point he seems to notice the negatives.] The top one. . . . If Jimmy doesn't go to White he'll go to Red. (How do you know?) If he doesn't go to White he'll go to Red. (How do you know he doesn't go to Blue?) Jack goes to Blue.'

In his new attempt to handle the negatives, then, Michael is still making use of a conclusion derived from his earlier treatment of the negatives as positives. He goes on immediately: 'Well, there's two Dicks and I'm just missing one out. (Which one?) The bottom one. [He writes down 'Dick goes to White, Jimmy to Red, Jack to Blue.] (What about the other Dick?) [He laughs.] I don't think he goes to any school.'

This protocol illustrates several tendencies that are of interest, but the most striking is the failure to regard the two statements about Dick as statements about one and the same person, a failure which makes the problem strictly insoluble on the basis of the information given. How is this failure to be explained?

It is plain, in the first place, that Michael understands the principle of combining positive statements so that allocation of 'the only one that's left' is possible. Equally, he appears to be able to use an earlier conclusion of his own in combination with other information to derive further conclusions. The great stumbling block for him lies in the combining of negative statements.

Yet to say merely this is to give an inadequate account of his difficulty. It is not simply that he fails to understand how, precisely, the statements are to be combined, as was the case when children made the error we have called 'irrelevance', or as seemed to happen in the answer given by Robin (quoted on page 64). The difficulty goes deeper than that. It would seem to be relevant to an understanding of it to notice in what way the combining of negative statements differs from the combining of positive statements so that the principle of elimination of all but one may be applied. The combining of negative statements involves grouping together two or more statements about one subject in order to draw a conclusion about that same subject. The combining of positive statements, on the other hand, involves grouping together two or more statements about different subjects in order to draw a conclusion about yet another subject. Michael can handle the latter operation, where one statement per subject is involved. But he is unable to handle the former, apparently because of a failure to envisage the possibility of being given two or more statements about one subject.

76

Now the expectation of only one statement per subject may result partly from habits acquired in the handling of positive information. It is probably relevant to Michael's belief in 'two Dicks' that he treats the negative statements as positives. He begins by assigning the boys to those schools to which he has been told they do not go. Naturally, this leaves him with a superfluous Dick. However, when he realizes his mistake and attempts to treat the negatives as negatives, he does not abandon his belief in the two Dicks. Also, in a protocol which we shall quote shortly, the 'two Dicks' appear momentarily although the negatives are treated as negatives throughout. Finally, a very similar error occurs in another problem where no negative information is involved at all (see pages 117 to 120).

Can any other explanation be offered of Michael's difficulty? We shall see later that there are widespread indications in children's thinking of a tendency to hold quite separate what are conceived as the elements or components of the problem, associated with a failure not only to perceive inconsistencies (though this also occurs, as might be expected) but to perceive consistencies – a failure to recognize that a given statement of relationship does not necessarily preclude all other statements of relationship involving the same object. Within the conditions of the matching problem, a positive statement of association does, of course, preclude any other positive statement involving the same objects. So if the child takes negatives to be positives, he is almost driven to the conclusion that 'Dick number 1' is not the same person as 'Dick number 2'. But there is an alternative route to this conclusion, namely, to fail to realize that what is true of a positive statement in this respect is not true of a negative one. A statement of dissociation does not preclude other statements of dissociation. However, if one thinks it does – or, perhaps better, fails to see that it does not – then again one may reasonably enough arrive at the conclusion that there must be two boys called Dick.

This conclusion, of course, involves contradiction of the opening statement that there are *three* boys, Jack, Dick and Jimmy. Here is a child who, on this ground, rejects the view that there are two Dicks, though she does not successfully resolve her difficulties.

*Inga:* 'Jack goes to the Red School, Dick to White, and Jimmy to Blue. (Why?) It says, "Dick does not go to Red, Jimmy does not go to White, Dick does not go to White". . . . I think the answer is given up here. [She looks at the drawings and hesitates.] It says it up on the top – Jack's on top at Red School.'

Thus Inga seems to realize that she should use the information provided in the three negative statements, but instead of doing so she falls back on the association suggested by the diagram. However, it seemed as if Inga vaguely thought that the statements and the pairing in the diagram were in accord, so the experimenter decided to try to make her face the contradiction:

'(But down below here it tells you Dick does *not* go to the White School.) Oh! Well, Dick goes to the Blue, because he doesn't go to the Red or the White. . . . Yes . . . Jimmy to Red because not to White, and not Blue because Dick goes there. So Jack – well, it says Dick here [pointing to the second mention of Dick] but I think it's just Jack – there's just one school left, so Jack must go to White. (What do you mean when you say, "I think it's just Jack"?) Well, Dick goes to Blue School, and there's another Dick – but he does not go to the White. (Another Dick? Do you mean there are two boys called Dick?) No – well, I don't think so. It says "three boys" and there's just three schools, and if there were two Dicks it would leave out Jack.'

So, in spite of the solution she initially offered, Inga shows a fairly good awareness of the need to pay regard to the stated conditions of the problem. And she treats negatives as negatives, even managing to combine them at one point and thus evidently treating Dick as one person. But her grasp of this is very insecure and cannot be fully maintained in the face of her very clear expectation that for each boy involved there will be one statement provided.

This expectation did not always lead to a belief in 'two Dicks' but could show itself merely in the form of surprised comment either on the fact that 'Dick is in twice' or on the fact that 'it doesn't say Jack in it'. Remarks of this sort can hardly be held to constitute error, though they presumably do indicate a weakness in understanding of the structure of the problem. Sometimes, however, awareness that one boy and one school are not mentioned leads directly, if it is unaccompanied by understanding of structure, to the following faulty reasoning.

*Barbara:* 'Jack goes to Blue. (How do you know?) Because Jack is not mentioned and Blue is not mentioned.'

So one finds, in the answers of the children of Groups S1 and S2, a cluster of errors, varying in their precise form, but all related apparently to difficulty in understanding that, when the information is negative, it may be necessary to provide more than one statement about any given school or boy.[1]

In addition, there were one or two cases where a child failed to bring negative statements into strong combination yet did not show any sign that he expected to have to handle one positive statement per subject – that is, did not treat negatives as positives, or speak of 'two Dicks', or link the boy not mentioned with the school not mentioned. Cases of this kind have been classified separately.

These errors, then, are clearly structural. It is true that they may involve some arbitrariness, as when Michael (page 76) says: 'I'm just missing one out.' But in this case there is a specific incomprehension of structure which forces the child into arbitrariness.

Arbitrariness of the more usual kinds was also found in the answers of these children. However, because the statement of the problem did not exclude the possibility that more than one child might go to a given school (cf. page 72), it was sometimes difficult to tell whether or not a child's answers contained an arbitrary error. Thus the statement that Jack 'can go to any one he wants' may be arbitrary; but it may be based on a recognition that the premisses do not in fact strictly establish a link between Jack and

---

[1] In spite of this, the findings obtained with Problem A1 show that, when the problem is presented in a way that offers fewer structural difficulties, the principle of elimination can be applied and negatives can be used in combination, with no evident difficulty, by children of the same age as these.

any particular school. So in such a case – there were two instances of this kind – no error has been recorded.

Incidental illustration of the error of arbitrary rule has already been given in the answer by Inga (quoted on page 78), and her basis for solution – namely, order of presentation – was the most common of the arbitrary type, as indeed had been anticipated when the problem was designed. However, two others were also observed:

*Janet:* 'Jimmy goes to White School. (How do we know?) Jack goes to Blue School and Dick goes to the Red one. (How do you know Jimmy goes to White School?) It's because of the size, he fits in the school. . . . Jimmy's the smallest and he fits in the smallest. Jack is medium and he will go. . . . I'm not sure. . . . I think he goes to the Blue. So that leaves Dick for the Red one.' It is not surprising that Janet was not sure, for the differences in size were extremely small.

Here is an even more extraordinary argument:

*Joyce:* 'Jack goes to White School. (Why is that?) Jack can't go to Red. (Why?) It's got Jack and the Red School underneath – it's a lower school. [This is a strange inversion of the more common reasoning.] (Why can't Jack go there?) He's too clever, I think. (What about Jimmy?) He goes to Red School. (Why is that?) He doesn't go to White School. (Why does he not go to Blue School?) He has only come out of his primary classes. . . . That's where all the people go when they pass their qualifying.[1] (How do you know that?) You wear a blue blazer at the High School. (Where do you wear a red blazer?) At ———— [the local primary school]. (What about the White School?) It's going to be ———— [she names the new Junior Secondary School].'

So Joyce endows the three boys with different levels of intelligence, identifies each school with one known to her, and allocates accordingly. However, it should be added that, at the beginning of her answer, which has not been quoted, she deduced quite correctly and explicitly that Dick goes to the Blue School because it says he does not go to the Red School or the White.

---

[1] The 'qualifying' is the secondary school allocation examination.

It was only when she got into difficulties subsequently that the other basis for reasoning was introduced and she began to invent details of the boys' lives and circumstances. She would fall, then, at the second of the three levels which we have suggested that it may be possible to distinguish (see page 66).

*Table 6* gives the error frequencies for Groups S1 and S2 combined, that is, for fifty children between the ages of nine years ten months and ten years ten months.

TABLE 6    GROUPS S1 AND S2—PROBLEM A2

| Error | Frequency of error |
|---|---|
| (a)  Incomplete elimination | 5 |
| (b)  Loss of hold | 7 |
| (c)  Arbitrary allocation | 4 |
| (d)  Arbitrary rule | 8 |
| (e)  Failure to use solutions | 1 |
| (f)  Irrelevance | 1 |
| (g)  Difficulty with negative statement | 1 |
| (h)  Expectation of one positive statement per subject | 12 |
| (i)  Failure to combine negatives (in the absence of any evidence of expectation of one positive statement per subject) | 2 |

These figures may be compared with those given in *Table 5* (page 71) in respect of Group Y(i), since the ages of the children are similar. When this is done, it appears that the frequencies of the executive errors are appreciably lower in the case of S1 and and S2 (for incomplete elimination, 5 cases in 50 as against 10 in 20; and for loss of hold, 7 cases in 50 as against 10 in 20), while for the arbitrary errors the proportions are roughly the same. The position in respect of the structural errors is a little more complex. The four errors which we classified as structural in considering the answers to Problem A1 – that is, the answers given by Groups Y and O – have not become more common. One, indeed, namely 'expectation of five questions', has vanished –

but this is simply because the structure of A2 renders it impossible: in A2 there are as many questions as there are pairs of terms. The other three errors occur less frequently, and this fact, considered alone, might seem to suggest that it was false to suppose that Problem A2 would invite more structural errors than A1. However, the relative infrequency of these errors is probably due to the fact that the increased demands made by A2 gave rise to the new cluster of structural errors which seemed to have as their common feature the expectation that each term would figure once and once only in a statement of relationship.

This, so far as our inquiries show, is the fundamental difficulty of principle which arises when children attempt to use information in order to establish a pairing of terms. Other errors arise either from some failure of 'loyalty to the given', in Bartlett's phrase, or from some lapse of immediate memory or attention which has the effect of introducing inaccuracy into the manipulations that have to be performed.

# CHAPTER 5

## Three-term Series Problems

THE NAME 'three-term series' was proposed by Dr. I. M. L. Hunter in 1957. The type of problem, however, is not new, having been studied as early as 1919 by Burt, and shortly after by Piaget.

As the term is used here, it will apply not only to the problems with which Burt, Piaget, and Hunter worked, but also to some others of very closely related kinds.

We define a 'three-term series problem' as any one in which, from information provided, the subject must assign absolute or relative values to one or more of three objects which stand in serial relationship to one another.

Let us take first an example of the type of problem which Burt used, namely:

Harry is taller than Tom.
Harry is smaller than Dick.
Who is tallest: Tom, Dick, or Harry?

Here the problem is to assign relative values – and it is with this type of problem that Burt, Piaget, and Hunter were concerned. Our definition includes also the assigning of absolute values. An example of a problem in which the latter task is set would be:

Harry is 5 foot tall.
Harry is 2 inches taller than Tom.

Harry is 6 inches taller than Dick.
What are the heights of Dick and Tom?

We have thus a distinction to draw between problems which are unquantified and admit only of determination of order, and those which in addition include information which makes possible the calculation of magnitudes.

There is a third, intermediate possibility: that of a partially quantified problem. For instance, the information given might be:

Harry is 2 inches taller than Tom.
Harry is 6 inches taller than Dick.

This is simply the quantified problem that has already been quoted, with omission of the information concerning the height of Harry. The 'anchor' is removed, so to speak, and in consequence one can no longer ask: what are the heights of Dick and Tom? However, one can put a question additional to those that can be asked where there is no quantification at all. As well as asking whether Dick or Tom is the smallest, one can inquire about the difference in height between Dick and Tom. One has enough information to determine fully not only the order of the three terms of the series but the size of the differences between them. The absolute values of the terms, however, are not known.

Notice that, in the statement of all three-term series problems, one term of the series must be mentioned twice. Following Hunter, we shall call this term the 'link' of the series.

Now, in all completely unquantified problems the link must be the middle term for order to be fully determined. If the link is one of the end terms, the unquantified information is inadequate to determine order. If we know that Harry is taller than Tom and that Harry is taller than Dick, we still do not know whether Tom or Dick is smallest. But as soon as there is even partial quantification, the link may be in the middle or at either end.

Taking account of both the position of the link and the measure of quantification, we have, then, five possibilities, which may be represented thus:

| | Link in middle<br>←— *x* —→ | Link at end<br>*x* =⟶ |
|---|---|---|
| *Unquantified* | $x > \ldots$<br>$x < \ldots$ (1) | — |
| *Partially quantified* | $x > \ldots$ by b units<br>$x < \ldots$ by c units (2) | $x > \ldots$ by b units<br>$x > \ldots$ by c units (4) |
| *Fully quantified* | *x* has value a<br>$x > \ldots$ by b units<br>$x < \ldots$ by c units (3) | *x* has value a<br>$x > \ldots$ by b units<br>$x > \ldots$ by c units (5) |

It is evident that each of these five basic types may be varied in a number of ways. One possibility of variation arises from the fact that any asymmetrical relationship may be stated in two ways: $x > y$ or $y < x$. Thus, in a problem of type (1), we may say:

Tom is taller than Dick.
Tom is smaller than Harry.

or we may express precisely the same relationships in the form:

Dick is smaller than Tom.
Harry is taller than Tom.

Hunter, who worked with problems of type (1), varied the statement of the problem systematically in respect of this variable, taking into account not only the actual form of the premisses but also the question of which premiss is stated first. In addition, he had regard to two other variables: the question asked; and the content of the problem. Here his variations were not exhaustive, as indeed for the second of these at least they could not possibly be. He used the two questions: 'Who is tallest?' and 'Who is shortest?' And he varied the content by using the relations 'taller–shorter', 'happier–sadder', 'warmer–colder'.

There are many other possible variables, for instance:

(i) whether it is stated at any point in the problem, as it was in all of Hunter's, that there are three terms involved (the significance of this will appear later – see page 120);

(ii) whether the terms are named in any introductory statement, such as: 'There are three boys called Tom, Dick, and
Harry'; and, if so, whether the names appear in an order
corresponding to that of the correct solution;

(iii) whether the link is actually named twice, or whether it is
referred to pronominally in respect of the second relation
in which it figures – for example, one might say 'Dick is
taller than Harry, who is taller than Tom'; or, 'Dick, who
is taller than Harry, is smaller than Tom'.

In quantified problems, even more possibilities arise. Computational difficulty can of course be varied. It is also possible to
provide multiple-choice solutions and, if this is done, the choice
of distractors offers the usual virtually limitless scope for variation.
The critical question is then whether the errors to which the
subjects are prone are or are not provided for. The importance
of this will be discussed later (see pages 109 ff.).

The problems which were used with Group O[1] were basically
of type (5), but certain further complications were added. Here
is one of the two problems in question:

### PROBLEM B2

Tom, Dick, and Harry are 3 boys. Dick, who is 5' 4" tall,
is 6 inches taller than one of the other boys and 2 inches
taller than the remaining one. Harry is taller than Tom.
Therefore:

(1) Tom is 5' 2" tall.
(2) Harry is 4' 10" tall.
(3) Harry is 5' 0" tall.
(4) Tom is 4' 10" tall.
(5) Harry is 5' 2" tall.

The subject is instructed to say which two of these 'solutions'
are correct.

[1] It will be recalled that in Group O(i) there were twenty children, aged eleven years
nine months to twelve years three months. In Group O(ii) there were nineteen of the
original twenty, now aged fourteen years to fourteen years six months.

Thus, in effect, a third statement of relationship (namely, 'Harry is taller than Tom') is introduced to resolve an ambiguity caused by the absence in the other two of a named object or 'referee', as Hunter would call the second term of such a relationship. Schematically, we have:

$$x > (y \text{ or } z) \text{ by b units}$$
$$x > (z \text{ or } y) \text{ by c units}$$
$$y > z$$

Before this problem was given, however, the children of Group O were asked to tackle another similar task, Problem B1, in which the final piece of information, $y > z$, was *not* provided. The subjects were told that one more piece of information was necessary for solution and were asked to say what it was. The exact statement of the problem was as follows:

### PROBLEM B1

We want to find out the ages of two girls called Jean and May. We know that a third girl, Betty, is 15, and that she is 3 years older than one of the two girls and 5 years older than the other. If we had one more piece of information we could calculate the ages of Jean and May. What is that piece of information?

*Results: Group O(i)*

The question in Problem B1, as it stands, at once divided the children into two groups: those who appreciated the nature of the task set them and those who did not. Some had difficulty in understanding that they were not being asked to discover the ages of Jean and May but only to say what additional information would be necessary before this could be done. Most of the children who understood what was required of them did not seem to have great difficulty in producing an adequate solution, though they differed in the ease and confidence of their explanations. The 'piece of information' can, of course, be given in a variety of ways. Thirteen solutions that were judged acceptable were received.

87

Here are some examples of them:

*Jean:* 'You need to know which is the youngest of the two.'

*Pam:* 'If they said one of them . . . I don't know . . . if they said one girl was the older.'

*Ruth:* 'What girl she was three years older than.'

*Moira:* 'We need to know which is which.'

Of the seven children who did not give acceptable solutions, two could not make any reply, one said that no more information was necessary, and the rest made suggestions such as that we would need to know 'the ages of Jean and May combined', or 'the age of one of the girls', which latter was disallowed on the ground that this was what the 'piece of information' was to enable one to discover.

When the problem in its initial form had been considered, each child was asked: 'If May is older than Jean, what are the ages of May and Jean?'

Twelve children were able to answer this question without error. Of these, nine had also been able to offer an acceptable statement of the missing piece of information.

In the answers to this second part of the problem, three types of error were observed. The first of these was the treatment of an asymmetrical relationship as if it were a symmetrical one. In this error, the statement that 'Betty is older than May' is taken as signifying that 'May is older than Betty'; just as 'John is the brother of Tom' might be taken, but correctly this time, as signifying that 'Tom is the brother of John'.

In saying that this error occurs we do not mean to assert that these twelve-year-old children 'really' think that if Betty is older than May, then May is older than Betty. All we are saying at the moment is that, in solving the problem, some of them act as if this were implied, and arrive at the conclusion that May is twenty years old and, similarly, that Jean is eighteen.

Two children reached these conclusions. Here their answers:

*Robert:* 'If it says she is three years older than May or Jean we would know [i.e. this is the missing information]. (Would it be enough if I said "May is older than Jean?") Yes. May would be [pause] twenty and Jean eighteen.'

So Robert does not invert the relationship in the first part of his answer, but only when he comes to carry out the calculation. The other child, however, has it turned round from the start:

*Susan:* 'You'd need to know which one was three years older and which one was five years older. (If May is older than Jean, what are the ages of May and Jean?) If May was older than Jean, May would be twenty and Jean eighteen.'

There was one instance where a child reached the conclusion that May must be twenty and Jean twelve, appearing to treat the 'five-year' relation as symmetrical and the 'three-year' one as asymmetrical. This may merely indicate that the child's conception of the relationship was poorly established and fluctuating; but it might possibly be a function of the order in which the names appear in the problem. That is, the child might establish some link between the first-mentioned age-interval and the first-mentioned name. If then, before being told that May is older than Jean, he had associated Jean with the three-year interval and could not dissolve this association, he would have to reverse the five-year interval in order to satisfy the requirement that May is older.

We have evidence from other problems of the importance of the order in which names are mentioned; and one child showed in this problem that he regarded the order as of some consequence. When he was given the first part of the problem, he managed to say that it would be necessary to know which girl was the older; but he then went on promptly to advance a theory as to which one would be the older, thus:

*John:* 'I think Jean is twelve because she comes first. When my aunt talks about my two cousins she says the older one first.'

So here once again we encounter the appeal to ordinary experience which at once makes the problem a 'real-life' one and introduces considerations other than those that constitute the given of the problem. The error, then, belongs in the category of 'arbitrary rule'.

Another error in the calculation of the ages concerned the

overlap of the two age-intervals: the fact that the three-year one is included within the five-year one.

Some children failed to appreciate this fact. In terms of the formal description which has been offered (see page 85), they may be said to have acted as if they were dealing with a problem of type (3), instead of with one of type (5), that is, as if the middle member of the series of three were the 'link' of the problem. Typically, in this error May is said to be twelve years old $(15 - 3)$ and Jean to be seven years old $(12 - 5)$. But variants are also observed. One girl, for instance, attempted the division of five into two and three, but that only led her further astray because it apparently caused her to allocate the two-year interval wrongly, making May two years younger than Betty instead of three years younger; and in spite of this attempt she then subtracted the entire age-interval from May's age to find Jean's.

There would seem to be two very different possible interpretations of this error. The first is that it is essentially structural in nature, related to a difficulty in envisaging one interval as contained within the other. On this view, it might prove to be related to the tendency which we have already mentioned (page 77) to hold separate and distinct the components of a problem, a tendency which is certainly pervasive.

On the other hand, this error might be related rather to what we have been calling loss of hold, what is lost on this occasion being the subject to which the statement refers. This would not be loss of hold strictly as defined in consideration of the errors in Problem A1 (see page 47), for no immediate contradiction of something which has been said is generally involved. But it might be a kindred phenomenon. In this case it would have to be considered an executive error.

It is certainly true, in a sense, that when the overlap error occurs the child has 'lost hold' of the subject of the relational statement 'is $x$ inches taller than. . . .' But he may have lost hold of this – or never have gained hold of it – because of a false expectancy, because he anticipates a non-overlapping structure or rather, perhaps, fails to envisage any other kind. It will be recalled that in the matching problems we found it necessary to discuss whether a child who makes certain sorts of error does so because he expects that the information given will consist of one statement per boy or school. If there is some such false anticipation, then it would seem that the error ought to be regarded as structural.

What evidence could help us to decide which is the correct interpretation? In the first place, we might use a problem which avoided some of the complications of B1 and conformed more closely to the basic type (5) model (see page 85), with the given stated in short, simple sentences, where the risk that the subject of the sentence will become detached may be expected to be less; and we could then see whether the 'overlap' error still occurred.

Or, again, we might compare problems where the link is one of the end terms of the series with those where it is in the middle, and see whether any evidence of peculiar difficulty with the overlap structure of the former can be obtained. If the trouble is purely executive, it should be just as likely to occur when the link is in the middle.

Problems of types (2) and (4) seem particularly suitable for this purpose. Their partial quantification makes it possible to ask the subject to say how big is the difference between the two terms other than the link, without putting him in a position where he can work out absolute values for these two terms. Thus he must find the difference by appreciating the overlap or non-overlap of the two intervals. To illustrate this point, consider the type (4) problem which has already been quoted in the course of formal description of the various types:

Harry is 2 inches taller than Tom.   (i)
Harry is 6 inches taller than Dick.   (ii)
What is the difference between Tom's height and Dick's height?

If the height of Harry were also given, which would turn the problem into one of type (5), then the difference asked for could be arrived at in one of two ways: either by direct subtraction of two from six as in the partially quantified version; or by the – for this purpose – indirect procedure of calculating the heights of Tom and Dick and then taking the difference between them.

Now, suppose that a child were failing to integrate statements (i) and (ii) above into a three-term series at all; suppose, even, that he were regarding the two separate mentions of Harry as references to two different boys.[1] Then, if he were dealing with a type (5) problem, he might still arrive at a correct statement of the difference in height between Tom and Dick. But this would not appear to be possible in the case of a problem of type (4). In the latter instance, only if the two statements are correctly integrated to form a series and the overlap is correctly appreciated would it seem possible to answer the question asked.

It looks, then, as though a comparison of type (2) with type (4) should be more revealing of the nature of overlap error as observed originally in problems of type (5), than would a comparison of type (5) itself with type (3).

This is, of course, a formal statement of arguments which were developed only as the investigation proceeded. Appendix I gives an account of the manner in which we came to appreciate the need for evidence involving the partially quantified problems and describes some further studies which support the view that the overlap error should be regarded as structural.

One further error in Problem B1 remains to be reported. It is an already familiar one: the error of arbitrary allocation. It will be recalled that one child began by saying that there was no other information needed to solve the problem. Here is the relevant extract from her protocol:

*Morag:* 'One is five years older than ... One must be ten [pause] and the other's twelve. (But what do we have to know?) We *do* know. (Tell me how old May is?) She's twelve. (How do you know she's not ten?) Oh! [Morag looked very surprised. Then, after a pause] You have to know which is three years younger and which five years younger. (Suppose you knew May was older than Jean?) Well, May must be twelve, then, and Jean ten.'

It is worth remarking that Morag made this same error in Problem A1. When, after the very direct questioning just re-

---

[1] We shall see later that this certainly occurs with unquantified problems.

ported, she acknowledged her error, her surprise seemed completely genuine: it appeared that she had indeed had no awareness of the possibility she had ignored.

We now go on to consider the errors made on the second type (5) three-term series problem (quoted on page 86). It is printed again here for convenience of reference.

### PROBLEM B2

Tom, Dick, and Harry are 3 boys. Dick, who is 5′ 4″ tall, is 6 inches taller than one of the other boys and 2 inches taller than the remaining one. Harry is taller than Tom. Therefore:

(1) Tom is 5′ 2″ tall.
(2) Harry is 4′ 10″ tall.
(3) Harry is 5′ 0″ tall.
(4) Tom is 4′ 10″ tall.
(5) Harry is 5′ 2″ tall.

The errors observed in the answers to Problem B1 all occurred again in this second problem, but here the multiple-choice solutions introduced an added complication. For instance, Ruth begins by saying:

'Find one [that is, a solution] you could take six inches off and get five feet four inches. That would be five feet ten inches – but it's not there!'

Her distress at this discovery was considerable. However, with some encouragement she tried again, as follows:

'Well, Harry is taller than Tom, so Harry is the one Dick is six inches taller than, so Harry is four feet ten inches. Then Tom would be five feet two inches.'

The initial error, then, arose from a difficulty with the asymmetry of the relationships, but the multiple-choice form of the question forced on Ruth a reconsideration. Notice, however, that in her second attempt, though she treats the Dick:Harry relationship as asymmetrical, she still fails to do this with the Harry: Tom relationship. 'Harry is taller than Tom' is not converted to

'Tom is smaller than Harry'. It is almost as if 'taller than Tom' is taken to imply 'further away from Dick', which of course it would imply if Dick were the smallest of the three, as Ruth originally envisaged him.

So Ruth manages to cling to her error and yet still find a solution among those offered to her. Here, by contrast, is the answer given by Betty:

'So Tom is smallest – that's four feet ten inches. . . two inches smaller than the remaining one – that's four feet eight inches. I must be wrong somewhere.'

But Betty was quite unable to see where she was wrong. Finally, she chose one solution – 'Harry is five feet tall' – but could not justify it. It was plain that the multiple-choice form had driven her to offer a solution with which she could not be satisfied.

There were a few cases where the subject's inability to reconcile the offered solutions with his own reasoning led to great confusion and final rejection of the former rather than the latter. Thus Moira reasons: 'If Harry is taller than Tom, Tom can't be five feet two inches tall – so number (1) is wrong. "Harry is four feet ten inches tall" is right. Number (3) is wrong. "Tom is . . ."' (What's the matter?) Harry and Tom can't both be the same, so that means number (5) is right because it's the only one left. [She showed no sign of recognition of the impossibility of Harry's being two heights at one and the same time, and seemed quite prepared to select (2) and (5). But the experimenter decided to question her further.] (Is that true, then?) Well, if Dick is five feet four inches and he's tallest, Harry must be four feet ten inches and Tom must be four feet eight inches [overlap] so there's only one of them right. So number (2) is true, but it's the only one.'

Some children were successful in establishing the sequence Dick–Harry–Tom, and appreciated that the gap between Dick and Tom was six inches. They then decided that Harry was two inches taller than Tom instead of realizing that he must be two inches smaller than Dick. We shall classify this as a variety of overlap error, leaving discussion of the reason for doing so until the results for Group O(ii) have been presented, since some of the relevant evidence was not obtained until the second occasion of testing.

The only error that was made in Problem B2, but not in B1, was loss of hold. And this occurred only once, when Alice, having concluded that Tom was four feet ten inches, talked a few seconds later of Harry's height as being four feet ten.

*Results: Group O(ii)*

When the children of Group O were given these problems two years and three months later, all of them could successfully provide the missing information in B1. In the second part of B1 and in B2, no new types of error appeared. *Table 7* (page 97) shows the pattern of occurrence of error on the two occasions. (See *Tables 2* and *3* on pages 54 and 62 where the same is done for the errors in Problem A1, and pages 53 ff. where the procedure is explained.) One new issue arises here, however, in connection with the manner of recording data. For the first time, we are considering a situation where the same subjects have attempted more than one example of a given type of problem – that is, we have the two separate three-term series, B1 and B2. In recording error changes from occasion to occasion, should these problems be treated separately or together? If a child makes a given error in B1 on the first occasion but not on the second, and the same error in B2 on the second occasion but not the first, should this be recorded as one entry in column A – that is, error made on both occasions – or, on the other hand, as an entry in column B in respect of Problem B1 and another in column C in respect of Problem B2? The second of these alternatives, which involves recording results for B1 and B2 separately, might seem, on the face of it, more detailed and therefore better. But if a child does make the same error on both occasions, even though in different problems, then it might be preferable not to record this as two movements in opposing directions. Also, the first procedure has in its favour that it lets one see clearly how many of the children were quite free of the error. The main shortcoming of the first procedure, on the other hand, is that it makes no distinction between a child who, on one occasion, makes a given error in one of the problems and another child who, on the same occasion, makes the same error in more than one of the problems: each will contribute one unit to the total. However, this objection can largely be met by the provision of a very little supplementary information.

It will be recalled that, when Problem A1 was discussed, tables showing total error frequencies were provided in addition to tables showing patterns of change from occasion to occasion. Now when only one problem is involved, these total frequencies can of course be arrived at from the tables of patterns of change. They were printed separately in the case of A1 only for ease of reference, for they provide no extra information. But when more than one problem is involved, and when patterns of change are based on treatment of the group of problems as a whole, then total error frequencies – that is, total number of *instances* of a given error – do involve additional information.

Consider the figures for overlap error in *Table 7*. These show that nine children (column A+column B) made this error in one or other *or both* of Problems B1 and B2 on the first occasion. But if we count the *instances* of occurrence of this error on the first occasion we discover that they add to eleven. This is because two of the nine children made the error twice – that is, made it in both problems. This can be deduced from the information given in *Table* 7 in conjunction with the further information about the total number of instances of error. Of course, if the number of problems being treated as a group were more than two, this supplementary information would not permit such exact deduction – certain alternative possibilities might be left open. However, a fairly good indication of the extent to which repetition of error was occurring would still be obtained without the provision of further excessively detailed tables. We therefore decided to adopt this procedure and, accordingly, *Table* 7 treats the problems as a group, and is followed by *Table 8* which gives total error frequencies.

TABLE 7    GROUP O—PROBLEMS B1 AND B2

| Error | A | B | C | D | IME | IMC | IDC |
|---|---|---|---|---|---|---|---|
| | Number of children making the error on occasions | | | | | | |
| | (i) and (ii) | (i) not (ii) | (ii) not (i) | not (i) nor (ii) | | | |
| (a) Asymmetry | 2 | 5 | 0 | 12 | ·37 | ·71 | −1·00 |
| (b) Overlap | 5 | 4 | 1 | 9 | ·53 | ·50 | − ·60 |
| (c) Arbitrary allocation | 0 | 4 | 1 | 14 | ·26 | 1·00 | − ·60 |
| (d) Arbitrary rule | 0 | 1 | 0 | 18 | ·05 | 1·00 | −1·00 |
| (e) Loss of hold | 1 | 0 | 1 | 17 | ·11 | ·50 | +1·00 |

TABLE 8    GROUP O—PROBLEMS B1 AND B2

| Error | Frequency of error on occasion | |
|---|---|---|
| | (i) | (ii) |
| (a) Asymmetry | 7 | 2 |
| (b) Overlap | 11 | 6 |
| (c) Arbitrary allocation | 4 | 1 |
| (d) Arbitrary rule | 1 | 0 |
| (e) Loss of hold | 1 | 2 |

Three of the errors in *Table 7* figure also in *Tables 3* and *4*. We can therefore consider whether similar trends appear. The three in question are arbitrary allocation, arbitrary rule, and loss of hold. In the case of the first two of these, we may certainly say that the tendency for few new instances of the error to arise on the second occasion is maintained in Problems B1 and B2, there being, indeed, only one such instance, while there are five cases of change in the opposite direction. Further, the IMC continues at the maximum value of 1·00 for both errors: that is, no child makes either error on both the first and the second occasions. The general picture is of errors which are diminishing in frequency quite sharply and consistently.

Loss of hold, on the other hand, has a pattern in *Table 7* which is rather different from that shown in *Tables 3* and *4*, the chief difference being that the IME is much smaller in *Table 7*: the error occurs much less frequently in the responses of Group O to three-term series than it did in either group in the matching problems. The IDC differs also; but since the IDC of $+1\cdot00$ in *Table 7* is produced by one isolated case of increase, it need receive no special consideration.

The two new types of error – that is to say, the two which occur in Problems B1 and B2 without having been observed in problems of type A, namely, overlap and asymmetry – both diminish in frequency from the first occasion to the second. In the case of difficulty with asymmetry of relationship, the IDC reaches the negative maximum, there being no entry in column C. In the case of overlap, one entry appears.

In the course of earlier discussion of overlap error (see page 94) a group of mistakes was included in this category with the promise that the reasons for their inclusion would be given when the results for Group O(ii) were presented. The relevant evidence is of the following kind.

The answer given by Betty to B2 on the first occasion has already been quoted. It involved an unambiguous overlap error: 'So Tom is smallest – that's four feet ten inches . . . two inches smaller than the remaining one – that's four feet eight inches.'

Compare with this Betty's answer on the second occasion:

'Dick is six inches taller than one of the boys. One of the boys must be four feet ten inches. [At this point she notices the offered solution "Harry is four feet ten inches" but she is wise enough to check that "Tom is four feet ten inches" is offered as well.] Harry is taller than Tom – two inches taller – so there is somebody who is four feet eight inches – no, two inches *taller*, five feet. Harry is five feet. Therefore Tom is four feet ten inches. That's number (3) and (4).'

Betty, on this occasion, begins with a full overlap error just as she did on the first occasion, and it is the attempt to correct this which leads to the final choice of solutions (3) and (4). But can we learn anything further from her second-occasion answer about the source or sources of her difficulty? The main trouble on a first inspection seems to be that the subject of the sentence is lost from view. The phrase 'two inches taller than' floats, subjectless, in a kind of void. How does this happen? Betty has advanced far enough to be able to hold open in her mind the initial possibility that *either* Harry *or* Tom is six inches smaller than Dick: 'one of the boys must be four feet ten inches'. The phrase 'two inches taller than' is then without a subject, precisely, it would seem, because she envisages no possibility except measurement of this two-inch interval from the point four feet ten inches, yet recognizes the uncertainty of allocation at that point. It does not seem to occur to her to return to the initial starting-point, Dick's height, and calculate the two-inch interval from there.

On this interpretation, the main difference between Betty's first- and second-occasion answers is that she has achieved a greater capacity for suspension of judgement, and this capacity enables her to reconcile her error with the multiple-choice responses offered her. But the fundamental error on both occasions is the same, and consists in failure to return to the link term of the series when the second calculation of interval has to be made.

One can then compare Betty's two solutions with the correct solution as follows:

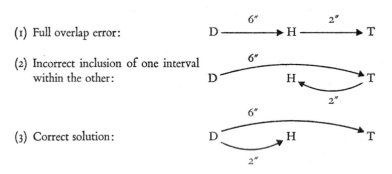

(1) Full overlap error:

(2) Incorrect inclusion of one interval within the other:

(3) Correct solution:

That is to say, in (1) the movement is from D to H, then from H to T; in (2) from D to T, then from T to H; and in (3) from D to H, then from D to T. Thus only in (3) is the necessary return to the initial point of departure made.

Now, from a study of the occurrence of these three solutions on both occasions, the following emerges: there are cases of movement from solution (1) above to solution (2), and from (2) to (3), and from (1) to (3); but no case occurs of movement in the reverse direction, except for the one already indicated in *Table* 7, which is an instance of movement from (3), the correct solution, to (1), the full error. It may be worth recording that this child succeeded in correcting his error, and made this comment:

'I hadn't read it properly . . . that the second one was two inches shorter. . . . I was thinking the second one was two inches shorter than the one who was six inches shorter than Dick. (What made you think that?) I am not sure.'

An interestingly similar comment came from Moira who, on the second occasion, reasoned as follows:

'Dick is five feet four inches tall – six inches taller than the taller one, which is Harry, so Harry is four feet ten inches. . . .'

This is a most explicit statement of the 'overlap error' interpretation of the problem. Moira, however, also corrects her error this time (cf. her first-occasion answer quoted on page 94), explaining: 'I thought he was six inches taller than Harry and he is only two inches taller than Harry.' Asked what made her think this, she replied:

'I think it was because I didn't read it properly. (How did you read it?) I understood that Dick was six inches taller than Harry and Harry was six inches taller than Tom. (And Harry was six inches taller than Tom?) I mean two inches taller than Tom. (How did you find it out?) I read it over again.'

So are we in the end to decide that overlap error is due to a misreading? Even if we do, we leave the question of the nature of the error still unresolved. Whenever there is failure to grasp the relationships involved in a problem there has, in a sense, been a 'misreading'. However, it does not follow that whenever there is a misreading there is a failure to comprehend the relationships: this depends on the nature of the misreading.

It might be said, in comment on the two protocols just quoted, that the two children 'did not understand the question'. Certainly they did not; but the question is whether their misunderstanding was the result of a brief failure to attend – perhaps some incapacity of the nervous system to 'hold' all the information in the sentence for a sufficient length of time – or whether it arose rather from a difficulty in conceiving the appropriate system of relations. Is the difficulty one of interpreting – making sense of – the information, or simply one of holding on to it long enough for the necessary manipulations to be performed?

When a given misreading persistently arises, this in itself suggests that the trouble is of the former kind. Loss of hold, as we observed it in the matching problems, gave rise to no predictable wrong steps or wrong conclusions. When it occurred it was at various points, and with various consequences for the course of the reasoning, and this seems to be fully in accord with what we conceive to be its nature.

In view of these considerations, then, and on the evidence which we have so far presented, there would seem to be grounds for thinking that the overlap error is due to a false expectation, a 'set' to perceive something other than what is there. As has already been stated, Appendix I contains further supporting evidence derived from the study of younger children and the use of problems of less complicated sentence form.

The final quotation from the results for Group O(ii) is in illustration of the asymmetry error. We include it because it is again very explicit. Ruth reasons as follows:

'Dick is five feet four inches and it doesn't say anything about two inches smaller, so number (1) [i.e. the first multiple-choice solution] is not true. Number (2) . . . Dick is five feet four inches and it says "Harry is four feet ten inches" . . . but it doesn't say anything about six inches smaller so that one's not true. [She works through all the choices offered in the same manner.] (What do you think the answers ought to be?) One would be five feet ten inches and the other would be five feet six inches.'

Ruth was then encouraged to represent the heights schematically on a piece of paper, and was questioned as follows:

'(If I said that you were taller than another girl in your class, who would be the taller – you or the other girl?) Me. (If I say that Dick is taller than the other boy, who would be taller?) Dick. (Who's the tallest in your picture?) The other boy. (What do you think has happened?) [Long pause.] It's Dick who is six inches taller than one of the boys and two inches taller than the other one. (Who did you think it was?) [To this question there was no reply.]'

Ruth's failure, then, is a failure to realize, within the context of this problem at any rate, the equivalence of the statements 'Dick is taller than Harry (or Tom)' and 'Harry (or Tom) is smaller than Dick'. She does not realize that 'taller than' and 'smaller than' are alternative ways of describing the same relation: that, with appropriate interchange of subject, the statements are in fact interchangeable. So since the expression 'smaller than' is not used, she must add to Dick's height to find the heights of the other two.

*Results: Group Y(i)*

The next stage in the inquiry, as with the matching problems, was to give B1 and B2 to a group of ten-year-olds. The composition of this group, Group Y, has been described (page 62). The results of giving Problems B1 and B2 to this group will now be examined.

The first point to notice is that, in comparison with the results of Group O(i) and, *a fortiori*, of Group O(ii), there is a substantial increase, among the younger children, of difficulty with the first part of B1: the discovery of the missing piece of information that is necessary for solution. Only six children in Group Y(i) were able to supply this without help; whereas of the thirteen in Group O(i) who are reported (page 87) as having produced an adequate statement, only one had had any help in doing so. More help was given to the younger children because the difficulty many of them experienced was very evident, and if they had been left feeling totally confused this might have had a harmful effect on their handling of the problem that followed. Even with considerable assistance, however, seven of them were unable to state adequately what further information would be required.

Here is an example of the incomprehension encountered:

*Alex:* 'One must be ten and one is twelve. What other piece of information? I got their ages but I can't get a bit of information. No, I don't get it. (Well, which one is twelve and which one is ten?) [Pause.] If Jean is twelve . . . [pause] Jean is twelve and May is ten. (Why?) [Pause, then he read the question in a whisper.] It says that she is three years older than one and five years older than the other. Well, the first one will be Jean and the second May. (Why will the first one be Jean?) [Pause.] I'm stuck. (Can you really tell who is older?) You would have to know which was the first person.'

Does Alex regard 'first' and 'oldest' as synonymous in this context? It looks as though he does; and, if so, he is not alone. Five other children were ready to assume that one or other girl was the older and, of these, three explicitly based their decision on the order in which the names were mentioned. (It will be recalled that there was one solitary indication of a tendency to do this in Group O(i) – see page 89.) Thus Robin, having decided that Jean is eight and May is seven, is asked:

'(How do you know that it is Jean who is eight? Why isn't it May?) Because she [i.e. May] is younger than the other two girls. (But how do you know?) Well, I thought it would be Jean since she's the first girl.'

Robin's calculation of eight and seven as the ages of the two girls may seem very curious to the adult eye. Here, to show how he arrived at this conclusion, is the earlier part of his protocol:

'[Long pause.] You could add the two ages, the five and the three, and then once you had got the two ages, you could subtract from fifteen. And that would make one of the girls older than the others. (And how do you do it that way, Robin?) Well, you know that one of the girls is fifteen, and it tells you that one girl is three years *younger* than Betty, and the other girl is five years younger [note that he does not specifically say 'than Betty'], and if you add these two you get seven – (You get seven?) – *eight*, and eight from fifteen is seven. (What then?) And the one who is five years younger will be seven and the one who is three years younger will be eight.' He then went on to the arbitrary assigning of age eight to Jean and seven to May which has already been reported.

So Robin is conscious of the asymmetry issue and able to handle it nicely – notice his emphasis on the word 'younger'. But the calculation of the intervals between the terms of the series defeats him entirely.

His initial idea about adding 'the five and the three' and sub-tracting the sum from fifteen is, of course, strongly reminiscent of overlap error. Robin, like most of the children who made the overlap error in Group O, thinks that this gives him the age of the youngest child – that is, the terminal member of the series. But he then comes to the curious conclusion that the total which he has just subtracted can itself be taken as the value of the middle term. Let us look back now to a protocol from Group O(i) which has not yet been quoted. Here is Brenda's attempt:

'You have the three years and the five years, and you add them and that gives the years of the difference between them. Then take the eight from the fifteen and you get seven. Find three years off seven – no! . . . Then take the three from seven and the five from seven – you'd have four and two. (And then what?) Then you've got to fix out which age is Jean and which May.'

Brenda, in fact, subsequently went on to do still more sub-tracting, but the main point of resemblance to Robin's protocol emerges from what we have quoted. Notice, incidentally, that starting from the value seven, once she had arrived there by this curious process of addition and subtraction, Brenda made a perfectly good 'overlapping' calculation. (However, in Problem B2 she made a quite typical overlap error.)

And now here is another example from Group Y:

*Jane:* 'If Betty was five years older than the other and three years younger, take five and three and add them, which gives you eight.

Well, if May was older than Jean she must be eight. Then Jean was three years younger, take three from five (sic) and that gives you two.'

These errors are puzzling, but the most probable interpretation of them would seem to be that they are, once again, forms of overlap difficulty. The addition of the two intervals is strongly suggestive of this. Indeed, the 'classical' overlap error solution could be arrived at in precisely this way, if the age thus calculated were taken as that of the youngest girl and the intermediate age subsequently calculated by subtraction of five years from the age of the oldest. But, of course, to take this last step would be to go back to the point of departure which, we have suggested, is precisely the difficulty which lies at the source of overlap error. Suppose, then, that a child, envisaging the two intervals without appreciating the inclusion of one within the other, proceeds, instead of subtracting first one and then the other, to add them and subtract the total,[1] what is his next move to be? If he cannot go back to the point of departure, he must move on from where he is: either 'upward' or 'downward'. But, naturally enough in these circumstances, the precise nature of the move he should take is likely to perplex him; and the variety of different moves we have just observed is not surprising.

Robin, whose first-occasion answer has been quoted (page 103) was still making this kind of error two years later and was very explicit about it. Here is what he says:

'Betty is fifteen and she is eight years older than one – *five* years older than one and three years older than the other. And that makes eight and you subtract them – fifteen from eight and you get seven. And then you add on the two years for the . . . [pause] and that'll make it nine. (Why do you add on two?) One's two years older than the other. (How do you know to add the five and the three in the first place?) It says that Betty is fifteen and that she is three years older than the one and five years older than the other. (So how do you know to add the five and

---

[1] He may even have been taught that if one has two figures to subtract in succession, this is often a good way to proceed.

the three?) If you want to find the youngest girl.'

One other case from Group O(i) provides evidence which can now be seen to bear on this issue. Mary concluded that Jean was seven, while May could be either twelve or ten. When she was asked to explain why May could be either twelve or ten, she said: 'She'd be either five years or three years older than Jean.' It appeared that she had first calculated the age of one girl by subtracting the combined intervals, three and five, from the age of the eldest; and then, instead of finding the age of the third one by further subtraction, either from the initial starting-point or from the point she had then arrived at, she had attempted to proceed upwards, but did not know how the eight years should be divided – that is to say, whether it was three or five that she should add on.

There is, then, in problems of this kind a whole complex of errors, of which the distinguishing characteristic is failure to return to the starting-point for the second step in the calculation. We can classify them according as:

(i) the first move is to subtract one interval only, or both added together;
(ii) the second move is upward or downward from the point thus reached.

Combination of these two criteria gives four classes, as follows:

|  |  | First Move | |
|---|---|---|---|
|  |  | *Subtract one interval* | *Subtract two intervals combined* |
| Second Move | 'Upward' (*add*) | a | b |
|  | 'Downward' (*subtract*) | c | d |

Instances in all four of these categories have been observed.

One may add that, theoretically, if the overlap error were combined with asymmetry difficulty, this whole set of relationships might be reversed or, so to speak, mirror-imaged, the first move being to add instead of subtract, and so on. But this combination of errors did not occur in the answers of any of our subjects.[1]

One more comment must be made before we go on to consideration of Problem B2. It concerns Brenda's protocol (quoted on page 104). According to the classification we have just proposed, Brenda made an error of type *d*, which is perhaps the most gross of the four, in the sense that the solutions finally arrived at are most glaringly in conflict with the data of the problem. Yet, as we pointed out, Brenda performed a flawless calculation once she took as her point of departure seven instead of fifteen. This underlines the danger of asserting, on the sole basis of a child's failure to carry out a certain task, that the child is *unable* to carry it out.

Problem B2 is, for most children, more confusing than B1, the difference between the problems being more marked among the ten-year-olds tested than among the older children. Some of the members of Group Y had extreme difficulty with B2, and some interpreted the problem in ways that appeared very puzzling.

Here, for instance, is the answer given by Isabel:

'Tom must be bigger than Dick because he [?] is the one who is left out. When you add them [?] up, they must both be the same height. (Why?) [No reply.] Have we to find *all* the boys' heights, or just Harry and Tom? [The experimenter explained again that two statements among the five offered were correct and she was to find these two.] Dick must really be tallest. [Pause.] Number (5) because Harry is the tallest; and number (4).'

So Isabel chose the correct solution, but with how much understanding is far from clear. The opening argument is puzzling. What is meant by 'the one who is left out'? Is this a reference to the fact that Dick's name does not appear among the solutions offered? But, if so, how can it be thought to follow that Tom must be bigger than Dick? Also, *who* will be the same height when *what* is added? We have no basis for answering most of

[1] See, however, Appendix I, page 232.

these questions and can only say that Isabel obviously begins by entertaining some very curious notions. The question 'Have we to find *all* the boys' heights . . .?' does, however, suggest that Dick is indeed the 'one left out' and that it is his omission from the list of solutions that is being noted. This view is further supported by the fact that one or two other children made specific attempts to calculate Dick's height.

Thus, Frances:

'Have I to find out which one is five feet four inches? (Just read it and see.) [Pause.] Dick is six inches taller than one boy and two inches taller than the other. I'm trying to figure out this bit: "Harry is taller than Tom". What is it for? (Whose heights are you trying to find out?) Tom and Dick. I can't get this one at all!'

And Sheila:

'[Long initial pause.] Well, I'm trying to get the height of Dick. (Well, you know how tall Dick is, don't you?) Yes. Five feet ten inches. (Why is he five feet ten inches?) Well, he's five feet . . . four inches tall . . . Well, he's six inches . . . oh! [With decision.] He's five feet four inches, and he's six inches taller than one of the other boys. (So what do you know?) That one of the boys is four feet ten inches. (Good.) And two inches taller than the other boy . . . so one boy is four feet eight inches.'

Thus we end with the familiar overlap error in its most straightforward form. But what of the initial error: the attempt to find the height of Dick when this is in fact given and forms the indispensable starting-point of the problem?

To the child who does not understand this, the problem must seem confusing beyond all possibility of establishing order. Failure to understand it is possibly associated with the difficulty of the sentence structure, the fact that the critical information is given in a relative clause. Perhaps the relative pronoun is being treated as interrogative: '*Who* is five feet four inches tall?' Frances, it will be recalled, begins by asking: 'Have I to find out which one is five feet four inches?' This misunderstanding appears to account also for part of the confusion shown by Jane. Here is her answer:

'Tom and Harry. [That is, instead of giving the heights of Tom and Harry, she simply gives "Tom and Harry" as her solution. Asked to say which of the multiple-choices she selects, she goes on] Numbers (1) and (5). (Why do you choose these?) Because five feet two inches is nearer to five feet four inches. (How do you know this is the answer?) If he [?] was six inches taller, that would be five feet eight inches. And you've to take two inches away, so that would be Tom and Harry, because they're nearest to the five feet four inches. (How about this part here: "Harry is taller than Tom"?) [Looks surprised.] I've made a mistake. (You've made a mistake here – Tom and Harry are the same height, aren't they? Well, see if you can do it again so that Harry is taller than Tom.) [Pause.] Number (5) first and number (1) second. Because if you take five feet four inches and add on six inches that's five feet ten inches. Take away two inches, that's five feet four inches. Well, there's three Harrys and only two Toms, and I think it'll be Harry first and Tom second.'

The fact that Jane begins by saying simply 'Tom and Harry' suggests strongly that she is trying to answer a question in the form: 'Who is . . .?' It is reasonable, then, to interpret her later references to heights that are 'nearest to five feet four inches' as attempts to answer the question 'Who is five feet four inches?' in a situation where none of the choices open to her can be regarded as satisfactory. In other words, if she is not told who is five feet four inches she will take the next best solution. Later in her answer there are also signs of difficulty with asymmetry, as shown by her attempts to add six inches to five feet four inches, and once again the distractors do not include appropriate solutions. If these interpretations of Jane's errors are correct, the confusion in her answer may well result from her attempts to reconcile her thinking with the possibilities that are offered to her.

Now the advantages of a multiple-choice item from the test constructor's point of view are very obvious. The main one, of course, is that it makes possible the unambiguous determination of the rightness or wrongness of a solution; and this is convenient, to say the least, when tests are being scored. But there are certain disadvantages, some of which are illustrated by the answer we have just been considering. In general, we may say that, if it is any part of the tester's aim to know what kind of incomprehension or incompetence lies behind a given wrong solution, or if it is his aim to be reasonably certain that the desired comprehension and competence lie behind a given right one, then multiple-choice items have some very serious drawbacks. The inclusion of at least five choices in these items has been advocated – and is the practice in most reputable tests nowadays – on the ground that this number is sufficient to keep within bounds the occurrence of right solutions behind which comprehension and competence do not lie, these being identified with successes which a candidate might gain by chance alone.[1] But we are not dealing with beings who habitually solve problems by guesswork when they cannot solve them by flawless reasoning. We are dealing with beings who make very persistent 'efforts after meaning' – to borrow Bartlett's phrase – and equally persistent efforts after justification. It is false to suggest that the young child is not concerned to justify his reasoning. He does this frequently in very arbitrary ways, accepting the 'strait-jacket' of the problem situation very much less readily that the adult, as we have seen. But his wrong solutions are not for the most part the result of guesswork – they are the result of positive errors, and are not merely indicative of an absence of understanding.

What, then, of the use of multiple-choice items to test a being who makes errors and is, on the whole, unlikely to 'guess'? How can we deal in this case with the possibility of his getting right solutions for wrong reasons? The answer is that this can be done to some extent in items of multiple-choice form if their constructors are equipped with enough information to provide solutions that correspond to the errors which those for whom the test is intended are likely to make. But if a subject is prone to make an

---

[1] This emphasis on guarding against *chance* success is consistent with the failure on the part of theorists of test construction to pay a great deal of attention to the nature of the alternative choices offered. If one is guarding against chance success, any four wrong solutions will do.

error for which no appropriate solution is provided, then anything at all may happen, and all sorts of curious arguments may be produced in order that some solution may be arrived at and justified.

In the case we have been considering, Jane was not led by her confusion to choose the fully correct solution. But she *was* led to choose one part of the correct solution, this being presumably judged 'next best' to the solution she was searching for and failing to find. Now if, for some reason, the correct solution seems 'next best' to the one to which the child's reasoning leads him, then it will be chosen not randomly but systematically. And in this case no mere proliferation of other distractors will prevent 'the right solution' for the wrong reasons. This can only be prevented – or reduced to a minimum – by a careful inclusion of the critical distractors.

To this argument, test constructors of the traditional school will probably reply: 'But if the right answer is being chosen for the wrong reasons by an appreciable number of children, our procedures will show that something is wrong with the item and will lead us to reject it'.

This is true. But there are two further comments to make. The first concerns the word 'appreciable' and raises the question of whether it is held to 'matter' if the tests are inaccurate in a few cases, provided that, on the whole, they 'work'. We would only say that it does not seem to us satisfactory to be content with this rough success if greater precision is by any means possible. The second comment is closely related to this first. It is true that, if many children choose the right solution for inadequate reasons, current item-selection procedures – which would really be better described as 'item-rejection procedures' – will show that 'something is wrong'. But they will not show what is wrong. And while they may lead to the exclusion of an item from the finished test, they cannot lead to its improvement and ultimate retention, which may be most unfortunate if the item is potentially of value. We are here illustrating and reiterating our earlier contention that what is needed is study which will provide the test constructor with the kind of understanding which can lead to the construction of better tests than could be made before.

If multiple choices are to be used, then, they should offer the solutions to which the main systematic errors lead. Problem B2 is, by this criterion, a faulty question, since it does not provide either for overlap or for asymmetry errors: these simply were not envisaged when it was constructed.

Here is another protocol which illustrates this fault in B2 very simply and clearly:

*Alex:* 'If Harry is taller than Tom, take Harry first. Mm. There's three Harrys! [That is, he begins by enunciating the requirement that Harry is the taller of the two. Then he surveys the solutions offered.] Tom must be four feet ten inches. Numbers (4) and (5) are correct. (Why?) Well, Harry is taller than Tom, so Tom can't be five feet two inches. . . . Harry is two inches taller than Tom [puzzled tone] and that's four inches taller. . . .' So Alex thinks the 'two inches taller' is a statement of the relation between Harry and Tom, not of that between Dick and Harry, a belief which is typical of the children who make overlap error. His choice of the correct solutions is therefore not based on full understanding, and he is himself puzzled by what he sees as an inconsistency which he cannot avoid. (He could, of course, have avoided it by choosing 'Harry is five feet and Tom is four feet ten inches'.)

The protocols quoted illustrate difficulties and confusions of an order not encountered among the older children, but otherwise the errors made by Group Y on the first occasion were of the sorts we observed in Group O.

### Results: Group Y(ii)

*Tables 9* and *10* show how the errors made by Group Y on the first occasion relate to those made by the same children two years later.

If *Table 9* is compared with *Table 7*, which shows the changes in these errors that occurred between the ages of twelve and fourteen, it will be seen that the pattern looks less regular in the case of the younger than of the older age group. In *Table 7*, every

TABLE 9     GROUP Y—PROBLEMS B1 AND B2

| Error | A | B | C | D | IME | IMC | IDC |
|---|---|---|---|---|---|---|---|
| | Number of children making the error on occasions | | | | | | |
| | (i) and (ii) | (i) not (ii) | (ii) not (i) | not (i) nor (ii) | | | |
| (a) Asymmetry | 1 | 3 | 3 | 13 | ·35 | ·86 | ·00 |
| (b) Overlap | 2 | 6 | 4 | 8 | ·60 | ·83 | −·20 |
| (c) Arbitrary allocation | 1 | 7 | 1 | 11 | ·45 | ·89 | −·75 |
| (d) Arbitrary rule | 0 | 2 | 3 | 15 | ·25 | 1·00 | +·20 |
| (e) Loss of hold | 0 | 2 | 1 | 17 | ·15 | 1·00 | −·33 |
| (f) Attempt to calculate value of link term | 0 | 4 | 0 | 16 | ·20 | 1·00 | −1·00 |

TABLE 10     GROUP Y—PROBLEMS B1 AND B2

| Error | Frequency of error on occasion | |
|---|---|---|
| | (i) | (ii) |
| (a) Asymmetry | 4 | 5 |
| (b) Overlap | 10 | 6 |
| (c) Arbitrary allocation | 8 | 2 |
| (d) Arbitrary rule | 2 | 4 |
| (e) Loss of hold | 2 | 1 |
| (f) Attempt to calculate value of link term | 4 | 0 |

IDC is negative – except for the loss of hold error, of which there is only one isolated instance – and the negative values are high, reaching unity in two cases and ·6 in the other two. *Table 9,* on the other hand, reveals a greater and more widespread tendency for children to make on the second occasion an error which they did not make on the first.

One error, however, did vanish completely when Group Y was tested for the second time, namely, the error that does not figure at all in *Table 7*: 'attempt to calculate the value of the link term'. Some of the ten-year-olds, it will be recalled, revealed that they had a very imperfect grasp of the structure of B2 by setting out to find the height of Dick when that height was already given.

Now it is plain that, so long as this degree of incomprehension exists, the overlap error cannot occur. A child who is unable to identify the link term of the series cannot make the error of failing to relate the other terms to it in the correct way. If he cannot even find the 'point of departure', then he cannot make the error of failing to return to it. So it is interesting, in relation to these theoretical considerations, to discover that, of the four children who made the overlap error at age twelve, not having done so at age ten, three were recorded as having, at the earlier age, made the error of attempting to calculate the value of the link. Thus what looks in *Table 9* like a somewhat irregular fluctuation of the overlap error is produced by the imposition of one pattern upon another. And so at age twelve, for some children, the occurrence of overlap error represents progress, by comparison with their performance at age ten. This is yet another exemplification of the principle, stated earlier, that the occurrence of one error may prevent the occurrence of another one. This principle cannot be invoked, however, to explain the three fresh instances of difficulty with asymmetry, all of which occurred in Problem B1. One of the three children solved B1 with no errors at all on the first occasion. The other two made errors, but not of a kind to render impossible the occurrence of asymmetry error.

It will be observed that loss of hold continues to be infrequent as an error in three-term series problems, but that it behaves much as it did in the matching problems with respect to trend. There is no clear sign in any of the tables so far of any tendency for it to diminish – or to increase.

PROBLEM B3

At the beginning of this chapter we discussed the formal structure of three-term series problems and pointed out that degree of quantification is one of a number of possible ways in which these may vary. The experimental results that have been reported so far were derived from work with fully quantified problems. We now go on to discuss the results obtained when unquantified problems were given to the children of Group S2: that is, to forty children with ages ranging from nine years eleven months to ten years ten months.

As we have seen already, certain variations in the form of unquantified three-term series problems arise by virtue of the fact that any asymmetrical relation may be stated in two ways: 'A is greater than B' (A>B) or 'B is less than A' (B<A). It follows that, when two such relations are combined to form the premisses of a three-term series problem, this may be done in four ways,[1] namely:

$$\text{I} \quad A>B; \ B>C$$
$$\text{II} \quad A>B; \ C<B$$
$$\text{III} \quad B<A; \ C<B$$
$$\text{IV} \quad B<A; \ B>C$$

With each of these structures it is possible to ask the subject to name either the greatest or the least term of the series, so that eight formulations are obtained. Following Hunter (1957), we shall call these I.1; I.2; II.1; II.2; and so on.

Let us begin by considering an example of structure I.1.

> Tom is taller than Dick.
> Dick is taller than John.
> Which of these three boys is the tallest?

This particular formulation is generally recognized to be, for an adult, the simplest. In Hunter's terminology, the premisses are 'isotropic', that is, the link appears second in the first premiss

---

[1] There are, of course, eight possible structures if the order of presentation of the two premisses is varied. This was not done in our study.

and first in the second premiss. (Whenever this is not the case, Hunter calls the premisses heterotropic.) This makes the seriation seem obvious and without complication. However, it cannot be assumed that this logical structure is as easily handled by children.

*Results: Group S2*

It was quickly discovered, when this problem was given to the subjects of Group S2, that although a wrong solution was seldom offered, the reasons for choosing the correct solution were frequently unacceptable by adult standards. There was, however, no obviously distinct 'break' between those children who treated the problem with an impeccable logic and those who made glaring errors: various intermediate responses were observed.

Some children showed a prompt awareness of the seriation involved and handled the relationships easily. For example, John resolved the problem in this way:

'Tom is the tallest. (How do you know?) Tom is taller than Dick and Dick is taller than John. So John is smaller than Dick and it already says that Dick is smaller than Tom. So John is the shortest and Tom is the tallest.'

John, then, takes the premisses in reverse order and correctly restates them in terms of the relationship 'smaller'. (Hunter calls this latter operation 'converting the premisses'.) In so doing, John shows a facility that was not common.

Derek also gives evidence of his awareness of the seriation but reasons rather differently from John:

'It's Tom. That's an easy one (Why?) It's sort of straightforward. (Why is that?) If you read it out it joins up together all right. (How do you know that Tom is the tallest?) If Tom is taller than Dick then Tom is the tallest between Dick and him. Then Dick is taller than John but Tom is taller than Dick, so Tom is the tallest.'

Derek plainly structures the whole series, as John did ('it joins up together all right') but there is some indication in his answer of a tendency to deal with each premiss separately. This tendency is more clearly illustrated by Sandra:

'Tom is taller than Dick so Tom is tallest. Dick is taller than John so Dick is tallest. So Tom and Dick are tallest. But there [first premiss] Tom is taller than Dick, so Tom is tallest.'

The solution is thus arrived at by a process of paired comparison: the first premiss is read and that member of the series who can still be considered as a 'possible' correct answer is carefully remembered; the second premiss is then similarly treated. In this way it is possible for a child to arrive at a solution without ever envisaging the series of three terms as a whole (although, of course, the use of this method does not in any way prove that the child fails to conceive of the whole series).

When Sandra's method is adopted to deal with this particular problem structure (I.1), it is necessary, after dealing with the second premiss, to refer again to the first premiss in order to decide between the two 'intermediate' solutions. Sandra omitted to make explicit the fact that her intermediate solutions *were* intermediate; it was almost as if she had placed both Tom and Dick in a distinct category – 'tallest'. The tendency to classify the members of the series in this way was found to be common. James showed himself more naïve in this than Sandra: 'Tom is taller than Dick and Dick is taller than John. That means that Tom and Dick are tall and John is short. So John is the shortest, Dick is just in between the two, and Tom is the tallest.'

Both James and Sandra, then, tend to speak in terms not of seriation but of class membership. This might be thought to be of no importance, since it does not lead them into error in the handling of the relationships; but the answers which have been quoted so far are very clearly related to others where error is not avoided.

*Jessie:* 'It's Tom. Tom is taller than Dick so Dick is small. And Dick here [points to the second premiss] is taller than this Dick here [points to the first premiss] but not so much as Tom. So Tom is the tallest. (How many people are there?) Four. (Which order would you put the boys in?) Tom is first, then there's the second Dick, Dick in the first line is third, and John is last.'

The most interesting feature of Jessie's answer is the separation of the premisses, which is carried so far that she concludes that 'Dick' in the one premiss is not the same person as 'Dick' in the other. This is clearly associated with the attempt to translate the information given in the premisses into class membership terms: 'so Dick is small'.[1] Only if Dick can be seen to be 'small' in relation to one of the terms and 'large' in relation to the other can his position as the link be maintained. It will emerge in other connections how difficult it proves for some children to envisage this kind of 'double membership'. And if this cannot be achieved in the present case, then the conclusion that there are two boys called Dick is inescapable.

When a child treats the premisses separately, acting on the assumption of four terms, he is at once in a position where he lacks information. If there were indeed 'two Dicks' the problem would be insoluble. Thus we have a situation where structural error leads almost unavoidably to some element of arbitrariness in the final choice of a solution. (In this case, we still classify the error as structural – see pages 68 and 79.) There may, however, be a greater or lesser degree of awareness of the difficulty which arises from the assumption of four terms. Jessie, for instance, makes her decision confidently: the second Dick is taller than the

---

[1] Burt (1919) and Piaget (1921) note the tendency for the translation of relative into absolute statements to occur in the solving of a three-term series problem of structure IV, viz. 'Edith is fairer than Suzanne; Edith is darker than Lili'. Piaget claims that: 'Instead of tackling the matter by means of judgements of relation, i.e. by making use of such expressions as 'fairer than', the child deals simply in judgements of membership and tries to find out with regard to the three girls whether they are dark or fair (absolutely speaking). It is as though he reasoned as follows: Edith is fairer than Suzanne so they are both fair. Edith is darker than Lili so they are both dark. Therefore Lili is dark, Suzanne is fair, and Edith is between the two. . . . The child by substituting the judgement of membership for the judgement of relation . . . comes to a conclusion which is exactly the opposite of ours.'

In Burt's words, the statement ' "Edith is darker than Lili" suggests that both Edith and Lili belong to the dark group, Edith being more intensely marked by the special character of this group.'

These analyses, more especially since they were in close agreement, led us to expect many instances of such reasoning. But, while our group of children often proceeded by 'judgements of class membership', the interpretation of 'Tom is taller than Dick' was more often 'Tom is tall and Dick is short' than 'Both are tall'. Sometimes, however, two interpretations were offered by one child in swift succession – see, for instance, pages 130 and 131.

first Dick, 'but not so much as Tom'. She appears to be in no doubt about Tom's being the tallest. Her certainty may derive from the fact that the 'tall Dick' shares his name with the 'small Dick' – that they are, to some extent at least, associated. That some connection of this kind influences Norma is, in turn, suggested by her answer:

'Tom is taller than Dick and Dick is taller than John. Now it can't be John because John is smaller than Dick. And the first Dick is smaller, so Tom will be tallest. (Why can't it be Dick?) Well, one is smaller and one is bigger. It can't be Dick, you see, because there are two of them and one is smaller.'

Robert, however, is much less sure of the ground of his final decision:

'It's Dick. (How do we know that?) Well, there's only one Tom and only one John, so Dick must be it. (Why is that?) [Long pause: no answer.] (How many boys are there here, Robert?) Four. There's Tom and John and the two Dicks. (Who is the shortest?) John. (How do we know that?) I don't really know. It says Tom is taller than Dick and then it stops. Then it says Dick is taller than John. (It stops?) Yes, there's a full stop; and that's the end of a sentence. [Robert grinned his triumph after this remark.] (Who is the tallest, then?) Dick in the second line. (Why is that?) It says Tom is taller than Dick and Dick is taller than John, so I said Dick is short there [first premiss] and Dick is tall there [second premiss] so I just said Dick. (Why did you do that?) Because Dick is tall in the second sentence. (Is anyone else tall?) Tom. (How do we know that Dick is taller than Tom?) It says he's short in the first sentence but he's tall in the second. Dick is in the *second* sentence so Tom could be a bit smaller than Dick.'

So an element of more or less conscious arbitrariness is involved in the final choice when the two premises are separated to the point where four terms are envisaged in place of three. But, given the precise wording of the problem, answers based on the assumption of four terms must be regarded as arbitrary also in another way. We have spoken of arbitrary error as arising whenever part of the given of the problem is ignored. The child who decides that there are four terms is therefore behaving arbitrarily – even before he actually produces his solution – in so far as he thereby ignores the fact that he is asked 'Which of these *three* boys is the tallest?' However, it is plain once again that the arbitrariness is a necessary consequence of the failure to understand the relationships involved in the problem – the child who works in terms of class membership without envisaging double membership is virtually driven to conclude that there are four terms, as we have seen.

Once the 'four term' error had shown itself in a few protocols, the children were invited to comment on the possibility of there being 'two Dicks', even where they had dealt successfully with the problem. Those who had shown a sure hold of the structure of seriation were quite clear that, if there were 'two Dicks', they would be unable to answer the question without more information. Others were less sure and rejected the possibility only on the ground that the question specifically mentioned 'three boys'. For instance, Roberta:

'(Could there be two Dicks here?) Yes, sir. (Why do you think that there are not two, then?) Because it is only "three boys" that is written down here.'

When, on another occasion, the group was required to find the shortest boy and not the tallest,[1] the strategies which have already been noted were, generally speaking, reaffirmed. In particular, those children who had reasoned by paired comparison maintained that strategy. Among the others, however, there was

[1] For half the children, the question as to the shortest preceded that as to the tallest boy. The other twenty children met these questions of structure I in the order in which they are discussed here.

All eight problems were presented to the children in randomized order, the orders of structures and of questions within each structure being systematically varied. In an effort to counteract the influence of memory on reasoning in different problems we used four different sets of names. (In each structure, however, the same names were used, but no child met both questions for each structure with fewer than three other problems intervening.)

Quotations in the text have been adapted, for the convenience of the reader, so that only the names Tom, Dick, and John appear.

some regrouping. Several children who had reasoned to find the tallest in much the same way as John had done (see page 116) now – while still retaining a firm hold on the seriation involved – tended rather to treat the premises one by one than to structure the complete series. John himself seemed unconcerned by the change of question, except that he did not this time confirm his solution by converting the premises, but simply said:

'Tom is taller than Dick and Dick is taller than John. So Tom must be taller than Dick and John, and Dick is taller than John anyway. So John is the smallest.'

Unlike John, however, some children, asked to find the shortest, found it necessary to convert the premises so that they contained only the relation 'shorter'. Stephen explained:

'This means Dick is shorter than Tom, John is shorter than Dick. So that gives the answer – it's John. (You changed the lines round?) Yes. (Why?) I thought it would help. (How would it help?) It would be 'shorter' on the top line and on the bottom line. (How does that help?) It makes it easier. (In what way?) I don't know.'

Similarly, Bryan assured the experimenter that it was easier in this problem to find the tallest one:

'(Why?) You don't have to turn it round or anything. (Why might you have to turn it round?) It's easier when it wants the shortest.'

In one case in which the change of question led immediately to conversion of the premises, inquiry after the reasons for this conversion brought in its wake a realization that it was, after all, unnecessary.

*Alec:* 'John is shorter than Dick. Dick is shorter than Tom. So John is the shortest. (Why did you start with the bottom line?) I don't know . . . no reason . . . I could start from the top. (Why did you change the lines round?) It makes it easier. (How?) I . . . well, not really this time. (Why not?) It tells you it both ways. Tom is taller than Dick. Dick is taller than John, so John will be shortest. . . . It gives you them all in their order from top to bottom.'

Sometimes, the attempt to convert the premisses led to mis-handling of the asymmetrical relationship. Janet's protocol reads:

'I would change these two "taller" ones to "shorter" ones. Dick is the shortest one. (How do you know?) When you change them it becomes: "Tom is shorter than Dick and Dick is shorter than John". (Who will be the shortest?) I think it's going to be Tom, and Dick must be nearest him.'

Among the group of children who not only proceeded by paired comparison but assigned the members of the series to two distinct classes, it was generally held that it was easier to find the shortest than the tallest: Tom and Dick were 'obviously' tall and so the shortest was equally 'obvious'. 'John is the only short one' and 'John must be smallest – it hasn't got that he's tall' were typical comments.

Robert (see page 119) maintained his method of reasoning despite the change of question: he still failed to link the premisses and still talked of the four boys in the problem. His solution – though in fact correct on this occasion – was reached arbitrarily as before:

'[Covers up the names of Tom and of Dick in the second premiss.] It's John. (How did you work that out?) I just put out Tom and the second Dick. They're tallest. And John is in the second sentence, so it's John. (Is the boy in the second sentence always smallest?) Oh, no. I had to choose one of them between Dick here [points to first premiss] and John, and so it's John. He comes last.'

There seems to be some indication here of the operation of an arbitrary rule: 'the child who is last named is smallest'. Even though Robert specifically denies that 'the boy in the second sentence' is always smallest, he does seem to use some such notion, not as the entire basis of solution, but as a means of decid-ing between the alternatives with which he finds himself left when he has eliminated the two boys who, in his reasoning, are 'tallest'. Robert repeatedly reached his solutions in this way.

Jessie, on the other hand, found the change of question much more troublesome:

'You don't know the shortest. (Why is that?) It doesn't have any . . . [Long pause.] . . . (Who *might* be the shortest one here?) Dick. (Where did you find that out?) [Jessie points to the first premiss.] (Is anyone else going to be short?) John. (How do we know?) It says Dick is taller than John so John will be short too. . . . [Looks very puzzled indeed.] . . . (Who do you think will be the shortest boy, then?) [Long pause: no answer.]'

These, then, were the difficulties encountered by the children of Group S2 in dealing with structure I – both when they were asked to identify the greatest term of the series (problem I.1) and when they were asked to identify the least (problem I.2). The same group was set also the remaining six forms of Problem B3. These were:

*Structure II*       Tom is taller than Dick.
                John is shorter than Dick.

            Which of these three boys is tallest? (II.1)
                                        shortest? (II.2)

*Structure III*     Dick is shorter than Tom.
                John is shorter than Dick.

            Which of these three boys is tallest? (III.1)
                                        shortest? (III.2)

*Structure IV*     Dick is shorter than Tom.
                Dick is taller than John.

            Which of these three boys is tallest? (IV.1)
                                        shortest? (IV.2)

Hunter in his article describes how – in his attempt to identify the 'covert psychological performances presumed to be involved in deriving a series from a set of two-term premisses' – he made a number of assumptions. One was 'that seriating necessitates the successive judging of premisses which are not only linked (this is a logically necessary condition) but also isotropic. . . . If two linked premisses are not isotropic, the thinker must therefore make them isotropic by reorganizing one or other of the pre-misses.' Another assumption was that, 'where reorganizing is required, it is the second encountered premiss which tends to be reorganized rather than the first. That is, the first premiss establishes the direction of the series, and predisposes the thinker to make the second premiss isotropic with the first.' Now these assump-tions may well be valid in analysing the reasoning of adults faced with unquantified three-term series. If they were to be substan-tiated for children's reasoning, our researches would have had to show none of the converting and reordering of premisses which we have already seen in the protocols for structure I, since that is already isotropic. We shall now see what methods are adopted to deal with problems which are not presented in isotropic form.

Structure III may be rendered isotropic in two different ways: either by reordering the premisses so that the second comes first, to give 'John is shorter than Dick, Dick is shorter than Tom'; or by restating both premisses in terms of the relation 'taller than', that is, in Hunter's terminology, by 'converting' them. If both premisses in structure III are converted (with no change in the order of their succession) then the problem becomes identical with structure I.

The first of these procedures would seem at first glance the easiest way to produce isotropy. But we found no instance in which a child adopted this method systematically in dealing with structure III – no instance, that is to say, where both III.1 and III.2 were solved in this manner.

We did, however, discover that several children reordered the premisses of structure III when they had to solve for the tallest boy. Jean's protocol shows very clearly why she did so:

'It's Tom [after a long pause]. It helps you if you start at the second line; you don't have to go back to the first line again. I read it through and if I don't know the answer at once then I know to start at the second line and go up the way. It says here "John is shorter than Dick" so Dick is tallest there. But Dick is shorter than Tom, so Tom is tallest.'

Jean, then, proceeds by paired comparison: that is, she asks the question separately in relation to each premiss, and thus reaches her final answer stepwise, by successive stages.

Now, if one takes the statement 'Dick is shorter than Tom' and asks the question 'Who is taller?', there are two answers which are formally equivalent: the positive answer 'Tom' and the negative answer 'not Dick'. But formal equivalence, as may be observed again and again, does not imply psychological equivalence. It may therefore be important to draw a distinction between those cases where the child makes paired comparisons and explicitly retains a term at each stage in his reasoning (with implied rejection of another term, of course) and those where he does so with explicit rejection of a term. Thus we shall speak of paired comparison by retention and paired comparison by rejection.[1]

Jean, then, makes her comparisons and retains possible solutions. Where this method is adopted, it is helpful if the answer to the first question asked is the link term. If this occurs, one can proceed easily to the second premiss and solve the problem in two stages only. Consider the two premisses of structure III – namely, 'Dick is shorter than Tom. John is shorter than Dick' – and suppose that the question is 'Who is shortest?' Then, asking this question and considering only the first premiss, one gets the answer 'Dick'. If one turns next to the second premiss, one finds that Dick figures there and so one can go straight on to a solution. But suppose the question to be 'Who is tallest?' If this is asked in relation to the first premiss the answer is Tom – and Tom does not figure in the second premiss so there is no single further step that can lead to a solution.

The situation may be indicated schematically in the following way. Let A, B, and C be the terms of the series and suppose B to be the middle or link term. Then the unfavourable case, when the answer to the first question asked is not the link term, may be represented thus:

[1] The first of these procedures has already been illustrated by Sandra's protocol (quoted on page 117).

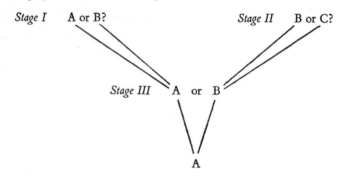

Stage I and stage III are, then, in fact identical but, since stage II intervenes, I and III have to be separately performed.

When, on the other hand, the link is the answer to the first question asked, we have:

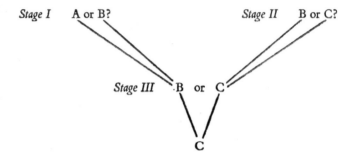

Here it is stage II and stage III which are identical and, since there is nothing to separate them, they are, in an actual process of solution, fused into one.

Now, in any unquantified three-term series problem that admits of solution, the link must be the answer to the question in the case of one of the premises. Thus, if one deals with this premiss first, one can always reach the solution in two stages. Jean was explicit in her description of her reasoning for all structures that the problems were easy 'once you know which line to start at'; so she, and those who reasoned in the same way, found that they could always find 'the shortest' without reordering but had to begin with the second premiss when asked to find the tallest boy. This was because, in all four of the structures which we used, the tallest boy and the link term figured in the first premiss. However, if the other four structures (see page 115) had been used, the opposite would have been the case. It would seem, then, that the two sets of structures are not psychologically equivalent.

Thus the order of treatment of the premisses is important if one makes paired comparisons and retains 'possible' solutions. It is less so if one uses the rejection method. The latter procedure may be schematized thus:

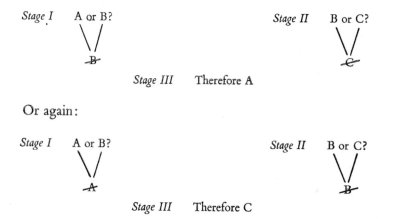

*Stage I*    A or B?            *Stage II*    B or C?

*Stage III*    Therefore A

Or again:

*Stage I*    A or B?            *Stage II*    B or C?

*Stage III*    Therefore C

It is at once plain that the answer which is obtained from the first question asked has less effect on the subsequent course of reasoning. There may be a slight advantage if the sequence of events is as portrayed in the first schema – that is, if the link term figures negatively in the answer to the first question. But it is doubtful if this will make much difference. In either case, two of the terms are ruled out by two successive steps, and the third one is then the solution.

The rejection procedure seems to be unlike the retention one in that the former could, in principle at least, be adopted by someone who kept the three-term and serial nature of the problem very well in mind throughout – though it is certainly in practice adopted by some children who fail to do so, and notably by some of those who make the 'two Dicks' error.

It is clear, then, that the form of question may affect the frequency with which reordering of premisses takes place. It may also affect the frequency with which premisses are converted. It is true that three children made both problems III.1 and III.2 isotropic by converting both premisses and thus turning structure III into structure I; but a further two converted in III.1 yet elected to leave the premisses as they were when asked to identify the shortest boy. That the conversion of III.1 was on account of the question asked was underlined by Susan who stated that she changed both premisses to 'taller than' because 'when they are both the same it seems easier'.

With structures II and IV there were again some cases of conversion of premisses to isotropic form, but again few children restructured the premisses in the same way for both questions.

Structures II and IV, unlike III, cannot be rendered isotropic by reordering of the premisses alone: one or other premiss must be converted. Whether reordering is also necessary depends on which premiss is chosen for restatement. To make structure II isotropic one may either (a) convert the second premiss or (b) convert the first premiss and reorder. With structure IV one may either (a) convert the first premiss or (b) convert the second premiss and reorder.

We found that, in structure II, only two children converted the second premiss for both forms of question, and none converted the first premiss and reordered for both forms; and, in structure IV, only five children converted the first premiss for both forms of question, while none converted the second premiss and reordered for both forms. (This difference in numbers using the (a) procedure is in the direction opposite to that which Hunter's hypothesis would lead one to expect: he thought the second premiss more likely to be converted than the first.) But a further four children in the case of structure II and a further five in the case of structure IV made the premises isotropic by one or other method when asked to find the tallest boy, though they adopted different strategies when asked to find the shortest.[1]

Although the foregoing discussion has been primarily concerned with differences in strategy, it has necessarily involved some mention of all the main errors. The accounts of these will now be drawn together and amplified.

The most prevalent type of error was that which involved the assigning of the terms to distinct classes – the 'tall' and the 'short'. Piaget speaks in this connection of the substitution of 'judgements of membership' for 'judgements of relation', and his terminology will be adopted here, although the most common procedure observed was not the one described in his detailed account of how the 'judgements of membership' are made (see footnote on page 118).

We have already seen that the making of judgements of membership does not necessarily lead to the choice of a wrong solution and sometimes seems hardly to impede the progress of the thought. Sometimes, on the other hand, it clearly underlies a serious breakdown of reasoning. There can be no doubt that a full appreciation of the strictly relative nature of the information given in the premises would preclude the judgement that any of the terms is absolutely 'tall' or 'short', so whenever this judgement is made we hold that, in our sense of the term, there has been error. At the same time, we have drawn a distinction between those cases in which the tendency to sort into classes leads to the introduction of a fourth term, thus unquestionably affecting the

---

[1] Burt and Hunter were surprised to find that children answered problems of structure II more quickly and more successfully than problems of structure I, and explained this as being due to the 'direct statement' or the 'atmosphere effect' of the premisses in structure II. For example, in our problem II.2, Burt would say that 'with the statement "John is shorter . . ." ringing in the memory, a child asked "who is shortest" naturally tends to say "John is shortest".' But our evidence shows no such unthinking acceptance of John as shortest because, as it were, the words 'John' and 'shorter' are floating together on the surface of a child's mind. The greater speed and ease of solution in problems of structure II were, for our group of ten-year-olds, rather due to the particular strategies they used. The majority solved both II.1 and II.2 in two stages.

course of the reasoning, and those cases in which the child manages by one means or another to proceed without resort to a second 'Dick'.

Both varieties of the error have already been illustrated in the course of the discussion of responses to structure I. However, some interesting examples arose in answers to the other structures, and a few extracts from them now follow:

*Tommy* (III.2): 'John. Dick is shorter than Tom so Tom must be small and Dick is small. Then John is shorter than Dick and so Dick must still be big. And that makes Tom small and John small and John will be the smallest one. (Why is it John?) It says Dick is shorter than Tom so Tom must be tall and then John is shorter than Dick so Dick is small and Tom is big and John is short. And so John is the shortest. (Why is Dick small?) Well, because it has John is shorter than Dick. . . . No, sir, I've made a mistake. . . . It means Dick is big. So Dick is big and Tom is big and then John is shortest. (But doesn't it tell us that Dick is shorter than Tom?) Yes, sir . . . [pause] . . . that makes Dick small . . . and then in the next line he's tall. But I think he's really small.'

*Tommy* (IV.2): 'It's John. Dick is shorter than Tom and Dick is taller than J. . . . Well, now, Dick is short first and then he's tall. So I have to find the difference between Tom and John. Dick is shorter than Tom so Tom must be big: and Dick is taller than John so John must be small. (It says that Dick is shorter than Tom. Why isn't Dick the shortest one?) It's because he's had two "shots" and Tom and John have only had one. It wouldn't be fair otherwise. Dick has been short once and tall once: he's had two turns. (How many boys are there?) Three. (How do you know?) It says "Which of the three boys . . ." (Might there be four boys?) Oh, yes, there could be two Dicks, but I think there's really just one having two turns.'

So Tommy avoids the 'two Dicks' error – but only just avoids it. Norma made it consistently. Here is her answer to II.2. Immediately before she was presented with this problem, the experimenter drew her attention to the phrasing, made her repeat it, and heard her remark to herself that there were only three boys. She then proceeded to reason in this fashion:

'John. (Why is that?) Tom is taller than Dick. John is smaller than Dick. So it can't be Tom because he's taller and it can't be the second Dick for he's taller. It can't be the first Dick, for one of the Dicks is bigger and so it must be John. (How many people are there here?) Three. (How do you know?) There are three names. (Will you put the boys in order for me?) Well, John's the shortest and then there's the first Dick and then the second Dick and then Tom.'

Finally, here are Jessie's answers to IV.1 and IV.2.

(IV.1): 'Dick. It says that Dick is shorter than Tom so Dick is short and Tom is short too. And Dick is taller than John so Dick is tall and John is short. (What order would the boys be in?) This Dick [second premiss] is the tallest, John is the next tallest, Tom is third, and then it's Dick [first premiss].'

(IV.2): 'Dick. Dick is shorter than Tom so Dick is short and Tom is tall. Dick is taller than John so Dick is tall and John is tall too. So that makes Dick [first premiss] the shortest. . . . There's Dick [first premiss], then Tom, then this Dick [second premiss], then John. (So John is the tallest one?) Yes. (But it says here that Dick is taller than John.) . . . [Pause.] That makes John third and this Dick [second premiss] the biggest.'

It is evident, then, that a child may shift from moment to moment in the way in which he assigns to classes. The statement 'x is taller than y' may be taken to mean that both are 'tall' in the way Piaget and Burt describe, then in the next breath another formally similar statement may be made the basis for assigning the terms to opposing categories. So far as we have been able to observe, these different interpretations are not systematically related to the formulation of the premisses.

These quotations give some indication of the main ways in which the tendency to substitute absolute for relative values showed itself. They illustrate also the arbitrariness in reasoning which the substitution almost invariably brought in its wake: 'I think he's really small'; it can't be Dick because 'he's had two turns'. In *Table 11* we list separately those instances where, as in the latter of these two examples, the child invokes some arbitrary rule to support his choice. But it is important to stress that the error of arbitrary rule had no independent occurrence in the unquantified three-term series: it arose only in conjunction with judgements of membership. The arbitrary rules which were employed were two in number: the rejection of the link term because it appeared twice; and, where the issue was between two terms in different premisses, the basing of choice on the order of presentation.

Two further errors remain. The first of these arose in connection with attempts to convert the premisses and has already been illustrated by the quotation from Janet's protocol (page 122). Janet tries to convert 'Tom is taller than Dick' and produces 'Tom is shorter than Dick' as the equivalent statement. This seems to be closely akin to the error observed in the quantified three-term series, where 'Dick is two inches taller than Harry' is taken as synonymous with 'Harry is two inches taller than Dick'. In both cases, the difficulty lies in manipulating the statements of asymmetrical relationships, though the precise forms of error are not the same: in the one instance, the position of the terms is reversed while the relation is not; in the other, the opposite is the case. Successful conversion requires, of course, that both these changes be made. We shall describe both forms of error as 'difficulty in handling asymmetry'.[1] It is curious, however, that only the form illustrated by Janet arose in the unquantified problems, and only the other arose in the quantified ones. (The subjects were, of course, different children.)

The final error was loss of hold, of which there were only a very few instances here. The error frequencies are shown in *Table 11*.

---

[1] Success in dealing with statements of asymmetrical relationship could be variable in the responses of any one child. For example, Andrew constantly converted and re-ordered the premisses in reaching his solutions and made no errors. Yet, after he had correctly answered both problems II.1 and II.2, he was asked which he had found easier: 'This one [II.2]. (Why is that?) Well, Dick is shorter than Tom and John is shorter than Dick. (You turned the first line round?) Yes, it makes it easier when you've got two the same. (Could you have turned the second line round?) No, it would say that John is taller than Dick when he's shorter.'

TABLE II    GROUP S2—PROBLEM B3

| Error | Structure | | | | | | | | All (out of 320 answers) |
|---|---|---|---|---|---|---|---|---|---|
| | I | | II | | III | | IV | | |
| | 1 | 2 | 1 | 2 | 1 | 2 | 1 | 2 | |
| (a) Judgements of membership | | | | | | | | | |
| (i) without addition of a fourth term | 5 | 5 | 5 | 9 | 5 | 5 | 8 | 7 | 49 |
| (ii) with addition of a fourth term | 3 | 3 | 3 | 3 | 3 | 3 | 3 | 5 | 26 |
| (b) Arbitrary rule | 2 | 2 | 2 | 2 | 3 | 3 | 4 | 4 | 22 |
| (c) Asymmetry | 0 | 1 | 0 | 2 | 0 | 0 | 2 | 1 | 6 |
| (d) Loss of hold | 0 | 0 | 1 | 0 | 1 | 0 | 1 | 1 | 4 |

By far the most common error, then, was 'judgements of membership'. Where this involved the addition of a fourth term, there was great consistency in response from structure to structure: the same three children made the error in each problem that they encountered. In structure IV.2, however, they were joined by two more, who did not make the error elsewhere.

There was more variability in the case of judgements of membership without a fourth term: sixteen children were involved in the forty-nine instances of this error which are shown in the table, so that there was an average of three instances per child. But four children made the error six times or more.

# CHAPTER 6

## *Series Extrapolation Problems*

THE THREE-TERM series problems which have been discussed are to be solved by the integration of the given pieces of information, one with another. No extension or extrapolation of the series beyond its three terms is called for, nor would such extension be possible in any of the examples we have considered, since in none of them is there a rule or principle of serial relationship to be discovered. A type of problem that has been much used in intelligence tests, however, is one which provides a few terms of a series where some such principle is involved, and requires the subject to supply others, in either direction – or in both directions – from the terms given.

The main variables in these series extrapolation problems, to which we now turn, would appear to be:

(a) the content, that is to say, the nature of the terms of the series;
(b) the complexity of these terms;
(c) the complexity of the relationships between the terms, that is, of the principle that is to be discovered;
(d) the computational difficulty involved in calculating the terms which are to be supplied.

The first of these refers to the possibility that numbers, or letters of the alphabet, or months of the year, and so on, may be the stuff of which the series is made. 'The complexity of the terms' refers to the fact that each term may consist simply of, say, one letter or number, or may be composed of two or more of these; and there is also, of course, the possibility of a series of mixed content, with terms that are complex in the sense that they each include, say, both a number and a letter of the alphabet. The third variable is obviously the crux of the matter and is the only one which usually receives much attention. At the moment only one comment need be made, and that is on the difference between a series which develops in non-recurrent progression, the obvious example being the series of natural numbers itself, and a series which consists in the repetition of a certain pattern. Thus, OXOOXOOXO . . . is, in one sense of the word at least, a series which can be extrapolated. But it is probable that ability to repeat a brief pattern of this kind is far from being identifiable with ability to extrapolate a non-recurrent series. The former is within the power of the average child of seven; the latter, as this chapter will show, presents severe difficulties years later.

The distinction between the third and the fourth variables is one which has already been used in the discussion of errors: that between structure or principle and execution or application. In series extrapolation the distinction is very clear: it is perfectly possible to understand the principle, yet calculate the terms wrongly. And different problems can vary in the extent to which they invite this occurrence. For instance, the end from which the series has to be extended may affect the difficulty. Compare:

$$10, 12, 16, 18, \ldots, \ldots, \ldots, \ldots$$

with

$$\ldots, \ldots, \ldots, 10, 12, 16, 18.$$

There is no difference in the principle which must guide extrapolation in the two cases but the actual tasks set are not the same.

What differences these and other variations make must, of course, be decided empirically for different subjects. We have been concerned up to this point only with the preliminary formal analysis in terms of which discussion of the experimental work can later take place.

For many years, series items having as 'content' the letters of the alphabet have been used in Moray House tests, and it was with examples of this type of problem that the first study of series extrapolation was concerned. As in Moray House tests, the alphabet was printed above the problems. This probably serves both to facilitate the discovery of the principle and to reduce executive error, but it does not by any means eliminate the latter. Indeed, as in the case of the matching problems, almost all the errors made by Group O(i) had to be placed in this category.

The children in Group O(i) were asked to complete the blank spaces in the following three series:

C1    ..., Q, N, K, ...

C2    XC, VE, TG, ..., ...

C3    KL, JK, IJ, ..., ...

Thus, in all three problems, letters of the alphabet provide the content of the series, but the terms of C2 and C3 are more complex than those of C1, since the former are pairs of letters, the latter single letters only. Further, in C2 and C3 the principles to be discovered are more complex, in the sense that two-directional movement is involved – C2 converges on the middle of the alphabet, and in C3 the rule is 'two back, one forward' – whereas in C1 there is a simple one-directional progression. However, C1 gives rise to its own peculiar computational difficulties, since, although it progresses in one direction only, this direction runs counter to that of the printed alphabet and extrapolation at both ends is required.

*Results: Group O(i)*

All the children in Group O(i) showed a general understanding of what it is to extend a series. There were, however, some differences in mode of procedure. The main distinction was between those children who tried to establish a principle, explicitly stated, and those who relied on rhythmic chanting, as did, for instance, Susan: '*K'* L M *N'* O P *Q'* R S *T'* – *K'* J I *H'* '. The same child solved Problem C2 by this method, treating it as two separate series. She was the only one to attempt C2 in this way, but chanting was very common in C3 where it seemed to be particularly helpful. Children who read aloud 'KL, JK, IJ' were usually able to continue 'HI, GH' without much hesitation. A count shows that thirteen of the twenty children chanted C3 with little or no statement of principle. Of these, ten reached the correct solution, while, of the seven who tried to state the full principle, only four were finally correct. It should be added, however, that most of the attempted statements were inadequate, like the following from Charles: 'It's just one forward all the time – the first letter of what you did last time.' It is hardly surprising that this did not help much. But it is interesting that successful solution should so often have been based on an inarticulate feeling for rhythm.

One other method difference is to be noted. It concerns C2, where there was a division between children who established the 'miss one' principle and applied it directly and those who, realizing that the numerical series 3, 5, 7, 9 was involved, laboriously counted nine and then eleven letters from the beginning and from the end of the alphabet. Six children were notably laborious 'counters'. Obviously, the procedure is time-consuming and liable to lead to error, but beyond this the significance of the tendency is not clear. However, it is suggestive of a lack of confidence in certain arithmetical equivalences – in this case, for instance, in $7+2=9$. The relevant addition facts are certainly known by the children but it is possible that they are not felt to be quite 'safe'. So the ninth letter is found, not by moving two on from the seventh, but by starting all over again at the beginning.

Two errors were of frequent occurrence. The first of these consisted in a failure in the estimation of intervals between terms, and will be referred to as 'miscounting'. The source of the error was not always plain but it seemed to derive most commonly from inconsistency about the inclusion in the count of the final letter. Thus O might sometimes be said to be two letters from L and sometimes three. For instance, Sarah reasons thus: 'How far Q is from N – three places. So another three from K will be G.' It looks, then, as if the child is falling victim to the ambiguity of the language she is using, and is not recognizing that 'three places from' may be varyingly interpreted. What must be appreciated, of course, if the error is to be avoided, is the need for consistency. Whether we count inclusively or exclusively is conventional, and the convention varies in different circumstances. The French call a week *huit jours* while we call it 'seven days'; on the other hand, we use the inclusive convention in music and talk of an octave. There is therefore no unvarying rule for the child to apply.

A second error, which almost equalled this first one in frequency of occurrence but was, by its nature, confined to Problems C2 and C3, showed itself in reversal of the correct order of the two letters selected as solution: IR was written instead of RI, and KP instead of PK. Whenever this happened, the child was asked whether it mattered which letter came first. Only one child, Pam, replied that it did not matter, and she added quickly: 'Oh, well – here it's got the end one before the beginning. I didn't notice that.' It appears, then, that this error arises because the child is not sufficiently alive to the importance of exactness. Under the pressure of adult questioning, however, he acknowledges the desirability of a sterner discipline. It seems probable that something of this kind is the source of the trouble, for the error is, in most cases, very quickly and easily corrected. However, the frequency of its occurrence in the first instance may have had something to do with the two-directional progression of the series. Possibly it would not have arisen at all if C2 had been CX, EV, GT, ... instead of XC, VE, TG, ...; and if C3 had been KL, LM, MN, ...

Difficulty with direction, manifesting itself in the single-letter series, C1, constitutes a third error. The trouble in C1 arises from conflict between the direction of the series and the direction of the printed alphabet. Only two children in Group O(i) gave a wrong solution which seemed to be attributable to this, but three others showed signs of hesitation, one of them of hesitation sufficiently severe to be classed as error.[1] It was noticed that the first space in C1 gave more trouble than the last. It seemed to be easier to read 'Q, N, K, *H'* ' than to fill a blank space coming before Q with a letter which comes after Q in the alphabet. Clare gives an answer which illustrates this: 'Q to N – two letters; N to K – two letters. So two letters back from Q – N. No! I don't think it could be. H is the second one all right. Two letters before Q – that's N.' The final conclusion, 'that's N', was spoken in a puzzled tone, but she wrote N on her answer sheet. Thus she accepted a conclusion with which she was plainly dissatisfied. It was clear that she was not happy about having the series read N, Q, N, . . . (There is no suggestion that she had envisaged the possible complicated series N, Q, N, K, N, K, H, K, H, . . .) Yet she did not persist in the attempt to discover what had gone wrong.

Each of these three errors appears to arise in the course of attempts to apply a principle. In so far as this occurs, the errors must be considered to belong in the category we have called executive. However, they differ to some extent from previous instances of this class. The most common of the executive errors, and the one chiefly discussed so far, namely loss of hold, involves a failure of immediate memory of a kind which seems to have no counterpart in the errors we are now considering. The failure in these must be described rather as arising from some lack of precision and exactness in applying the principle. Now it might of course be argued that this lack of exactness, especially in the case of 'reversal of pairs', indicates an inadequacy in the conception of the principle rather than in the application of it. That is, one might maintain that the principle has not been understood in a sufficiently precise manner. However, the ease and readiness with which the children corrected this error, when they were questioned, argue for its inclusion in the executive rather than the structural category and, for the time being, this classification has been adopted.

[1] In such a case, the decision is of course arbitrary.

The error of difficulty with direction (Clare, page 139) resembles miscounting in so far as it is a somewhat ambiguous and misleading formulation ('... back from Q ... two letters before Q') which apparently leads Clare to go back *in the printed alphabet* to N. But this confusion presumably arises because she has seen that she must go 'back from Q' in the series as it is printed, yet is unable to translate this instruction into its 'mirror-image' – forward in the alphabet – when she comes to carry it out.

A fourth error was one that could arise only in dealing with C3, for it consisted in a failure to handle successfully the overlap of the terms. This failure might be complete, so that GH and EF were offered to fill the blanks; or it might be partial, as in the case of Flora, who offered GH and FG as her solution. Discussion of the significance of this error will be left till later, but it probably has to be considered as a failure to understand the principle.

There was one clear case in C3, apart from this particular difficulty, of application of an inappropriate principle, though it was hard to understand what this principle was. Morag gave as her solution LI and MH. She seemed to be moving out on either side of the pair JK, but her explanation was confused to the point of incoherence and it was not really possible to discover how she arrived at this conclusion.


*Results: Group O(ii)*

As was the case with the other problems so far considered, no new types of error appeared when the children were tested for the second time at the age of fourteen. *Table 12* shows the pattern of occurrence of error on the two occasions.[1]

The first three errors in *Table 12* are alike in having IDC in the neighbourhood of zero: that is, they show little or no sign of becoming less common from one occasion to the next. And they are, overall, of rather frequent occurrence – especially miscount-

---

[1] See pages 95 ff. for a discussion of the reasons why we do not give the patterns of change for each of the three series problems separately.

TABLE 12    GROUP O—PROBLEMS C1, C2, AND C3

| Error | A | B | C | D | IME | IMC | IDC |
|---|---|---|---|---|---|---|---|
| | Number of children making the error on occasions | | | | | | |
| | (i) and (ii) | (i) not (ii) | (ii) not (i) | not (i) nor (ii) | | | |
| (a) Miscounting | 3 | 6 | 5 | 5 | ·74 | ·79 | − ·09 |
| (b) Reversal of pairs | 4 | 4 | 3 | 8 | ·58 | ·64 | − ·14 |
| (c) Difficulty with direction | 0 | 3 | 3 | 13 | ·32 | 1·00 | ·00 |
| (d) Wrong principle | | | | | | | |
| (i) Overlap | 0 | 2 | 0 | 17 | ·11 | 1·00 | −1·00 |
| (ii) Other | 0 | 1 | 2 | 16 | ·16 | 1·00 | + ·33 |

ing, which has an IME of ·74. The 'overlap' wrong principle error, on the other hand, though infrequent, has an IDC of −1·00.

Once again, there is one IDC with a positive value. On one or two previous occasions, when this occurred, it was found possible to explain the somewhat surprising fact of an error's becoming more rather than less common with increasing age by showing that there existed some other error which by its nature rendered impossible – or at least improbable – the error in which increase was observed. It was also possible to show that most of the children whose responses produced the increase had on the previous occasion made the other 'inhibiting' error. However, in this case, the explanation of increase seems to be somewhat different. If one studies the protocols of the two children who made a wrong principle error on the second occasion, not having done so on the first, one finds that both tried the second time to formulate the principle more articulately. They both produced the correct solutions on the first occasion with little hesitation and little formal statement. There seems to be no doubt that this problem can often be solved more readily by subjects who do not attempt to formulate explicitly the relationships that are involved, provided that the general idea of extension of a series is adequately grasped.

*Table 13* gives the total numbers of errors made in the series problems on the two occasions.

TABLE 13    GROUP O—PROBLEMS C1, C2, AND C3

| Error | Frequency of error on occasion | |
| --- | --- | --- |
| | (i) | (ii) |
| (a)  Miscounting | 11 | 10 |
| (b)  Reversal of pairs | 9 | 7 |
| (c)  Difficulty with direction | 3 | 3 |
| (d)  Wrong principle | | |
| (i) Overlap | 2 | 0 |
| (ii) Other | 1 | 2 |

*Results: Group Y(i)*

Comparison of the performance of the twelve- and fourteen-year-olds with that of the group of ten-year-olds reveals one very striking difference: there are many more wrong principle errors among the younger children. This may seem surprising in view of the fact that a slight increase in errors of this kind between the ages of twelve and fourteen was found. However, the wrong principle errors of the ten-year-olds have certain features which distinguish them from those made by the older children. Most of those observed to occur at age ten fell into two classes, instances of which were entirely lacking in the answers given by the children of Group O.

First, wrong principle errors arose through what seemed to be a failure to generalize at a sufficiently high level of abstraction. Instead of grasping the fact that these problems were alike in that the series could all be extrapolated according to some principle but not necessarily the same principle in each case, some of the children concluded that the principle which they discovered – or believed – to be applicable in the first problem encountered would be applicable in all. Thus the notion 'this rule' took for them the place of the more general notion 'some rule'. Now with these younger children it had been considered necessary to begin by offering an example of series extrapolation. The simple example 'A, B, C, . . .' was used. Perhaps this very simplicity was unfortunate. It may be that 'find the letter which comes next' is more tempting as a rule that will be applicable in all cases than a more complex principle would be. At any rate, our experience suggested that examples may quite often mislead in this way, if they are not regarded by the children in a sufficiently abstract manner – if, in fact, the principle illustrated is not grasped in its widest generality.

Here is an answer typical of those in which the example was taken as a much more closely fitting model than it was intended to be.

*Tom:* [solving C1 – '. . ., Q, N, K, . . .'] 'The first one's P. And the second is L. (Why is it P?) Well, this one's Q, so it must be P. (Why is it L?) K, L.'

[Solving C2 – 'XC, VE, TG, . . . , . . .'] 'I think this one [first blank] is U and this one [second blank] is H.'

[Solving C3 – 'KL, JK, IJ, . . . , . . .'] 'That one should be J [first blank] and this one is K [second blank].'

So Tom in each case simply chooses the letter which comes next. Notice, also, that in the double-letter series he puts only one letter in each blank space.

Here is an instance of another way in which the model of the example could be misapplied. It is a little less straightforward but it involves essentially the same error.

*Gwen:* [solving C1 – '. . ., Q, N, K, . . .'] 'It's L in the first space and P in the second. (Why?) Because A is two letters before C in the example, so L is two letters before N. P is two letters after N, just as E is two letters after C in the example.'

So the principle in the example is differently – in fact less adequately – conceived, but the model, as understood, is being followed just as closely. However, this girl managed to solve C2 and C3 correctly.

Seven children in Group Y(i) made this error in at least one of the three problems. Eight children made the other error of principle which will now be considered.

Here is the answer given by Frances: [solving C1 – '..., Q, N, K, ...'] 'Have we just to find out which letters go *between* these ones? [pointing to Q, N, and K.] I don't get this one as good as I did the last one [i.e. Problem A1]. [Pause.] (Have you any ideas?) [Pause. The experimenter then solved C1 for Frances, explaining the principle.]'

[Solving C2 – 'XC, VE, TG, ..., ...'] 'Have you to find out how many letters are between X and C? (See if you can work it out for yourself.) [Pause. Frances wrote DW, FU.] (Why?) D comes between C and E, W comes between X and V, F comes between E and G, and U comes between T and V.'

[Solving C3 – 'KL, JK, IJ, ..., ...'] 'I don't think there's any letter between K and L. Shall I just leave the first one out? (If you like.) No letters between the second one either! (Well, see if you can find another way of doing it.) J comes between K and I, and K comes between J and L.'

So Frances has one hypothesis and only one: that the letters which fill the blank spaces must 'come between' the letters which are given. And the working out of the first problem by the experimenter does not bring her to abandon this idea.

Again, here is the answer given by Isabel: [solving C1 – '..., Q, N, K, ..., ...'] 'Are they to be words? (No, letters.) Are we to work it out with numbers? [Pause.] (Do you see how it works?) I still don't see. [The experimenter explained the principle, but Isabel supplied the letters M and O.]'

[Solving C2 – 'XC, VE, TG, ..., ...'] '[Pause. She seemed quite at a loss.] Find out how far each letter is from the other in the group? – how far T is from G and take the middle one? [The experimenter again explained the notion of extending a series, stressing that all the letters given must be taken into account. Isabel then wrote UW on her answer sheet.] (Why is it U?)

Well, U comes between V and T, and W comes between X and V. [So Isabel was now evidently trying to take all three given pairs into account but still could only think of inserting letters. She filled in the second blank with the letters DF.] D is between C and E, and F is between E and G.'

[Solving C3 – 'KL, JK, IJ, . . ., . . .'] 'K, J, I go backwards and so do L, K, J. Have I to get two letters here as well? [She writes IK and LJ.] (Why is it IK?) They are the two outside ones in the letters here [i.e. in the sequence K, J, I] and L and J are the two outside ones here [i.e. in the sequence L, K, J].'

Isabel, then, was under much the same impression as Frances and, again, the impression was a singularly persistent one. The error made by both children may be described as the substitution of interpolation for extrapolation: they did not appear to understand the notion of extending the series beyond the limits of that section of it which was given them.[1] Even children who appeared to understand that extension was called for would often retain traces of what might be called interpolative notions.

Thus Robin: [solving C2 – 'XC, VE, TG, . . ., . . .'] 'All the . . . X, V, and T are all near the end. And C, E, and G are all near the beginning. So the two that we want will be near the middle [pause]. The first one's X and C. It'll be N for the first part. (Why?) Well, C is two from the beginning and X is two from the end. And that will give you twenty-two letters altogether, and you could halve the twenty-two, that'll give you eleven. And if you count along eleven that gives you N. I've still to find the other one. (How are you going to do it?) [Pause.] You would have to add on the other eleven, but if you did that you would just come back to N again.'

Robin seems to begin by trying to treat his problem as one of serial extension, but what is probably the most primitive of all interpolative ideas – 'put it in the middle' – intervenes, and prevents him from extracting the rule of relationship. We may perhaps say of these errors in general that they indicate that the

---

[1] Bartlett (1958) observes that extrapolation is commonly thought to be more difficult than interpolation, and considers that his own results support this view.

child understands the desirability of introducing some kind of pattern but does not appreciate the serial nature of the pattern that is offered to him.

Other errors made by these children, apart from a few cases of such misunderstandings as that a letter was to be provided for each dot,[1] were of the same kinds as those encountered in the answers of the older children.

## Results: Group Y(ii)

*Table 14* shows the numbers of children in Group Y who made errors in the series extrapolation problems on the first and second occasions.

TABLE 14    GROUP Y—PROBLEMS C1, C2, AND C3

| Error | A | B | C | D | IME | IMC | IDC |
|---|---|---|---|---|---|---|---|
| | Number of children making the error on occasions | | | | | | |
| | (i) and (ii) | (i) not (ii) | (ii) not (i) | not (i) nor (ii) | IME | IMC | IDC |
| (a) Miscounting | 4 | 3 | 6 | 7 | ·65 | ·69 | +·33 |
| (b) Reversal of pairs | 0 | 3 | 6 | 11 | ·45 | 1·00 | +·33 |
| (c) Difficulty with direction | 3 | 3 | 6 | 8 | ·60 | ·75 | +·33 |
| (d) Wrong principle | | | | | | | |
| (i) Faulty generalization | 0 | 6 | 0 | 14 | ·30 | 1·00 | −1·00 |
| (ii) Interpolation | 2 | 6 | 0 | 12 | ·40 | ·75 | −1·00 |
| (iii) Overlap | 1 | 1 | 0 | 18 | ·10 | ·50 | −1·00 |
| (iv) Others | 0 | 6 | 0 | 14 | ·30 | 1·00 | −1·00 |

The fourth category of wrong principle errors, headed 'others', includes such errors as supposing that each dot in the underlining

[1] This suggests that blanks in tests should be indicated by a solid line.

146

of the answer space indicates a missing letter, or that each gap must be filled by a single letter even in a double-letter series, as well as any errors where some misunderstanding of principle is clearly involved but where the exact nature of the misunderstanding is obscure.

The pattern in *Table 14*, then, is quite clear and consistent. The last four errors, that is, the different varieties of failure to understand the principle, diminish very sharply. The first three, on the other hand, all increase a little in frequency. It seems that there is here yet another instance of the release of one set of errors by the disappearance of another set. The errors of principle on the first occasion were often such as to exclude the possibility of miscounting (as when the faulty generalization 'next letter in the alphabet' was applied), or of reversal of pairs (as when one letter instead of a pair was put in each gap), or of difficulty with direction (as when interpolation was substituted for extrapolation). Sometimes, however, the situation was slightly ambiguous. Consider the answer given by Frances to C2 and already quoted (page 144). She offers DW because 'D comes between C and E, and W comes between X and V'. Now, Frances is not working on a principle of serial extension at all; yet a case could perhaps be made for the opinion that, if one accepts her attempt to develop a pattern of a different kind, W should come first. On the other hand, it would not be impossible to formulate a principle whereby inversion would take place and D would come first after all. This illustrates the increased freedom from restriction which accompanies the substitution of some variety of interpolative patterning for serial extension in these problems. On this reasoning, then, it seemed that Frances could not be regarded as having made the error 'reversal of pairs' in addition to her basic error of principle.

In these and other similar ways, the increase in executive errors is related to the overall decrease in the other errors. Of the thirteen children who provide the eighteen fresh instances of executive error in *Table 14*, all but one had made the error of faulty generalization or interpolation on the first occasion of testing.

It remains now to consider the absolute frequencies of errors on the two occasions for the subjects of Group Y. These are reported in *Table 15*, which also contains the comparable figures for Group O (already shown in *Table 13*) so that a survey of the complete age-range is provided.

TABLE 15    PROBLEMS C1, C2, AND C3

| Error | Frequency of error among children in Groups | | | |
| | Y (i) (age 10) | Y (ii) (age 12) | O (i) (age 12) | O (ii) (age 14) |
|---|---|---|---|---|
| (a) Miscounting | 7 | 10 | 11 | 10 |
| (b) Reversal of pairs | 3 | 6 | 9 | 7 |
| (c) Difficulty with direction | 6 | 9 | 3 | 3 |
| (d) Wrong principle | | | | |
| (i) Faulty generalization | 12 | 0 | 0 | 0 |
| (ii) Interpolation | 14 | 2 | 0 | 0 |
| (iii) Overlap | 2 | 1 | 2 | 0 |
| (iv) Others | 8 | 0 | 1 | 2 |

The most striking feature of *Table 15* is the very sharp drop in the frequency of wrong principle errors between the ages of ten and twelve. It seems that, in the course of this period, these children came to understand what it is to extend a series. At the age of ten, only five of the group of twenty were wholly free from failure to understand the principle. But, although by age twelve almost all of the children of both groups have come to understand what is required, they are very far indeed, as the figures for the other errors show, from an ability to carry this out flawlessly. And the children of Group O have not made very marked progress in this respect even by the age of fourteen, at which point our study of them ends.

# CHAPTER 7

## *Related Series Problems*

THIS TYPE OF problem is less well known than the others we have been discussing, so it will perhaps be best to begin by giving an example:

### PROBLEM D1

If all fast-moving animals were smaller than slower-moving ones, which of the following would be the largest?

(cat/snail/horse/squirrel/elephant)

The problem states a general rule of relatedness between two series: animals arranged in order of speed and animals arranged in order of size. It postulates, in fact, a perfect correlation between speed and size in animals, and the subject is required to make an inference on this basis from one series to the other: from what may be called the independent series to the dependent one. The dependent series is, of course, the one to which the question-mark applies – in this case, the series according to size. The arrangement of the offered alternatives in series according to the other – the independent – quality, speed, must then form the basis of the inference; and the final step, once this arrangement is made, is the selection of the appropriate extreme.

We do not, of course, suggest that any such procedure is articulately gone through by those solving the problems – but this analysis seems to help in the study and classification of the errors which arise. The conscious formulation which most favours correct solution is probably something like: 'Fast ones are small, so slow ones are big. That means "find the biggest" equals "find the slowest".'

The main variables, in problems of this kind, are the following:

(a) the content, in the double sense of (i) the nature of the objects to be arranged in series (in the example, animals); and (ii) the nature of the qualities whereby this arrangement is determined (in the example, speed and size);

(b) how the postulated correlation stands in relation to the real state of affairs – that is, whether there is in fact a measure of the same correlation in reality, whether there is none at all, or whether an inverse relationship really exists;

(c) whether both extremes of the dependent series are mentioned or only one – compare 'if all fast-moving animals were *smaller* . . . which . . . would be the *largest*?' with 'if all slow-moving animals were *larger* . . . which . . . would be the *largest*?'

The four problems used were:

D1: If all fast-moving animals were smaller than slower-moving ones, which of the following would be the largest?

(cat/snail/horse/squirrel/elephant)

D2: If all rough cloth were thicker than smoother cloth, which of the following would be the thickest?

(silk/blanket/sacking/nylon/velvet)

D3: If all light-coloured foodstuffs were sweeter than darker-coloured ones, which of the following would be the sweetest?

(honey/treacle/jam/brown sugar/milk)

D4: If all small articles weighed less than larger ones, which of the following would be the heaviest?

(an alarm clock/an iron/a cushion/a teacup/a nail)

*Results: Group O(i)*

The errors in these problems fall into seven main categories. Some of these categories were infrequently represented in the answers of the children of Group O; and, indeed, the few instances of them were not recognized for what they were, until analysis of the answers of the younger children had thrown light on the development of the ability to solve these problems. It then became clear that the main distinctions are to be drawn in terms of (a) the use of the dependent and the independent series; and (b) the choice of one extreme or other of the series used. The correct answer, as the formal analysis has already shown, is arrived at by using the independent series as criterion and selecting the appropriate extreme. But the child may use the dependent one instead, or else he may try to take account of both series; and in either case he may fix his attention on the wrong end of the series.

The first error, then, consists in using only the dependent series, but selecting the appropriate end term. This amounts, in fact, to answering the question: 'Which of the following *would be* the largest?' as if it asked: 'Which of the following *is* the largest?' When this error occurs the child simply answers, to use as illustration Problem D1: 'The elephant – it's the biggest.' We shall call this error 1(a).

However, it is possible for choice to be based on the dependent series, as in the above example, but for the wrong extreme to be chosen. The child may select the snail 'because it's the smallest'.[1] When this occurs, the child's comments frequently show that he has gained, from his reading of the problem, some dim idea that things are to be other than they are in reality – that he is dealing with some sort of topsy-turvy world. Consequently, he simply reverses the quality to which the question refers and, asked which would be largest, names the smallest. This error occurred only once in Group O(i), and that in a very complicated

[1] Notice that 'snail' is the correct solution. So the problem allows choice of the right solution for a wrong and quite common reason – indeed for more than one wrong reason, as we shall see later – and is in this respect faulty.

answer, containing other errors also. So for clear illustration we take an instance from Group Y(i) where it was common. Jim, giving his reason for choosing 'snail' as the solution to D1, said: 'It's the smallest, and it would be the biggest of them if it were sort of changed around.' Several other children spoke of 'changing round' or 'turning round about'.

When this sort of comment is made, the error – which will be called error 1(b) – is plainly an error of principle: there is a quite systematic and intentional reversing of values, resulting from an inadequate grasp of the problem. However, it is possible that occasionally a child might choose the wrong end of one of the series as a result of a brief loss of hold – a momentary confusion. This would seem much more likely to happen when the independent series is being used, as we shall see in a moment. But it cannot be excluded even when it is reversal of the dependent series that is in question, except in cases where remarks of the kind which have just been quoted show that the child conceives himself to be applying a rule.

Errors 1(a) and 1(b), then, involve the use of the dependent series, with choice of either the correct or the wrong extreme. Next, there occurs a type of error in which the child attempts to take into account both the dependent and the independent series. Thus John, answering D1, says:

'Well . . . elephant. (Why?) Because it's slow and it's large and if it was fast-moving it would be small like a snail.'

So instead of finding the slowest and inferring that, in terms of the premiss, it would be the largest, John picks an animal which is both large and slow. It is as if he is trying somehow to effect a compromise.

In some of the answers this error took a slightly different and rather more extreme form than in the case just quoted. The child would begin by dividing the alternative solutions into two groups according to real possession of either the dependent or the independent property. Then he would choose one of these groups as lying towards the appropriate end of the series and make a final selection from within this group according to real possession of the *other* property. Thus, Robert, answering D2: 'Blanket, because blanket and sacking are rough, and the blanket is thicker than the sacking.'

This boy starts with the independent series – divides the alternatives into the rough and, by implication, the smooth – and ends by selecting in terms of the dependent series; that is, instead of choosing sacking because it is rougher than blanket, he chooses blanket because it is thicker than sacking. An example of the reverse procedure – initial division according to the dependent series, final choice in terms of the independent one – is given by Joy, answering D1: 'The horse and elephant are larger, the others are smaller. If a horse is faster than an elephant that makes it smaller, so the elephant's the largest.'

These last errors clearly belong to the group which we have defined as involving the use of both series, but they have as their distinctive feature the explicit division of one or other series into two parts so that the terms are assigned to two distinct classes. This so closely resembles what happens when a child makes judgements of membership in the unquantified three-term series that it would seem appropriate to use the same term in referring to it.

These, then, constitute the errors of type 2(a). Type 2(b) is the same in that both series are used – but the wrong extreme of one or other or both is chosen. Thus, in D1, the child making this error might choose the squirrel because it is small and fast; or the horse because it is large and fast; or the snail because it is small and slow.

Next come answers where the independent series is the criterion of choice. This, when the correct extreme is chosen, produces the right solution. However, there occurs an error which falls somewhere between the correct procedure and the errors of type 2. It sometimes happens that a child claims to be choosing on the basis of the property of the independent series but in fact is influenced by the property of the dependent series also. John, whose answer to D1 has already been quoted, gave the following answer to D4:

'An alarm clock. (Why?) Because it's the largest. (Is it larger than a cushion?) No, it isn't – no, "cushion" is the answer. (Why did you choose "alarm clock"?) I just thought in my mind: an alarm clock would weigh heavier than a cushion.'

This will be called an error of type 3(a). Proceeding on the same basis as before, one could define a type 3(b) which would be the same as the example we have just quoted, except that the wrong end of the series would be chosen. No instance of this occurred in either of the groups.

Errors of what may be called type 4(b) were, however, quite frequent (4(a) being, of course, the correct solution). That is, it sometimes happened that a child used only the independent criterion but picked the wrong extreme. In Problem D4, for instance, Jean gave as her answer: 'A nail, because it's smallest,' whereas she should have said: 'A cushion, because it's largest.'

In the discussion of error 1(b) (page 152 above), the suggestion was made that the element of reversal in that error might sometimes arise from the deliberate attempt to apply a principle, but, on the other hand, might sometimes be the result of a brief loss of hold; also, that this second explanation would perhaps be more frequently appropriate when reversal of the independent rather than the dependent series was in question: that is to say, in the case of the error we are now considering.

There are two grounds for this belief. First, there is the *a priori* consideration that choice based on the independent series is formally a more complex operation than choice based on the dependent one. It requires that the precise form of a correlation be apprehended, and that an inference be made from one series to the other. More information has to be handled, more manipulations have to be performed, than when the dependent series alone is involved. It therefore seems more probable that a loss of hold error should occur.

It is, of course, dangerous to base any psychological conclusion upon a consideration of the merely formal characteristics of a problem situation, because psychological complexity and formal complexity are not always coincident. However, in this case there is some evidence to support the view that more 4(b) than 1(b) errors are of an executive kind. This evidence consists in the relative lack of comments like 'you have to change it around', which, as already reported, were very common accompaniments of reversal of the dependent series. In the case of 4(b), the child would often make the error and then quite quickly correct himself. Thus, Peter (Group O(ii) ), answering D1, says: 'Well, if the fast-moving ones were smaller, the fastest would be the biggest and the fastest there would be the horse. Oh, no! – it's the slower ones – so that would be the snail.' Peter made no other errors on this occasion and had made none at all in dealing with these problems on the previous occasion. This looks, then, not like a failure to comprehend a principle, but rather like a failure to put it into practice without flaw. It is quite clear, at the same time, that reversal of the independent series does sometimes arise in a way that has more in common with the majority of the errors of type 1(b). For instance, Clare, giving an account of her attempt to solve D4, says that she first thought of 'nail' as the solution because she expected to be told that small objects would be heavier than larger ones. In her own words, 'I thought it might say "more than larger ones" so I thought of "nail".' Then she realized to her surprise that the stated relationship is 'just as it is now'.

If it were possible to distinguish confidently between a 4(b) error arising from a false expectation or an inappropriate principle and one occasioned by loss of hold, it would, of course, be desirable to do so, setting up two categories of error instead of one. However, sometimes the answers given were more ambiguous than those of Peter and Clare, and it was impossible to decide whether the error was of one kind or the other. The category was therefore left undivided.

There remains for brief mention a further error, which lies outside the two-way classificatory schema. It consists in a confusion of the dependent with the independent series so that the child actually answers the wrong question. For instance, Charles, attempting D1, where he is asked which animal would be the largest, gives 'elephant' as the solution because: 'We know the elephant is largest, so we know it would be the slowest.' Thus he correctly establishes the connection 'large-slow', but appears to get confused and think he is to infer speed from size instead of making the inference in the other direction.

*Results: Group O(ii)*

The pattern of change from the first to the second occasion is shown in *Table 16*.

TABLE 16    GROUP O—PROBLEMS D1, D2, D3, AND D4

| Error | A | B | C | D | IME | IMC | IDC |
|---|---|---|---|---|---|---|---|
| | Number of children making the error on occasions | | | | | | |
| | (i) and (ii) | (i) not (ii) | (ii) not (i) | not (i) nor (ii) | | | |
| 1(a) Dependent series—no reversal | 0 | 1 | 2 | 16 | ·16 | 1·00 | +·33 |
| 1(b) Dependent series—reversal | 1 | 0 | 1 | 17 | ·11 | ·50 | +1·00 |
| 2(a) Both series—no reversal | 2 | 3 | 0 | 14 | ·26 | ·60 | −1·00 |
| 2(b) Both series—reversal | 0 | 2 | 0 | 17 | ·11 | 1·00 | −1·00 |
| 3(a) Claims to judge by independent series—actually uses dependent series; no reversal | 1 | 2 | 3 | 13 | ·32 | ·83 | +·20 |
| 4(b) Independent series—reversal | 3 | 1 | 3 | 12 | ·37 | ·57 | +·50 |
| 5 Confusion of dependent and independent series | 0 | 0 | 1 | 18 | ·05 | 1·00 | +1·00 |

From this table by itself no very clear picture of development emerges. The only diminishing errors are those of type 2, the errors in which the child makes use of both series as criteria of choice. It might seem, then, that these are the most primitive errors and that, as they disappear, others are taking their place. However, in spite of the positive indices obtained with Group O, the findings from the study of the younger children suggest strongly that the errors of type 1 are even more primitive. The presentation of these findings will therefore precede further discussion of the developmental trends.

*Results: Group Y(i) and (ii)*

All the types of error found in either group have already been discussed, so we can proceed directly to the table of patterns of change for Group Y *Table 17*.

*Table 17* shows why errors of type 1 – and especially those of type 1(a) – are judged the most primitive: it is obviously these that show the sharpest decline in frequency as one passes from the youngest age-group studied to the next. Type 1(a) is an error made by as many as twelve of the children on the first occasion of testing (column A + column B). Three of the twelve continue to make the error on the second occasion, but the remaining nine have ceased to do so and there are no fresh instances, so the diminution is very marked. Further than this, there is evidence that the principle of error replacement is operating and that the fresh instances of errors 1(b), 2(a), and 2(b) (see column C) are linked with the diminution of this most primitive error of all. All three of the new 'second-occasion' occurrences of 1(b) were by children who made error 1(a) on the first occasion, two having made this error only and having made it on all four problems. Again, the two fresh instances of 2(a) were by children both of whom had made error 1(a) – and this error only – the first time; and the two fresh instances of 2(b) were produced by children who had made errors 1(a) and 1(b) on the first occasion.

So it seems clear that, in this group at any rate, errors of type 2 are tending to replace those of type 1: the use of the dependent

TABLE 17    GROUP Y—PROBLEMS D1, D2, D3, AND D4

| Error | A | B | C | D | IME | IMC | IDC |
|---|---|---|---|---|---|---|---|
| | Number of children making the error on occasions | | | | | | |
| | (i) and (ii) | (i) not (ii) | (ii) not (i) | not (i) nor (ii) | | | |
| 1(a) Dependent series—no reversal | 3 | 9 | 0 | 8 | ·60 | ·75 | −1·00 |
| 1(b) Dependent series—reversal | 0 | 6 | 3 | 11 | ·45 | 1·00 | −·33 |
| 2(a) Both series—no reversal | 2 | 3 | 2 | 13 | ·35 | ·71 | −·20 |
| 2(b) Both series—reversal | 1 | 6 | 2 | 11 | ·45 | ·89 | −·50 |
| 3(a) Claims to judge by independent series—actually uses dependent series; no reversal | 0 | 3 | 2 | 15 | ·25 | 1·00 | −·20 |
| 4(b) Independent series—reversal | 1 | 0 | 5 | 14 | ·30 | ·83 | +1·00 |
| 5 Confusion of dependent and independent series | 0 | 1 | 0 | 19 | ·05 | 1·00 | −1·00 |

series only is giving way before the attempt to make some use at least of the independent one.

Further, the evidence from Group O suggests, as we have already seen (cf. *Table 16*), that the next stage consists in a diminution of errors of type 2 (which both have IDC of − 1·00 in Group

O) and their replacement by errors of type 3 or by the correct solution: in other words, that there is a continuation of the tendency to move from use of the dependent towards use of the independent series. Two of the three children in Group O who make error 2(a) on the first occasion make error 3(a) on the second, the third making no errors the second time. And one of the two who make error 2(b) the first time makes error 3(a) the next time. The other one, however, reverts to error 1(a) and helps to contribute to the positive IDC for that error which *Table 16* contains. About this and the other two cases of 'regression' to type 1 errors, one can say only that they run counter to the general trend: the protocols afford no indication of why the errors should have arisen. It has, of course, proved to be the case throughout this study, even when there is a trend which seems very marked, that one or two contrary instances arise. For some considerable time after an error has ceased to be prevalent it remains possible that an occasional child who appeared to have moved beyond it will produce it again.

We now give in *Table 18* the total error frequencies for both groups on both occasions.

TABLE 18    Problems D1, D2, D3, and D4

| Error | Frequency of error among children in Groups | | | |
|---|---|---|---|---|
| | Y (i) (age 10) | (Y ii) (age 12) | O (i) (age 12) | O (ii) (age 14) |
| 1(a) | 21 | 3 | 1 | 2 |
| 1(b) | 11 | 5 | 1 | 2 |
| 2(a) | 8 | 6 | 8 | 2 |
| 2(b) | 11 | 3 | 3 | 0 |
| 3(a) | 3 | 2 | 3 | 4 |
| 4(b) | 1 | 7 | 6 | 7 |
| 5 | 1 | 0 | 0 | 1 |

By far the sharpest drop in total frequency occurs in error 1(a) between the ages of ten and twelve. On the other hand, error

4(b) shows a substantial rise over the same period of time, and gives no sign of diminishing again. The increase is consistent with the view that it is an 'advanced' error, which begins to occur as the more immature responses disappear.

# CHAPTER 8

## Formal Deductive Reasoning

So far, discussion of each type of problem has started with a brief analysis of the main ways in which it may be varied. Discussion of the formal variants of the syllogism is traditionally a task for the textbooks of logic and no attempt will be made to usurp their function. But there are four types of variation (not all of them logical or formal ones) which are of particular interest here.

1. The first concerns the number of premisses in the argument and thus raises the question of the distinction between the syllogism proper and the sorites. Quine (1952) defines syllogisms as 'arguments wherein a categorical statement is derived as conclusion from two categorical statements as premisses, the three statements being so related that there are altogether just three terms, each of which appears in two of the statements'. The sorites is an argument of the same kind but with one or more additional premisses – that is to say, with four or more related terms instead of three. This difference will be illustrated later when the problems used are quoted.

2. The second variable is that of content, and here the main issues are two in number:
   (a) whether the terms of the premisses are symbols such as a, b, c, or whether they are the names of objects and classes of objects;
   (b) if the latter is the case, whether the premisses are true or false.

3. The third variable is that of the form in which the premises are stated, and particularly whether they are in conditional or categorical form. It must be noted at this point that to state the premises of an ordinary categorical syllogism in hypothetical form – that is, simply to preface them by the word 'if' – is not to turn the syllogism into what is traditionally described as a conditional syllogism. The latter has the form: 'If A, then B. But A. Therefore B.' Consequently, it is different in its structure from the ordinary or categorical syllogism.

4. The fourth variable is that of the form in which the answer is to be given: whether the subject has to draw a conclusion for himself; or say of one stated conclusion whether it is valid or invalid; or select a valid conclusion from a number of offered alternatives.

The first of these variables is important in that the problems include two syllogisms and one four-term (three-premiss) sorites. The other three are relevant in the following ways.

It is of the very essence of formal reasoning that content is unimportant in the sense that the validity of the inference drawn is independent of it. But psychologically it seems evident, and has indeed been demonstrated,[1] that content matters considerably. This amounts, of course, to saying that reasoning based only on the form of the relations between premises (that is, 'pure' formal reasoning) is not a very common event. Most of the work which demonstrates this shows that meaningful content in the premises produces 'bias' and hence invalid deduction. It might therefore be urged that, if one wants to give capacity for formal reasoning a good chance to show itself, one should use as terms only symbols. From the point of view of a study of errors, however, the important thing is not so much to reduce the likelihood of choices based on considerations other than those of deduction from the pre-

---

[1] See, for instance, I. L. Janis and F. Frick (1943), A. Lefford (1946), and J. J. B. Morgan and J. T. Morton (1944). But see also Henle and Michael (1956), who criticize some of the earlier work.

misses as to make sure one is in a position to recognize such choices when they do occur – to distinguish them, in other words, from genuine (even if perhaps fallacious) inference. And there is the further consideration that if one uses symbols one risks putting the problems so far beyond the understanding of some children that they cannot attempt them at all.

So it seemed best to use meaningful terms – ordinary words – but to make the premises obviously false, on the ground that this makes it much easier for the experimenter to recognize genuine deduction when it happens. Then there is a new danger – namely, that the child with only a limited ability to adopt the formal attitude might be very unwilling to base any reasoning at all on a manifestly false statement. It was in order to lessen this risk that the statements were put in hypothetical form in the two syllogisms. (The premises of the sorites were left in categorical form for reasons that will be given in a moment when the problems have been quoted.) As has already been indicated, this does not turn a categorical syllogism into a conditional one: it was used simply as a means of emphasizing for the child's benefit the essentially hypothetical nature of all formal deductive reasoning. It is doubtful, however, if it had much effect.

The three problems used were as follows:

### PROBLEM EI

If all people who were born in July were lazy, and Bob was lazy, then:
  (1) We would know that Bob had been born in July.
  (2) Bob's teacher would tell him to try harder.
  (3) We would not know that Bob had been born in July.
  (4) Bob would not want to tell anyone when his birthday was.
  (5) Bob might learn to work harder.

### PROBLEM E2

If all boys with red hair played football well and Tommy did not have red hair, then:

163

(1) Tommy would not play football well.
(2) Tommy might still play football well.
(3) Tommy would have no hope of playing in the school team.
(4) Tommy would probably play other games.
(5) Tommy would wish his hair was red.

### PROBLEM E3

No animals that can only move slowly can climb trees.
A hedgehog is a prickly animal.
All prickly animals can only move slowly.
Therefore:
(1) All animals that can only move slowly are prickly.
(2) A hedgehog has no need to climb trees because it can curl into a prickly ball.
(3) All animals that can move quickly can climb trees.
(4) A hedgehog can move quite fast sometimes.
(5) No hedgehogs can climb trees.

Thus there are two syllogisms, E1 and E2, and one sorites, E3. And in all three problems the correct solution has to be selected from a number of possibilities – that is, the problems are in multiple-choice form. This makes it possible to present, among other choices, an invalid conclusion and a statement rejecting it, which, it seemed, might be the best way of testing the child's recognition of fallacy – better, perhaps, than the other possible procedure of simply offering him one conclusion and asking him to pass a direct judgement on its validity.

In both E1 and E2, then, the first distractor is the conclusion of an invalid syllogism and the correct solution is a statement negating it. The sorites, on the other hand, permits of a valid conclusion, but two logical fallacy distractors are provided – numbers 1 and 3 – each of them being an invalid inference from one of the premisses. The remaining distractors in all three problems have no direct logical link with the premisses. They are all observations that accord fairly well with everyday experience and might be made by way of general comment on the situation. Some of them, however, may be said to have indirect logical links with the premisses by way of further unstated propositions. For instance, the second distractor in E1 may be said to rest on an implicit proposition to the effect that 'all teachers are people who tell lazy boys to work harder'. This distractor, of course, virtually ignores the stated major premiss and really derives from a combination of the minor premiss, 'Bob is lazy', and the implicit premiss to which we have just referred.

Attention has already been drawn to the fact that the premisses of the two syllogisms are stated hypothetically, while those of the sorites are stated categorically, and the reasons for using the hypothetical form of statement in the case of the syllogisms have been given. The categorical form was preferred for the sorites because it was felt that, with three premisses, repetition of the 'if' in front of each one would seem strange and forced. Nor did it seem possible to run the three premisses into one sentence, as was done in the case of the two premisses of the syllogisms, in order to avoid this repetition.

*Results: Group O(i)*

As we have seen, the choice of a solution in these problems offers a threefold possibility: the child may choose the correct solution; he may choose a solution which can be deduced fallaciously from the premisses; or he may choose a solution which is not deducible from the premisses at all. Later, when the results for Group O(ii) are presented, the numbers of choices which fell into these three categories on the different problems will be stated. Here, as usual, concern is with qualitative discussion of the children's answers. It may be said at once, though, that correct inference was rare.

The most common reason given for choice of a logical fallacy solution was that it was 'obvious'. Sometimes the premisses were simply read aloud along with the 'conclusion' as if the juxtaposition spoke for itself and there was nothing more to be said. Sometimes, however, although no further positive reason for the choice could be given, reasons were offered for rejection of the other four possibilities. Three examples follow to illustrate the kinds of reason that were proposed; they refer to the second distractor in Problem E1.

*Charles:* 'His teacher would know his birthday and wouldn't bother to tell him to work harder.'

*Mary:* 'Because it's a different subject. It's about Bob's teacher and we were talking about Bob.'

*Flora:* [Laughing.] 'You don't know Bob's teacher.'

The first of these reasons is a clear example of the introduction into reasoning of considerations based on 'real-life experience', and of accompanying neglect of the given. It is thus an instance of arbitrary error. By contrast, the second is expressive of a fairly rigorous insistence on connection between the premises and the conclusions to be drawn. But the third comes perhaps nearest of all to the formal attitude: we cannot draw this conclusion because we lack some necessary information. It is true that Flora says 'You don't know Bob's teacher', rather than, 'You don't know anything about Bob's teacher', which latter would be a more formal statement of the reason why the conclusion in question cannot be drawn from the premises. But her awareness of inadequacy indicates a regard for the given and its necessary implications which was rare in the children of her group when they were tackling these problems on this first occasion of testing.

It is a very striking fact, however, that, in many of these children, reasoning which approaches more or less closely to the standards of strict deduction is sharply followed or preceded by what one may perhaps call the 'common-sense' kind. Thus Flora herself, in spite of her rather formal treatment of E1, goes on to prefer distractor 2 to the correct solution (number 5) in E3, saying: 'I did have a temptation (sic) to choose 5 but I thought 2 was more common sense.' And when she was then asked: 'Why did you think it might be 5?' she replied: 'Well, it's true – no hedgehogs *can* climb trees.'

So it is possible for there to be swift alternations as one mode of reasoning jostles with the other for dominance. Only in a very few children, as we shall see later, was common-sense reasoning entirely absent from all three problems of this kind. Here are one or two further illustrations of the manner of its occurrence:

*Stewart* (answering E2): 'I'll take 5, because I would wish my hair was red.'

*John* (answering E3): 'It can't be 3, because a lion moves fast but it can't climb trees.'

In both of these examples, the criterion is not relation to the premisses, but everyday knowledge or everyday values. Reasons of precisely the kind that John advances – namely, that a case can be thought of which proves the generalization false – were very frequently given to justify rejection of the two logical fallacy distractors in E3. Pam rejects distractor 1 'because a snail moves slowly and *it's* not prickly'.

Many of the children were apparently quite satisfied when they offered reasons of this kind. Some, however, seemed to be aware that they should be deducing – or 'imagining it out of this', as one boy put it – even when they did not succeed in doing so. The boy just mentioned was Stewart, who made the remark quoted earlier about basing his choice on how he himself would feel. Here is his attempt at E3:

'I think 5 is the most sensible. (Why?) Well, they can't really. But if you're imagining it out of this [pointing to premisses] I'd say 1. (Why?) Well, the hedgehog *is* very slow and it *is* prickly.'

Here again the two modes of reasoning appear in rapid succession, if not conflict. Stewart is aware apparently that connection with the premisses matters. Yet even after basing his choice of the logical fallacy distractor on this awareness, he offers a common-sense justification for that choice: 'the hedgehog *is* very slow . . .'

Notice that Stewart thinks the correct solution is 'the most sensible' for a similar reason: hedgehogs 'can't really' climb trees. In other words, the premisses, false though they are, lead by correct inference to a true conclusion: and so, as in some of the other problems we have considered, the correct solution can be chosen for the wrong reason. Here is Brenda's reason:

'It might be 5. (Why?) Because they're fat and they have small feet and couldn't cling to trees.'

167

When Problem E3 was constructed at the start of the inquiry, this kind of reasoning was anticipated; but its extreme prevalence was not fully appreciated. False premisses were used so that genuine deduction could be recognized when it occurred. But the fact that the correct solution was true, and very attractive to the 'common-sense thinker', was not noticed. The moral for test constructors is obvious: before a test is used, the most detailed inquiry into its functioning is desirable. Without this, the risk that the right solution might be given for the wrong reasons is a major one. However, in this case it happened that distractor 2 was even more powerfully attractive, and, though 5 was often called 'true' for reasons such as Brenda's, it was seldom chosen for these reasons by the children of Group O.

We shall now turn to the answers of those few children who showed at least some interest in the correct solutions for genuinely deductive reasons. Jean immediately chose the right solution for E2, saying:

'I think the second one. (Why?) Because maybe it isn't that all boys . . . Maybe some other boys that didn't have red hair could play football too.' But she was alone in managing so firm a choice and so clear a justification in this problem. Yet she chose the fallacy for E1 and a common-sense distractor – number 2 – for E3.

Several children were prepared to allow that both the correct solution to E2 and the accompanying logical fallacy distractor were acceptable. There was, in these cases, no apparent concern about the fact that the two contradict one another.

The two most competent answers to E3 are perhaps worth quoting in full. They were given by Peter and by Mary.

*Peter:* 'Number 1, I think. Numbers 2 and 3 have nothing to do with it at all, so they're out. [Scornful tone.] Number 3 could be true. [He re-reads the premisses carefully.] I'm not so sure about 1 now. It just tells you . . . Well, there's more animals than prickly ones that can move slowly. I think it's 5 now. (Why?) Well, slow animals can't climb trees, and a hedgehog is a slow animal. (How do you know?) Because all prickly animals can only move slowly.'

The tone in which Peter dismisses the common-sense distractors is worthy of notice. This was the only sign of scorn.

*Mary:* 'Number 5. (Why?) Because it says no animals that can only move slowly can climb trees. And it says prickly animals move slowly, and the hedgehog is a prickly animal so it can't climb trees.'

## Results: Group O(ii)

As usual, the quantitative results for Group O(i) will be presented along with the comparable figures for Group O(ii); but the procedure will not be exactly as before. The question is whether the findings provide any evidence of regular developmental trends. Therefore, since the problems offer three types of solution – 'common-sense', deductive but fallacious, deductive and correct – one may take each possible pair of types of solution and see how often movement in each of these directions occurs: how many children move from common-sense to logical fallacy solutions, and how many in the reverse direction; how many from logical fallacies to the correct solutions, and vice versa; how many from common-sense choices to the correct solutions, and vice versa; and how frequently there is no change. This differs from the analysis of errors in previous problems, not only in being slightly more complicated, but also in that the data relate to the actual solutions offered rather than to characteristics of the reasoning that led up to the final choice.

The reason for this is the extraordinarily complex interweaving of different modes of reasoning which has already been mentioned. It is much less easy here than in the other problems to isolate 'an error'. It is certainly possible to say of any given child whether in his answers, whatever his final choice may be, common-sense reasoning does at some point or other occur – and this will be done later. But since there are so few children who are entirely free of common-sense reasoning and yet since its extent varies so widely from child to child in these problems, a mere record of occurrence or non-occurrence is not by itself very revealing. An obvious procedure, then, is to analyse by solution chosen, on the argument that the more pervasive and powerful the tendency to common-sense reasoning, the more likely it will be to lead to actual choice of a common-sense distractor. Yet this analysis of final solutions is a practice which has been avoided in other problems precisely on the ground that a given final choice may be arrived at in a variety of ways; and we have already seen that, at least in one of the problems now being discussed, this does in fact occur. So there is something of a dilemma. In fact, however, so far as this group of children is concerned, the difficulty is not in practice very serious. It will be recalled that, though the children were sometimes prepared to accept the correct solution to E3 as 'true' on common-sense grounds, the attraction of the second distractor was generally sufficiently strong to lure them away. With the children of Group Y, the problem becomes altogether more acute. Meanwhile, however, the analysis will be by solutions chosen.

*Table 19* shows in how many cases choice of a common-sense distractor on the first occasion was followed by choice of a logical fallacy distractor on the second, and so on. In this table, CSD stands for 'common-sense distractor', LFD for 'logical fallacy distractor', and CA for 'correct answer'. (Although the word 'solution' has been used for final choice throughout this book, the letters CA are used here to avoid confusion with CS, standing for 'common sense'.) The arrows indicate the direction of the movement the frequency of which is being recorded.

In *Table 19*, all pairs except number (3) involve the occurrence of error on one or other or both occasions. One may thus calculate an index of magnitude of error in the usual way, by dividing the summed frequencies for all pairs except (3) by the total frequency. Similarly, an index of magnitude of change may be arrived at if one divides the sum of pairs (4) to (9) (which involve both error at some point or another and change) by the total for all pairs except (3). So far as the calculation of an index of direction of change is concerned, one may, in such a case as this, postulate a directional sequence and select for comparison those pairs which are compatible with it on the one hand and those

TABLE 19    GROUP O—PROBLEMS E1, E2, AND E3

| Movement in choice of solutions occasion (i) | occasion (ii) | E1 | E2 | E3 | All |
|---|---|---|---|---|---|
| (1) CSD | →CSD | 1 | 0 | 2 | 3 |
| (2) LFD | →LFD | 14 | 8 | 1 | 23 |
| (3) CA | →CA | 0 | 1 | 6 | 7 |
| (4) CSD | →LFD | 2 | 4 | 1 | 7 |
| (5) LFD | →CSD | 0 | 2 | 0 | 2 |
| (6) CSD | →CA | 0 | 2 | 5 | 7 |
| (7) CA | →CSD | 0 | 0 | 1 | 1 |
| (8) LFD | →CA | 2 | 2 | 3 | 7 |
| (9) CA | →LFD | 0 | 0 | 0 | 0 |

Frequency in problems column header spans E1, E2, E3, All.

which are incompatible with it on the other. One can thus get some assessment of the evidence for or against a given order of events. It is equally possible, of course, to proceed by asking which combination of pairs will give the highest IDC and then claim that, in so far as there is any trend, it is in this rather than in any other direction. In adopting the latter course, however, one is not free to combine any pairs that one pleases, for it would be nonsense to combine contraries – for instance, pair (4) with pair (5).

The IDC will now be calculated for the sequence which seems most likely, on general theoretical grounds, to represent the course of development, namely, common-sense choice, followed by logical fallacy choice, followed by choice of the correct solution. Pairs (4), (6), and (8) are compatible with this sequence, since a move from common-sense to correct solution is in the right direction. Pairs (5), (7), and (9), however, represent movement in the opposite direction and must be regarded as evidence against this particular postulated trend.

Accordingly, *Table 20* gives the IDC for pairs (4), (6), and (8) calculated against (5), (7), and (9), separately for each problem and also for all three problems considered together. Pairs (4), (6), and (8) are given the negative sign in the calculation, so that a high negative IDC is evidence for the existence of the trend, and a high positive IDC is evidence for the existence of the opposing trend. In *Table 20* the IME and IMC for each problem separately and for all three combined are also shown.

TABLE 20    GROUP O—PROBLEMS E1, E2, AND E3

| Indices | Problems | | | |
|---|---|---|---|---|
| | E1 | E2 | E3 | *All* |
| IME | 1·00 | ·95 | ·68 | ·88 |
| IMC | ·21 | ·56 | ·77 | ·48 |
| IDC | −1·00 | −·60 | −·80 | −·75 |

It will be seen from *Table 20* that no child chose the correct solution in E1 on both occasions (IME = 1·00); but the IMC for that problem is markedly low. This arises because of the very large number of children who chose the logical fallacy solution on both occasions.

Perhaps the fact that the fallacy distractor in E2 contains a negative helps to explain why it is chosen relatively less often and less persistently. The same suggestion might explain the counter tendency for the correct solution in E2 to be chosen more often than the correct solution in E1, the latter again being a negative statement. In E2, however, it is still the fallacy distractor which accounts for most of the stability; whereas in E3 it is the correct solution. By this criterion, then, E3 is the easiest task, though this is the reverse of what might have been expected. But, on the other hand, E3 calls forth more common-sense reasoning, if the totality of choices is considered, than either of the other two, although only two common-sense distractors are offered in E3, compared with three in each of the other two problems. Any subject who appears in any of pairs (1), (4), (5), (6), or (7) has chosen a common-sense solution at one or other stage. For E3, nine children fall in these groups; for E2, eight do so; and for E1, only three.

Let us turn now to the evidence of the IDC. It is plain from *Tables 19* and *20* that evidence in favour of the postulated trend is fairly strong, especially in E1, where there is no single case running counter to it. In the other problems, however, there are a few contrary instances (three in all); and reference to *Table 19* shows that one of these represents what, in the terms of the hypothesis, must be regarded as a regression from the most advanced to the least advanced way of responding. It may be worth examining the contrary protocols in detail, to see whether an explanation suggests itself.

When this is done, it appears that, in two of the three cases (including the most severe retrogressive movement), trouble with one of the negative statements in the problem has brought confusion. Now it is an interesting fact that difficulty in the handling of negatives in these problems was something which increased between the first and second occasions, the increase not being confined to children who, in the end, 'regressed' in their actual choice of a solution. This increase in difficulty occurred chiefly in E3, there being in fact only one other instance. *Table 21* shows the pattern of change.[1]

TABLE 21    GROUP O—PROBLEMS E1, E2, AND E3

| Problem | A | B | C | D | IME | IMC | IDC |
|---|---|---|---|---|---|---|---|
| | Number of children having difficulty in handling negatives on occasions | | | | | | |
| | (i) and (ii) | (i) not (ii) | (ii) not (i) | not (i) nor (ii) | IME | IMC | IDC |
| E1 | 0 | 0 | 0 | 19 | ·00 | — | — |
| E2 | 0 | 0 | 1 | 18 | ·05 | 1·00 | +1·00 |
| E3 | 0 | 1 | 5 | 13 | ·32 | 1·00 | + ·66 |
| All | 0 | 1 | 6 | 50 | ·12 | 1·00 | + ·71 |

[1] Here we are of course concerned, as in earlier problems, with errors in reasoning rather than with final choices.

The overall IME is small (·12), but the IDC is + ·71. The explanation seems to be that the increase in perplexity is associated with the increase in attempts at genuine deduction. It is, after all, quite understandable that the negative in 'no animals that can only move slowly can climb trees' should give no trouble till one tries to deduce consequences from it; and that the negative in 'no hedgehogs can climb trees' should give no trouble till one wonders whether one is justified in drawing it as a conclusion.

The two protocols which offer the clearest illustration of the increase in perplexity and its nature are those of Sarah and Stewart. Sarah unhesitatingly chose distractor 2 for Problem E3 on the first occasion, her reason for doing so being 'because it has prickly spines and no animal could touch it or it would get jagged'. Thus she reasons in a very straightforward common-sense fashion. But on the second occasion, after a hesitant reading of the premisses, she says: 'I can't seem to understand this bit here [pointing to the first premiss]. I get muddled up with animals that move slowly *going* up trees': that is, she muddles the positive and the negative. She deduces correctly in the end, but with a great struggle.

Stewart, on occasion (i), begins by saying that 'no hedgehogs can climb trees' is 'the most sensible' on the ground that 'Well, they can't really', though he then goes on to choose the logical fallacy distractor on other grounds (see page 167 where the rest of his answer is quoted). On the second occasion, however, Stewart had this to say:

'Well, we would know that no hedgehogs can climb trees. Because a hedgehog is a prickly animal and all prickly animals can only move slowly and no animals that can only move slowly can climb trees. [Hesitates, looks very puzzled.] *Can* climb trees . . . Well, the more I read it, the more it seems to change. Well, no animals that can move slowly can climb trees, well, no animals that can only move slowly *can* climb trees, well, I thought that the "can" . . . that could do it too. The "can" seemed – well, at first it seemed no animals *can* climb trees, that is to say, they cannot, then I read it over and I thought it meant they can.'

Plainly, this kind of confusion must be expected to arise more frequently when the full demands of the problem are appreciated and an attempt is made to meet them, than when the given is treated in a more casual way. The more strictly a subject is trying to adhere to the given, the more probable this kind of tussle becomes. The two children who regressed from logical fallacy and correct solution choice respectively to common-sense distractor choices, and had difficulty with a negative statement, were not so articulate in their answers as Stewart, but their perplexities seemed to be of a similar kind. Robert, like Stewart, appeared to find trouble in grasping the import of the first premise in E3 – i.e. in appreciating that 'no animals can' means the same as 'all animals cannot'. Thereafter he fairly rapidly gave up the attempt to deal with the complexities of inference and chose as his solution the favourite common-sense distractor, number 2, which, be it observed, he had also allowed to be 'true' on occasion (i) when he gave as his choice, apparently by genuine deduction, the correct solution, number 5. What we are implying, of course, if we attribute Robert's regression in solution-choice to an advance in appreciation of the demands of the problem, is that he got the correct solution on occasion (i) without appreciating these demands fully. When we say that he seemed to arrive at the correct solution deductively on that occasion, we are using as evidence the fact that, when asked to justify his choice, he repeated the premises, instead of making some such remark as, 'Well, they can't!' But this does not, of course, exclude the possibility that there was at this stage room for further advance in his appreciation of formal reasoning.

It must be emphasized that these are very tentative explanations. One would not be justified in stating emphatically on the available evidence that the change in Robert's answer – or in the answers of either of the other 'regressers' – is definitely to be explained by the occurrence of advances in thinking. Nevertheless, this study indicates again and again that genuine advance can lead to fuller awareness of difficulty, and hence sometimes to errors which did not occur at an earlier stage. This is a feature of development which has tended to be overlooked and yet which is of considerable importance both theoretically and in the practice of test construction.

Having made this point, we need say only a word or two now about the other two children who 'regressed'. Joy appeared to have difficulty in grasping the negative import of distractor 1 in E2: 'Tommy would not play football well.' She treated it as a positive, and rejected it, thereby revealing, of course, that she accepted the logical fallacy. But since she thought distractor 1 was a positive and to be rejected, she had then no alternative left but one of the common-sense distractors, and she preferred number 4 'because Tommy did not have red hair and could not play football, so he would probably play other games'. Notice that she explicitly bases her choice of 4 on the fallacious inference. In a similar way, Charles, the third child, also shows his acceptance of the fallacy. On the second occasion, as on the first, he rejects the correct solution on the ground that: 'If that statement [the premisses] was true, he could not play football well.' However, on the first occasion he goes straight on to choose the appropriate logical fallacy distractor, while on the second he prefers 'Tommy would probably play other games' for the reason that: 'It doesn't say Tom played football or wished to play football.' One concludes that Charles is basing his preference on some criterion of relevance.

Both Joy and Charles, then, although they choose common-sense distractors on the second occasion, find room in their reasoning for the logical fallacy. It should be noted, moreover, that this is not in any way exceptional – a fact which can perhaps help to make the nature of common-sense reasoning more clear. It is not that the child who reasons in a common-sense way is unable to draw inferences. Inferences abound in his thinking, and indeed the common-sense solution is often inferentially more complex than the straightforward deduction because, as we have already seen, further implicit premisses are involved. The difference between common-sense and strictly logical thinking is a matter of rigour, of the ability to limit and restrict one's inference-drawing, to say 'this follows – but this and no more'. In many of the cases of common-sense reasoning in the three problems we have been considering, the fallacy is obviously accepted, but is not accepted in all its starkness. The child adds to it and embroiders upon it as seems to him most sensible and perhaps most interesting. So it is the relative lack of discipline and restraint which chiefly distinguishes less mature from more mature performances in these problems. This being so, the admixture of common-sense and logical reasoning which was found to be so prevalent is perhaps not particularly surprising. The process is one of pruning down. Logical inference is not, on this view, a new activity for the children at this stage, something built on top of an already existing and distinct substructure of other modes of reasoning. It emerges, rather, in 'pure' form as the outcome of a process of refinement.[1]

The section of this chapter which reports results for Group O(i) quotes a rejection of common-sense reasoning based on the admission of inadequacy of knowledge ('You don't know Bob's teacher') with the remark that, among the twelve-year-olds, this kind of reason was rarely given. Among the fourteen-year-olds, however, it was quite common, and this is perhaps as good an indication as any other of the nature of the change that had taken place. 'You are not sure.' 'We would not know.' 'We know nothing about Bob's life really.' These and the many other similar remarks by the children of Group O(ii) illustrate the very appreciable advance which has been made towards the standard which Bartlett (1958) proposes when he maintains that 'any process which can be called thinking is to some degree at least constrained'. If, however, one calculates the frequencies of occurrence of common-sense reasoning (at any point at all in the answers to the problems, irrespective now of solution finally chosen), one discovers that the children who are quite free of it – that is to say,

---

[1] But this is apparently not the end of the matter, for there is evidence that further changes of a regressive nature occur with ageing (see page 66).

whose thinking, on the available evidence, is fully constrained by the given – are still in a minority. The figures for all three problems considered together are given in *Table 22*.

TABLE 22    GROUP O—PROBLEMS E1, E2, AND E3

| Problems | A | B | C | D | IME | IMC | IDC |
|---|---|---|---|---|---|---|---|
| | Number of children in whose answers common-sense reasoning occurred on occasions | | | | | | |
| | (i) and (ii) | (i) not (ii) | (ii) not (i) | not (i) nor (ii) | | | |
| E1, E2, and E3 | 12 | 3 | 1 | 3 | ·84 | ·25 | − ·50 |

Thus even on the second occasion there were only six children in whose answers this did not occur at all.

*Results: Group Y(i) and (ii)*

No new ways of dealing with these problems appeared among the ten-year-olds. Like the children of Group O, those of Group Y reasoned sometimes on a basis of common sense, sometimes deductively but fallaciously, sometimes deductively and correctly. Instances of the last kind were, however, rare at age ten, as was to be expected.

Since there are no new types of error to be described, we can go on at once to a consideration of patterns of change from one occasion of testing to the other. Here, however, a difficulty arises. In the section giving results for Group O, we discussed the issue of whether we could, in these problems as in others, analyse errors, the trouble being the extent to which different modes of reasoning interweave in the production of a solution. In the case of Group O, the best procedure seemed to be to analyse solutions chosen rather than errors, supplementing this analysis by a statement of the number of children who, at some point or another, reasoned in a common-sense way. This was possible because there seemed to be very few cases where the choice of a given solution had been chiefly determined by reasoning in another mode – for instance, where common-sense reasoning had led to a correct choice. Among the children of Group Y, however, such cases were fairly common. On the first occasion, as many as five children made the correct choice in E3 and justified this in un-ambiguously common-sense ways. For instance, Florence took 'No hedgehogs can climb trees' to be the right solution 'because they like to live underground'. She made no reference to the pre-misses at all. To classify her as having made the right choice and leave the matter there would therefore be seriously misleading. So it has been necessary, for this group, to decide in each case what was the main determinant of the chosen solution: was it preferred chiefly on grounds of common-sense reasoning, or on grounds of acceptance of a fallacy, or as a consequence of correct deduction? This was frequently easy to decide, as in the instance we have just given. But here is an example of an answer that gave more difficulty.

*Mollie* (answering E3): 'Number 5 (Why?) Well, they can't climb trees according to this [premises] and it *is* true, too, that they can't.' The same girl rejected distractor 1 as 'not true – because the snail, for instance'. But she rejected distractor 4 because 'it's contradicting that [premises]'. The choice was classi-

TABLE 23    GROUP Y—PROBLEMS E1, E2, AND E3

Number of discrepancies between
final choice and determinant

| Occasion | Problems | | | All |
|---|---|---|---|---|
| | E1 | E2 | E3 | |
| (i) | 1 | 2 | 5 | 8 |
| (ii) | 0 | 1 | 2 | 3 |
| | 1 | 3 | 7 | 11 |

fied as determined in this case by correct deduction, but it is obvious that common-sense reasoning was being used at least as a support. In general, each child was given the benefit of any reasonable doubt there might be. The outcome was that in eleven cases, distributed as shown in *Table 23*, there was a discrepancy between final choice and determinant.

In ten of these eleven instances, the correct solution had been chosen, but the main determinant seemed to be common-sense reasoning. In the eleventh, choice of a logical fallacy distractor appeared similarly to be based on common-sense.

*Table 24* shows the patterns of change in the type of reasoning which acted as the main determinant of choice; and is followed

TABLE 24    GROUP Y—PROBLEMS E1, E2, AND E3

| | Movement in determinant | | Frequency in problems | | | |
|---|---|---|---|---|---|---|
| | occasion (i) | occasion (ii) | E1 | E2 | E3 | All |
| (1) | CSD | →CSD | 3 | 5 | 12 | 20 |
| (2) | LFD | →LFD | 10 | 5 | 0 | 15 |
| (3) | CA | →CA | 0 | 2 | 0 | 2 |
| (4) | CSD | →LFD | 3 | 4 | 0 | 7 |
| (5) | LFD | →CSD | 0 | 0 | 1 | 1 |
| (6) | CSD | →CA | 2 | 1 | 5 | 8 |
| (7) | CA | →CSD | 0 | 0 | 0 | 0 |
| (8) | LFD | →CA | 2 | 2 | 2 | 6 |
| (9) | CA | →LFD | 0 | 1 | 0 | 1 |

TABLE 25    GROUP Y—PROBLEMS E1, E2, AND E3

| | Problems | | | |
|---|---|---|---|---|
| Indices | E1 | E2 | E3 | All |
| IME | 1·00 | ·90 | 1·00 | ·97 |
| IMC | ·35 | ·44 | ·40 | ·40 |
| IDC | −1·00 | −·75 | −·75 | −·83 |

by *Table 25* giving the indices of magnitude of error and of magnitude and direction of change.

When these tables are compared with their counterparts for Group O (*Tables 19* and *20*), it appears that the indices are rather similar, though there is less inter-problem variation in IMC among the younger children. However, when all three problems are considered together, the magnitude of change is closely similar in the two groups. The difference lies in the nature of the cases of 'no change'. In Group Y, most of these are still at the 'common-sense' stage, whereas in Group O most are at the 'logical fallacy' level (see pairs (1), (2), and (3) in *Tables 19* and *24*). So far as direction of change is concerned, the two sets of results are in close agreement, and there would seem to be a continuation of the same trend over the whole age-range with which we are dealing. There are, indeed, in Group Y only two instances of movement running counter to the main trend – see the entries for pairs (5), (7), and (9) in *Table 24*. It will be recalled that, in the course of the discussion of Group O, the 'retrogressive' cases were considered individually, in an attempt to account for what had happened. It then appeared that increased difficulty with negative statements might be a related phenomenon. In Group Y, though increased difficulty with negatives is again a feature of the change from the first occasion to the second, this does not seem to serve as an explanation of the two instances of regression. Indeed, a study of the protocols yields no clue at all as to what occurred. One can do no more than report that both the children concerned gave less mature answers on the second occasion of testing than they had done two years earlier.

*Table 26* shows the increase in difficulty with negatives for Group Y, and is thus the counterpart of *Table 21*.

Of the five children who appear in column C of *Table 26*, one had difficulty rather closely akin to that experienced by Stewart in Group O (quoted on page 174).

*Jane:* 'I can't get the real meaning of the first sentence. "No animals . . ." I don't know. "No animals . . ." If the "no" wasn't there I could understand it.'

TABLE 26    GROUP Y—PROBLEMS E1, E2, AND E3

| Problem | A | B | C | D | IME | IMC | IDC |
|---|---|---|---|---|---|---|---|
| | *Number of children having difficulty in handling negatives on occasions* | | | | | | |
| | (i) and (ii) | (i) not (ii) | (ii) not (i) | not (i) nor (ii) | | | |
| E1 | 0 | 0 | 0 | 20 | ·00 | — | — |
| E2 | 0 | 0 | 3 | 17 | ·15 | 1·00 | +1·00 |
| E3 | 0 | 0 | 2 | 18 | ·10 | 1·00 | +1·00 |
| All | 0 | 0 | 5 | 55 | ·08 | 1·00 | +1·00 |

But the difficulty of the other four children took a different form. They each expressed *agreement* with a negative statement and then made some remark like: 'So it's not that one.' For instance, Alex (answering E2): ' "Tommy might still play football well" is out because if it's keeping to the rules [pointing to premisses] Tommy would not. So that's out, and so is number 1 for the same reason.'

Now distractor 1 states: 'Tommy would not play football well.' And it is *rejected* because 'Tommy would not'. This is a curious error, not encountered elsewhere.

It remains to record, for Group Y as for Group O, the number of children in whose answers, at some point or another, commonsense reasoning occurred. This is easy to do, since it occurred in the answers of every child in Group Y on both occasions of testing.

# CHAPTER 9

## *Conclusions*

IN THE preceding chapters the errors discussed have been sorted into three main categories. There are, first, the structural errors: errors which arise from some failure to appreciate the relationships involved in the problem or to grasp some principle essential to solution. An error of this kind occurs, for instance, when a child interpolates in a series extrapolation problem; or when he thinks that successive pieces of negative information about the same term in a matching problem are pieces of information about different terms (the belief that there are 'two Dicks' in Problem A2).

Most people would probably expect to find that it is the grasp of principle in some form or another which intelligence tests mainly assess. It is now clear, however, that at least in the case of the problems and the subjects figuring in the present study, this is not so. Many of the errors are not structural. They belong in two other categories.

First, there are the errors which have as their outstanding common feature a lack of loyalty to the given.[1] They have been called the arbitrary errors since the subject may be considered to behave arbitrarily with respect to the problem whenever he is not constrained by the conditions which it sets him. Arbitrariness in these errors may, however, be more or less glaring. Sometimes

---

[1] In the structural errors, the child is loyal to the given as he understands it. The distinction is sometimes very clear – but again, sometimes it is not easy to draw (see, for example, p. 189).

the subject appears to be constrained, if not by the problem, at least by his knowledge of what is 'true' – by some considerations drawn from 'real-life' experience. This is the case when in the matching problems the child invokes the principle that boys go to schools near their own homes, and thus makes the error which we have called arbitrary rule. On the other hand, in the error of arbitrary allocation observed in the matching and in the three-term series problems, there was no sign of constraint of any kind: the subject appeared simply to decide 'it is so'.

The structural and the arbitrary errors form two of the three groups. The third is constituted by the executive errors. As the term 'executive' is meant to imply, these errors arise not from any failure to understand *how* the problem should be tackled, but from some failure in the actual carrying out of the manipulations required. Some defect of concentration, of attention, or of immediate memory seems usually to lie at their origin. The most prevalent member of this class of errors is loss of hold on reasoning. Other errors which seem to be executive are miscounting, reversal of pairs, and difficulty with direction in the series extrapolation problems; and at least some instances of reversal or choice of inappropriate extreme in the related series are also of this kind.

Now it is plain that this tripartite division is not entirely free of difficulties and ambiguities. In particular, the position of the arbitrary errors in relation to the other two kinds is a little uncertain. It might be arguable that the arbitrary errors arise from failure to grasp the general principle that the stipulated conditions of a problem must be rigorously respected. In this case, it might then be asked why these errors should not be included in the structural class, since errors of the latter kind have been defined as involving failure to 'grasp some principle essential to solution'. However, there is a distinction to be drawn between principles of very wide generality, applicable to all problem-solving behaviour, and principles relevant to the form or structure of a particular problem. As the name 'structural' implies, it is failure to grasp a principle of the latter kind which is intended to define 'structural error'.

On the other hand, it would also be possible to argue that an arbitrary error indicates failure to attend closely enough to the stipulated conditions, and that, in this case, the error ought properly to be considered a member of the executive group. The objection to this is that brief failures of attention or memory of the loss of hold kind seem to have rather little in common with the total ignoring of some part of the given and the concomitant solving of the problem on some arbitrary basis, even if the one versatile word 'attend' may be used in reference to both of them.

However, we have no wish to claim that the classification which we propose is the only possible one. In any sorting task there are, as a rule, several reasonable bases for division. This is not to say that the bases must all be equally good: some may overlook important distinctions, others may take account of trivial ones. Plato spoke long ago in this connection of the importance of 'cutting at the joints'. We offer the tripartite division which we have just described as the outcome of our endeavours to find the joints in the case in question.

There follows a brief review of each of the three types of error in turn.

## 1. The Structural Errors

### PROBLEMS A1 AND A2 – MATCHING PROBLEMS

It will be recalled that the matching problems gave rise to few or no structural errors in Group O, the children tested at the ages of twelve and fourteen. However, the ten-year-olds showed signs of difficulties of a new kind, especially in dealing with Problem A2, and a cluster of errors occurred which certainly seemed indicative of failure to handle the relationships involved in the problem. These errors were thought to arise from a false expectation about the structure of the problem: more specifically, from the expectation that the information would consist of one positive statement in respect of each term in the one set, relating this term to a term in the second set and thus directly establishing a pairing. This expectation appeared to lead a child sometimes to treat negative statements as if they were positive; sometimes to conclude that the boy not mentioned must go to the school not mentioned; sometimes to regard two mentions of the same term as mentions of two different terms (the 'two Dicks' error).

### PROBLEMS B1, B2, AND B3 – THREE-TERM SERIES

The quantified three-term series problems gave rise to three errors which should probably be regarded as structural. There was, first, failure to appreciate the asymmetrical nature of the relationships 'taller than . . .' and 'older than . . .', the statement 'Betty is older than May' being taken to signify 'May is older than Betty', and so on. It is not necessary to interpret this as meaning that the children 'really' think that if Betty is older than May, then May is older than Betty. However, in the context of the problem, some of them act as if this were implied.

Second, the quantified three-term series provided occasion for the overlap error – or, rather, for the cluster of errors which all seemed to spring from a difficulty in correctly conceiving of the inclusion of one of the intervals within the other. It seemed probable that this difficulty too, like that occasioned to the young children by the matching problems, arose from a false expectation: in this case a strong tendency to see the relationships as

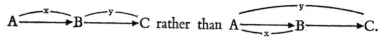

A further effort at analysis led to the suggestion that the difficulty may lie in taking one step and then having to return to the initial point of departure before taking a second one.

The third structural error in the quantified three-term series was the attempt to calculate the value of the link term – that is, an attempt to calculate a value which is directly given. This suggests a fundamental failure to come to grips with the problem and, indeed, whenever this error occurred there was a great deal of concomitant confusion. There seems to be no doubt that this error arises from a serious failure to grasp the relationships with which the problem is concerned.

The unquantified three-term series gave rise to a few instances of difficulty with asymmetrical relationships, though this took a form slightly different from that which was observed in the quantified problems.

However, the most prevalent structural error in the unquantified series was that of substituting a judgement of membership for a judgement of relation. This sometimes involved the assumption that the series contained four terms – that is, that the two separate references to the same term were references to two different terms. Thus there was obvious kinship with the error which led children to conclude that there must be 'two Dicks' in the matching problem, A2.

PROBLEMS C1, C2, AND C3 – SERIES EXTRAPOLATION

In these problems, errors of principle can occur on at least two levels of generality: they may arise in connection with the grasp of the general notion of extending a series in accordance with some rule of relationship between the terms; or they may arise in connection with the attempt to discover what, in any given instance, this rule may be. Apart from the failure to handle the overlapping nature of the terms in C3, these failures to discover the particular rule were all different, one from another, in their precise form.

A few errors of principle of the second kind occurred in the answers of the older children (Group O) as well as in those of Group Y. Errors of principle of the first kind mentioned above were confined exclusively to Group Y and occurred, with only two exceptions, on the first occasion of testing, when the children were ten years old. Indeed, one of the sharpest diminutions in error frequency observed in the whole investigation occurred for these errors between the ages of ten and twelve.

There were two main ways in which the children might fail to grasp the general principle of series extension. The first was to generalize inadequately from the example given and conclude that there was only one rule which could be applied to any series.[1] The other was to interpolate instead of extrapolating – to 'fill up the gaps' between the letters that were provided. Bartlett (1958) points out that interpolation is usually regarded as the less difficult task and states that his own results tend to support this view.

PROBLEMS D1, D2, D3, AND D4 – RELATED SERIES

It will be recalled that, to sort out the errors in these problems, a two-way classification was employed, the two bases for classification being use of one or other or both series, and choice of right or wrong extreme of the series in question. Thus we had, in effect, the following double-entry table:

|  | Use of dependent series | Use of both series | Acknowledged use of independent, actual use of dependent, series | Use of independent series |
|---|---|---|---|---|
| Right extreme | 1(a) | 2(a) | 3(a) | 4(a) |
| Wrong extreme | 1(b) | 2(b) | 3(b) | 4(b) |

No cases of 3(b) were observed and 4(a) is, of course, the correct solution. In addition, there was one error standing outside this scheme and consisting in confusion of the dependent and the independent series, so that in fact the wrong question was answered. This last seems to be clearly an executive error, akin to loss of hold.

The structural errors arise in connection with both the variables which, by their interaction, give rise to the double-entry table. Successful solution demands in the first place a grasp of the notion

[1] The subjects of Group O were not given an example, so they could not have made precisely this error. However, they could have attempted to apply one rule to all three problems, and none of them showed any sign of a tendency to do so.

that perfect correlation makes possible inference from the possession of one property to the possession of another. Only when this is at least in some measure comprehended can the question 'which is heaviest?' be answered on the basis of a consideration of, say, the property of size: in other words, only then can the independent series alone provide the criterion for choice. It is in error 2(a) that failure to grasp this notion results in what is most unmistakably a structural error. Instead of using the information about the related nature of the two series to make an inference from one of them to the other, the child tries to apply the principle that whichever one of the choices open to him possesses both relevant properties in the highest degree is the one to be preferred. Thus, if the inference should be from 'slowest' to 'largest', as in D1, the child chooses the animal which he conceives as best satisfying both of these criteria together – hence, not the slowest of all, but the slowest of those which he classifies as large or the largest of those which he classifies as slow. When this error involves sharp division of one or other series into two groups – e.g. the 'large' and the 'small' – so that some conception of absolute size replaces that of relative size, there is in it a further structural element, apparently closely akin to the substitution of judgements of membership for judgements of relation that occurs in the unquantified three-term series problems.

Error 3(a) has probably to be regarded as executive, since the child who makes it shows that he understands the principle of inferring one property from the other, but fails to carry out this project successfully.

The nature of error 1(a), however, is a little less certain. Clearly, the child who makes it fails to apply the correct principle. But can he be said to apply a wrong one that is based on some misunderstanding of the conditions of the problem? Or must one say rather that he simply ignores the conditions of the problem?[1] On the whole, the latter interpretation seems to be the more reasonable and so the error has been classified as arbitrary.

Error 1(b), on the other hand, is quite certainly structural in

[1] This illustrates the difficulty mentioned in the footnote on page 183.

many of its instances, but with respect to the second variable: the choice of one or other extreme of the series. As we saw in Chapter 7, the child who chooses the wrong end of the dependent series is often explicitly applying a wrong principle: the principle that you 'turn it round' or 'change it round about'. He completely ignores the independent series, however, and in this respect the error, like 1(a), must be said to contain a certain element of arbitrariness. It must also be recalled that in the original discussion of these problems (see pages 152 and 154–155) it became clear that choice of the wrong extreme of the series might arise through an executive failing. This probably happens rarely in the case of 1(b), but frequently in the case of 4(b). The former of these has therefore been regarded as predominantly structural and the latter as predominantly executive, but in both cases exceptions probably arise.

There remains for consideration error 2(b). Here the use of both series, which 2(b) has in common with 2(a), makes the error, in this respect at least, structural. The element of reversal may, once again, be either structural or the result of some loss of hold. But comments implying the operation of a principle of reversal were not infrequent and, on the whole, this, too, is probably best regarded as a structural error.

### PROBLEMS E1, E2, AND E3
#### FORMAL DEDUCTIVE REASONING

It proved less easy in these problems than in others to isolate 'an error'. This was chiefly because of the complex intertwining of two different modes of reasoning: on the one hand, reasoning which had regard for the premises and attempted to proceed by rigorous deduction from them; and, on the other, reasoning which ignored some part of the given or freely based itself on additional implicit premises of the subject's own devising. A great many of the children produced in their answers very curious admixtures of these two means of reaching a solution; few were wholly free of the second of them.

It is clear that this second mode of reasoning exactly fits the definition of arbitrary error: it is characterized by the fact that the child is not constrained by the given of the problem. Structural errors in these problems – as elsewhere – arise, then, only when the child is acting on the basis of the given in so far as he is able to comprehend it and grasp what it implies. In other words, they occur within the deductive mode: they occur whenever the child reasons deductively but fallaciously.

Now it has become clear that when a multiple-choice form of problem is used, this may to some extent affect the errors that occur. It may therefore be that fallacies other than those actually observed would have arisen but for the limitations imposed by the choice of distractors. On the other hand, we saw, in the context of Problem B2, that a child might show signs of a tendency to make an error for which the multiple-choice form did not in fact provide, and there were no indications of this in the problems of type E. The only fallacies which seemed to tempt the children were of the kinds familiar from logic textbooks and hence foreseen in the construction of the problems and specifically invited by the distractors.

These, then, are the errors which are grouped together on the ground that they reveal some misconception of the structure of the problem in which they arise. But some of them have certain further characteristics in common, beyond the property of being structural.

One might expect that failure to perceive inconsistency would be a common source of structural error. More surprising, perhaps, is the realization of the importance of failure to perceive consistency.

Consider the following errors:

(i) expectation of one positive statement per term (matching problems)
(ii) judgements of membership (unquantified three-term series and related series)

    (iii) overlap (quantified three-term series)
    (iv) overlap (series extrapolation)
    (v) the logical fallacy errors (formal deductive reasoning).

These errors are diverse. And yet, underlying them all is what can perhaps best be described as a failure to realize that the same term or element of a problem may quite consistently figure in more than one statement of relationship – or at least, since this represents the extreme, a failure to recognize in how many different statements the same term may, without incompatibility, appear.

For instance, when negative information is given in the matching problems, the same term in one of the sets is linked negatively with successive terms in the other set, and we have seen how hard it is for some of the younger children to deal with a group of statements of this kind. For such children, to encounter one statement about Dick is apparently to believe that Dick is disposed of – they have the information about him and they can move on. So if they encounter 'Dick' again, they may go so far as to decide that they must be dealing with another boy having the same name.

No negative information is involved in the unquantified three-term series problems, but a very similar error occurs. Again, the same term is mentioned twice in the premises and, again, some children conclude that they are dealing with two boys who have the same name. This time the difficulty arises in connection with the making of relative judgements, in the form 'x is taller than y': the child takes this to mean that x is tall, absolutely, and that y is either tall or short as the case may be. Thus he places the terms in distinct classes, in the same way that some children, trying to solve the related series problems, divide the members of the series into two clear-cut groups – for instance, the 'big' and the 'small'. This substitution of absolute for relative judgements appears to involve a failure to appreciate that a given object may be big in relation to certain objects and small in relation to others – hence that it may enter into different relationships at one and the same time. It is easy to see how this can lead in appropriate circumstances to the conclusion that two terms are involved; also how it relates to the expectation that the premisses will consist of one statement about each term, each statement having about it a certain separateness and independence.

A similar expectation of separateness seems to mark the overlap error in the quantified three-term series problems – the error, that is, which consists in failure to envisage one interval as included within the other. The child, starting from information about the height of Dick, calculates the height of Harry in relation to him. Then it seems that Dick is considered to have been dealt with: there is no thought of going back to the starting-point to see in what relation Dick stands to the remaining member of the trio. Of course, by virtue of the nature of the problem, this simply means that the middle term instead of the extreme is made to serve as the link – that is, to stand in stated relation to each of the other two. But this apparently has the psychological effect of conferring on each of the relationships that kind of separateness and absoluteness which the children expect to find.

Seen in this light, the overlap error in three-term series is quite closely akin to the one to which we have given the same name in series extrapolation. Here it is on each term of the series that separateness is bestowed, so that there is a failure to recognize the element common to succeeding terms. It is as if the fact that 'D' belongs in the term 'CD' excludes it from the following term. 'D' has been dealt with and, as before, one moves on.

The notion of 'moving on' is of less relevance to the logical fallacy errors in the syllogisms. However, failure to recognize that one statement of relationship need not preclude another is again present. For instance, 'All boys with red hair play football well' is perfectly compatible with 'Some boys who do not have red hair play football well', but this is not appreciated when the child reasons fallaciously so that the classes 'boys with red hair' and 'boys who play football well' are seen as coextensive instead of – possibly – included one within the other (i.e. over-lapping).

All these errors, then, show a restricted awareness of the relationships which may, without inconsistency, obtain between the terms of a problem: that is to say, they show a limited recognition of the possibilities which are open. It is in this light that we are inclined to view the fact that several of the errors appear as 'false expectations'. The too-rapid assumption that a problem will have a certain structure – for instance, that the stated intervals in a three-term series will not overlap – suggests an inadequate conception of the possible forms which relationships of the type in question may take, or of the possible ways in which a given pattern of relationships may be described (but see also page 207).

In this connection it is interesting to note that Inhelder and Paiget, in one of their recent works (1958), claim that the most fundamental property of formal thought is 'the subordination of reality to possibility'. According to Piaget's theories, 'formal thought' characterizes the mature adult mind, and the transition to this from the earlier stage of 'concrete thinking' occurs during precisely those age-intervals with which our studies have been concerned. It is obviously necessary, then, to consider whether our findings support his views about the nature of the changes which take place at that time.

Piaget, in the book which has just been quoted, considers a number of alternative ways of making the distinction between 'concrete' and 'formal' thinking. He recalls that at one time he tried to do this in terms of the capacity to deal with problems presented verbally as opposed to those where physical objects are offered for manipulation. But this would not do: he discovered that the role of formal thought is not simply to translate into words or propositions what could previously be done 'in the concrete'. On the contrary, around the age of twelve on the average, a whole new set of 'operations' comes into play when the subject is faced with actual experimental problems, problems involving the manipulation of physical objects and calling for the discovery of physical laws. (It is relevant to the present discussion that it is with this sort of problem that Piaget is chiefly concerned in the book in question.) These new operations, characteristic of formal thought, consist of disjunctions, implications, exclusions, and so on; and the reason why they now supervene, according to Piaget, is that formal thought – unlike concrete thought which is limited to the classification and ordering of 'matters of fact' (*les données de fait*) – 'starts from hypothesis, that is to say from the possible'.

Or perhaps this last statement should be turned around. It might be closer to Piaget's views to say that the reason why thought now 'starts from the possible' is that the mental structures which underlie these operations have come into being. At any rate, he appears to hold that a new recognition of the importance of the logically possible in all reasoning arises in close conjunction with the coming into existence – normally in early adolescence – of certain specific mental structures or groups of operations. The outstanding characteristic of these structures[1] is their combinatorial nature: they involve (or it may be that one should rather say, consist in) the ability to take into account all possible combinations of a given number of elements. Thus they can be observed in very direct manifestation if a subject is asked to combine in all possible ways a number of cards of different colours, or cards bearing different numbers or symbols. But, according to Piaget, it is the same underlying organization which makes possible the manipulation of the logical relationships of implication, exclusion, etc., to which we have already referred – as well as the understanding of a certain number of fundamental notions such as proportion, correlation, and mechanical equilibrium.[2]

Now, although limited recognition of possibilities seemed to emerge as the common feature in a number of the errors observed in our studies, it did not appear to be the case that successful solution of the problems required the use of the 'propositional combinatorial system' or any of Piaget's 'formal schemata'.[3] The question which then arises concerns the closeness of the links between the role of 'the possible' in thinking and the development of these structures.

[1] For an account of Piaget's logical analyses of their nature, see Piaget (1953).
[2] Inhelder and Piaget (1958) give a full account of their theories concerning the kinship of these seemingly diverse competences. See especially pages 307–29.
[3] We shall shortly discuss two apparent exceptions to this (see page 199).

There are at least two different ways in which the possible may be said to figure in formal thinking and it is important to distinguish them, though Piaget does not do so clearly. In the first place, it is characteristic of formal deductive reasoning that the premisses are treated as hypothetical, which is to say that, in drawing conclusions from them, one is not concerned with truth or correspondence with reality but only with what is possible, given these conditions. Without this initial attitude to the problem, one cannot reason formally – and this is certainly part of what Piaget wishes to stress when he says that formal thought 'starts from hypothesis, that is to say from the possible'.

However, though this attitude is a necessary condition of the drawing of correct conclusions (since without it, as the arbitrary errors illustrate, deductive rigour is not achieved), it obviously does not by itself produce correct conclusions: these have still to be drawn by the processes of deduction. And here 'the possible' is again, and in a second way, important. As Piaget points out, the conception of deductive necessity and the conception of the logically possible are closely bound up with one another. Necessity arises when all possibilities but one have been excluded. Therefore, in order to draw conclusions correctly, one must be able adequately to conceive what all the possibilities are: that is, what things do and what do not conflict with or contradict the premisses.

It is at this point that the 'formal schemata' which Piaget describes have obvious relevance. It is clear that in some – indeed in very many – deductive problem situations the possibilities cannot be adequately conceived unless the subject can exhaustively manipulate sets of combinations.

However, Piaget appears to make claims which assert more than just this. He seems to claim that *all* formal reasoning involves the combinatorial schemata and that the ability to treat the given as genuinely hypothetical arises only in conjunction with them.

There are a number of reasons why these claims – if this is a correct interpretation of them – should be treated with caution. In the first place, while it seems very reasonable to argue that the hypothetical attitude involves an attempt to fit the given into a whole set of relations conceived as merely possible, it is not clear why one should suppose that it involves the ability to do this fully and adequately (this ability being presumably what the existence of the 'schemata' implies). If it were indeed the case that the formal attitude could arise only in conjunction with the fully developed instruments of formal thought, then it is hard to see how the arbitrary and the structural errors could exist apart from one another. Nevertheless, children may reason rigorously but fallaciously (as, indeed, adults may do also) while, on the other hand, they may show signs of common-sense reasoning and yet in the next instant demonstrate that they can in fact handle the logical structure of the problem.

It is true that the problems with which this inquiry was concerned did not seem to call for the 'formal schemata' in Piaget's sense. But this leads directly to the second point of doubt: are we really to say that only in a situation where an exhaustive survey of the possibilities involves taking account of combinations – that only then can reasoning properly be called formal? Take, for instance:

> A goes either to School X or to School Y.
> He does not go to School X.
> Therefore he must go to School Y.

This is a very elementary piece of deductive reasoning but it is formally deductive none the less.

In a recent study, we presented a problem in this form to seventeen five-year-old children who had started school only a few weeks previously. (The school was in a working-class district in Edinburgh.) The problem was given wholly verbally, as follows:

> I am going to tell you a story. It is about two little boys called Bob and Jack. What are their names? . . . Yes, try to remember them. Now Bob and Jack live in a town where there are two schools called the Red School and the White School. What are they called? . . . Yes, Red and White. Now listen carefully: one of the boys goes to one of these schools and the other boy goes to the other one. Tell me

the names of the boys again . . . And the names of the schools . . . Now listen very carefully: if Bob does *not* go to the Red School, what school does he go to? . . . How do you know? . . . And what school does Jack go to? . . . How do you know?

Thirteen of the seventeen children assigned Bob and Jack to the correct schools. Four of these gave reasons as follows:

(a) In respect of the allocation of Bob:
'Because there's no more schools' (2 children)
'If he didn't go to the Red, he could go to the White'
(1 child)
'Because you said he didn't go to the Red School' (1 child)
(b) In respect of the allocation of Jack:
'Because the other one's in the White one' (2 children)
'Because the other goes to the White' (1 child)
'Because he couldn't go to the same one' (1 child)

A further three children – also among the thirteen who were correct – gave these reasons:[1]

'Because I *know* (How do you know?) 'Cos I know the both of them.'
'Because he *does*.'
'Because you told me. (What did I tell you?) You told me the two. I listened to the story.'

The remaining children – that is, six who produced the correct solution and four who did not – either gave such reasons as 'because he likes that school'; 'because my mummy told me' (3 children); 'because my big brother told me'; 'because I wrote it in my book at home'; or else could give no reason at all.

It seems clear, then, that deductive reasoning at a purely verbal level is not wholly beyond the capacity of five-year-old children. Certainly the four children whose explanations fall in the first

---

[1] In these cases, and in the next group, the same reason – or roughly the same one – was reiterated for the second question. In other words, there was less articulation and differentiation than in the answers of children of the first group.

group justified their choices in ways that could hardly be bettered by any adult.

So we may conclude that the making of a firm deduction on the basis of a survey of possibilities can on occasion happen long before the appearance of the formal schemata, given that the possibilities are of a sufficiently simple nature – and that no consideration of combinations is required.

At the same time, the fact that four at least of the five-year-old subjects showed every sign of tackling this problem deductively does not mean that these same children would always proceed this way even with equally simple tasks – or even with the same task on another occasion. There is no reason to suppose that they would consistently avoid arbitrary error even in the simplest problems – and, from this point of view, there is no ground for claiming that they have in any sense reached a 'formal stage'. But whether the advent of a full appreciation of the essentially hypothetical nature of premisses and of the need for rigour in deduction is necessarily linked to the development of the capacity to survey more complicated sets of possibilities is what it seems wise at the moment to doubt. It may be relevant here to mention again the evidence quoted by Welford (1958) of the tendency for there to be some loss of the capacity for deductive rigour in older subjects. It would be of great interest to see whether any decline in the ability to manipulate combinatorial systems accompanies the increasing tendency to comment on or question the pre-misses instead of drawing deductive conclusions from them.

Let us return now to the errors which were mentioned (in the footnote to page 195) as apparent exceptions to the state-ment that none of the errors observed here arose from any failure to manipulate a 'combinatorial schema' in Piaget's sense. These are the error which involves the attempt to use both series as criteria in the related series problems; and the logical fallacy errors in the syllogisms. The former does not, at first sight, seem to call for any surveying of combinatorial possibilities: it is discussed in this connection only because Piaget includes correla-tion as one of the schemata which, in his view, are manifestations of the capacity for formal thinking (Inhelder and Piaget, 1958, pages 324–6); and it will be recalled that, when a child failed to use the independent series as criterion for choice in the related series problems, he was held to be in effect failing to see that the given perfect positive correlation between the series made possible inference from one of them to the other. However, when Piaget explains his reasons for concluding that the notion of correlation is, in his sense, formal, he has in mind a situation where the subject is faced with actual related variables and is given the task of deciding on the nature of the relationship. For the subject to determine that this is correlational is for him to exclude other relationships, such as implication, which might possibly obtain between the variables. Thus, says Piaget, the *combinatoire propositionelle* is involved and hence the operation is a formal one. But in the related series problems the child is not required to determine the nature of the relationship, only to accept a given statement of its nature. It seems doubtful, then, whether the error of failure to comprehend this statement can be said to involve failure in the surveying of logical possibilities.

The fallacies have a more obvious claim to be judged a failure in formal reasoning by any criterion, for what is more formal than the syllogism? Moreover, the relation of implication, which is being mishandled when these errors occur, is one of the 'sixteen binary operations of two-valued propositional logic' on which Piaget lays such emphasis.

Yet Inhelder and Piaget (1958) say: 'In the case of implication, more than in that of any other propositional operation, we can get the illusion that it is found even at the concrete level' – and this because it corresponds in effect to the inclusion of one class within another, a relation which is already comprehended, at least in certain situations, by children of seven.[1] They claim that the difference between a 'true implication' and an 'inclusion' can be recognized *à la marche d'ensemble des raisonnements du sujet*. This may be true in the problems with which they were concerned – problems involving experiment and much inductive reasoning.

[1] See also Morf (1957).

Conclusions

But it is not at once clear how one would tell the difference in the case of the type of problem which figured in our inquiries. If, however, the nature of the limitations in thinking which are revealed by these fallacies is ambiguous in terms of Piagetian theory, it must be said that several of the structural errors were clearly such as to involve mishandling only of 'concrete level' relations. This is true, for instance, of the asymmetry error in the three-term series, since the relations which constitute transitive asymmetry form one of the eight elementary *groupements*.[1] We have, then, to say that we find evidence of difficulties which, according to Piaget, should be largely overcome in children of the ages in question.[2] And, on the other hand, there is little evidence of the sorts of difficulty which his theories suggest to be typical of the period – that is to say, difficulties in the handling of combinatorial possibilities. Presumably, however, this is merely because the problems used were inadequate to reveal them.

## 2. THE ARBITRARY ERRORS

The arbitrary errors took two main forms:

1. The child might ignore a part of the available information, while acting on the rest. Thus, in the matching problems, he might proceed by strict deduction for part of the way towards solution and then, when two possibilities remained open, simply pick one or other of these, with no attempt at justification and no apparent sense that justification was called for. This was called the error of arbitrary allocation.

Another error, which was like this one in so far as some information was ignored, was error 1(a) in the related series problems, where the child paid no attention to the independent series, acting on the basis of the dependent one only. But here

---

[1] See Piaget (1953, page 14).
[2] In saying this, we do not overlook Piaget's emphasis on the difficulty occasioned by purely verbal presentation.

no choice that was entirely without apparent justification was involved.

2. The child might add to the information provided, importing an additional premiss, a new rule or principle for which the data offered no basis.[1] The rule might be of a quite formal nature – and, in this case, as we shall see in a moment, uncertainty could sometimes arise about the drawing of the line between structural and arbitrary error. However, a clear example of an arbitrary error in this category is provided when, in a matching problem, the child solves on the basis of the order in which the terms are named. On the other hand, the importation might take the form of an appeal to real-life experience. An example of this is the error of common-sense reasoning which occurred so frequently in the answers to the syllogisms.

The arbitrary errors, then, can be surveyed summarily with much less difficulty than the structural errors. It is a matter of definition that the form taken by the arbitrary errors is less dependent on the form of the problem in which they arise than is the case with structural errors. The latter involve failure to grasp some principle 'relevant to the form or structure of a particular problem' (page 184); the former involve a lack of loyalty to the given from which it evidently follows that the given cannot determine them.

However, it must be added that the given may to some extent encourage or discourage loyalty. One of the types of problem which we studied was notably free of arbitrary error – namely, series extrapolation. Now, since the most tempting form of arbitrariness, for many children, is the appeal to 'real life', it seems reasonable to say that the less a problem refers to people or events, the less encouragement there is to disloyalty. So this may partly explain the absence of arbitrary error in the series extrapolation tasks. However, it does not explain the absence of the kind of arbitrariness that consists in ignoring part of the given, or in adding some formal rule. It must be acknowledged that

---

[1] Frequently, of course, the use of the added premiss was accompanied by the neglect of some part of the original given.

arbitrariness of these sorts may have occurred without being recognized for what it is. Some of the children who are shown as having made a wrong principle error may have been ignoring part of the data; or they may have been introducing some rule of their own which should have been called arbitrary. It is clear that here we have a situation where it is not always easy in practice to draw the line between ignoring the given and somehow 'getting it wrong'. The theoretical distinction remains quite clear: an error is arbitrary if the child is not *engaged* with – not struggling with – the given. If a child had completed the blanks in a series extrapolation problem by drawing faces instead of letters, or if he had put letters but had then observed, 'I put these because they are the initials of my name', then we would have called his behaviour arbitrary. But nothing of the kind occurred; and it seemed better not to record arbitrariness unless it was very clear. In all the other problems, there were unmistakable instances of arbitrary error.

It is interesting that the findings concerning the arbitrary errors are in close agreement with what is reported in a monograph by Morf (1957), one of Piaget's colleagues in Geneva. Morf used a number of deductive problems of which the following is an example:

'My brother and I went climbing in the mountains. When we reached the hut, we realized that we had forgotten to bring food. So we searched the hut and found some food which had been left there but it was no longer very fresh. We found some condensed milk, some soup, and an old tin of meat. My brother ate some meat and some soup and I ate some soup and some condensed milk. *Version A:* An hour later both of us had stomach pains. What could have caused that? *Version B:* One of the three things gave both of us stomach pains. Can you guess which?'

Morf reports that his subjects commonly based their solutions to this and other similar problems on what he calls 'causal' as opposed to 'formal' reasoning. For instance, they might choose meat as the source of the trouble 'because meat does not keep well'.

A *Study of Children's Thinking*

This is clearly an example of what is here called common-sense reasoning.[1]

Morf observes, moreover, that 'often causal and formal arguments are combined or confounded with one another in the same answer'. He, too, finds that there is no direct transition from the exclusive use of one mode to the exclusive use of the other. And the child who reasons 'causally' is not necessarily incapable of taking the deductive steps of the formal argument.

One is brought to conclude, on the available evidence, that the two modes of reasoning coexist over a long period – indeed, they probably coexist over the greater part of life. We have seen that some children of five will on occasion deal by strict deduction with a sufficiently simple formal problem. On the other hand, there is evidence that adults – even rather intelligent adults – are not always rigorous when a formal problem is offered to them. Henle (1960) reports that a group of graduate students of psychology, asked to evaluate the logical adequacy of deductions, made errors which, in the terminology of the present study, would clearly have to be classed as arbitrary; for they involved the omission of premises and the use of additional premises. A number of other studies have claimed to show that the difficulty of syllogisms for adult subjects is not independent of the content of the premises: value judgements, knowledge of 'how things really are' appear to intrude and affect the issue.[2] Also, there is the evidence quoted by Welford which has already been mentioned (page 66). In the study which Welford reports, the subjects were given some fairly complicated premises and asked to draw conclusions – or, again, to consider the compatibility of a number of statements one with the other. The subjects were university teachers and members of other professions or were in managerial or clerical jobs. They were divided, for purposes of analysing the results, into two age-groups: under and over thirty-five. In both age-groups and in all occupational grades,

[1] All Morf's problems are such as to invite this rather than any other form of arbitrariness.
[4] For references see the footnote on page 162.

204

there were subjects who, instead of reasoning deductively, commented on the premises and made observations on the general topic of the argument. There was, however, a clear association between age and commenting, with the subjects over thirty-five commenting more frequently than the younger ones.

It seems, then, that we must suppose a period early in life when the capacity for formal deductive thinking in the handling of a problem is wholly absent – say until age four or five; then a long period during which this capacity grows both with respect to the range and scope of logical relationships which can be understood and with respect to the rigour with which all considerations except the implications of the stated premises can be excluded. For most people, this rigour is probably never complete and utterly reliable in its operation in all circumstances. However, it seems that there is a time of peak efficiency from about adolescence onwards, with a subsequent decline after the age of thirty-five, if not before.

The question which now arises concerns the status of measures of this rigour in the assessment of intelligence: should we deliberately try to take account of it? The two criteria of high status suggested in an earlier chapter were that the ability in question should underlie a number of diverse skills, manifest itself in numerous different kinds of behaviour (and thus be of value for purposes of 'clairvoyant' prediction); and that it should be a 'growing point' (hence also useful for precognitive prediction). The notion of the growing point is perhaps more relevant to the grasp of the separate logical relationships themselves (which can be seen as building one upon another) than to the question of rigour in their manipulation. However, this rigour – or the lack of it – may prove to be importantly indicative, at certain ages, of growth to come.

What is now needed is an attempt to devise tests which will measure the rigour of a child's thinking and as little else as possible. These should be tests where the actual relationships and principles involved are not difficult for the subject, but where he may be tempted in various ways to ignore or add to the given. It will, of course, be desirable first to verify by the study of individual children that, when wrong answers are given to the problems which it is proposed to use, these do in fact usually result from arbitrary error. Then large group studies may give us the information we need concerning prognostic value.[1]

There is a monograph by Goldstein and Scheerer (1941) called 'Abstract and Concrete Behaviour' which appears to bear on the understanding of arbitrary behaviour in problem-solving. In this work, Goldstein and Scheerer are concerned chiefly with the behaviour of brain-damaged adults, but they themselves point to likenesses between this and the behaviour of normal children. It is, indeed, widely accepted that children, adults with impaired mental function, and primitive peoples often resemble one another in their thinking and perceiving, though it may be that the similarities have sometimes been exaggerated.

Goldstein and Scheerer report that analysis of the behaviour changes accompanying brain injury led to the making of a distinction between two modes of behaviour: the abstract and the concrete. These they call 'attitudes', meaning to imply that they are concerned with 'capacity levels of the total personality'.

Of the concrete attitude they say that it is realistic and unreflective. When it is dominant, 'our thinking and acting are directed by the immediate claims which one particular aspect of the object or of the outer-world situation makes'. Hence there may arise rigidity or 'lack of shifting': if the person apprehends an object or situation in one manner, then it is characteristic of the concrete attitude that he will be unable intentionally to conceive it anew and in some other aspect because of the claim upon him of his first 'immediate apprehension'. But, on the other hand, if intentional or volitional shifting is rendered difficult by the concrete attitude, intentional stability may also be hard to achieve,

[1] It seems probable, however, even in the absence of this confirmation, that a child's tendency to arbitrary error will be important as an indication of his readiness to learn mathematics. How it will compare in importance with his grasp of specific principles and forms of relationship – that is, with the degree of his liability to certain structural errors – it is impossible yet to say.

since the individual is extremely susceptible to the varying stimuli of the moment. The outstanding feature, then, is absence of control: the individual whose attitude is concrete is not in command.

On the other hand, when the abstract attitude prevails, 'we transcend the immediately given situation'. We are then able to shift reflectively from one aspect of that situation to another or hold various aspects in mind at once, to plan our actions in advance, and generally to exercise constraint, to limit and order our behaviour. Now we have seen that the outstanding feature of the arbitrary errors is lack of rigour. It is true that sometimes arbitrariness occurs when the manipulations which the problem demands appear to be beyond the child's capacity to perform. But not always. For instance, arbitrariness in the syllogisms may involve the introduction of additional premisses which make the actual deductive manoeuvres more complicated than they would have been. Yet the child may be able to handle these self-assigned complexities with success. What he lacks, then, is the ability to limit himself to the problem as stated and prevent the intrusion of other notions which the data may cause to leap to mind – or, on the other hand, to require himself to take account of all that is given. It is in this respect that the Goldstein-Scheerer descriptions of concrete behaviour appear to be relevant to the arbitrary errors.

But it is interesting to note that these same descriptions are not without possible relevance also to some of the structural errors, and especially to those which are marked by the occurrence of some over-rapid assumption which is not then readily abandoned.

In such cases it has seemed appropriate to describe the children as having 'false expectations' about the form which the problem would take. But it would be quite in keeping with our observations to speak of an immediate apprehension of the situation which, once established, was resistant to change. Thus the Goldstein-Scheerer notion of lack of shifting may not only contribute to the understanding of the arbitrary errors but be of value in the interpretation of some at least of the structural ones. (However, it does not appear that it can do anything to explain why one particular way of apprehending the situation should be specially common.)

A further contribution to this understanding, and one which bears closely on the observations of Goldstein and Scheerer, may come through Russian work on the development of speech. Reports of this work in English are still too few, but a recent book by Luria (1961) seems highly relevant to the Goldstein-Scheerer distinction between the abstract and the concrete attitudes. It is Luria's argument that the development of the ability of the human being to control and order his own behaviour is in the strictest sense dependent on the development of the speech function. He shows how verbal instructions and comments to a child can alter the 'natural' strength of stimuli and 'make the physically weaker component predominant'. He then argues that it is when one's own speech assumes the role of 're-shaping' one's 'significant perception' that one has become, in Pavlov's terms, the 'highest self-regulating system'.

On this view, then, someone in whom the speech function is not fulfilling this role (either through immaturity or brain damage or for some other reason) must be expected to be at the mercy of the immediate impact of the stimuli he encounters. He will not be able to limit himself to the given of a problem and prevent the intrusion of other notions not strictly relevant to the task in hand. His behaviour will be marked by precisely that lack of rigour which has been observed in the subjects who make errors of an arbitrary kind.

## 3. THE EXECUTIVE ERRORS

The executive errors fall somewhere between the structural and the arbitrary errors in respect of their dependence on the form or relational structure of the particular problem in which they arise. The nature of the manipulations to be performed in solving a problem is naturally not without influence on the errors which arise in the course of carrying out these manipulations. Thus, miscounting is an error specific to the extrapolation of a certain type of series. On the other hand, it is possible in any problem for a subject to lose hold on his reasoning so that this error at least is like the arbitrary errors in its relative independence of problem structure.

We saw in Chapter 4 that the notion of the nervous system as a 'communication channel' with a limited capacity for the conveying of information may be valuable in the attempt to understand executive error. It may, indeed, be valuable in the attempt to understand all forms of error; but it is in the case of executive error that the notion of 'overloading' or 'exceeding capacity' has the most obvious relevance. It seems intuitively reasonable to suppose that the sheer amount of information which the subject has to handle has some bearing on the likelihood of executive error; whereas it is the content of the information which appears chiefly relevant to the occurrence of structural error – that is to say, in order to describe structural errors it seems necessary to talk of some failure to comprehend the 'meaning' or 'implication' of the problem.

The present mathematical theory of communication deals only with the statistical probability of different sign sequences in certain given conditions: it offers no measure of information such as might throw any light on the difference in difficulty between, say, a series extrapolation problem based on a multiplicative relationship and an otherwise similar problem based on an additive relationship. Still less does it enable us to compare quantitatively the difficulty of a series problem with that of, say, a syllogism. And it is this sort of difference that is relevant to the occurrence of structural error.

On the other hand, communication theory as at present developed has been applied in psychological study in ways which seem to suggest that, where the question of difficulty of 'meaning' is not critical, one can perhaps reasonably speak of an individual's 'capacity' as a 'communication channel', and regard error as what happens when capacity is exceeded. If normal adult subjects in our culture are asked to observe a screen on which sequences of printed letters of the alphabet are flashed for short periods, and if the task for the subjects is simply to report what they see, then one has a situation where errors of principle will be at a minimum. In fact, one would hesitate to say that any 'problem' is involved: there is merely a perceptual task of a very straightforward kind. Miller, Bruner, and Postman (1954), working in this experimental situation and using sequences of letters at varying degrees of approximation to written English, found, as would be expected intuitively and has long been known to be the case, that the closer to English the greater the average number of correctly reported letters. However, the mathematical theory of communication developed by Shannon and Weaver (1949) takes into account the probability of any given signal or signal sequence: the more probable the signal, the less the information it conveys. (In the extreme, a signal which is certain conveys no information at all.) Now, as letter sequences come closer to the structure of the English language, certain transitions become highly probable – for instance, N follows I one time in five in ordinary English. So the amount of information contained in a given letter sequence is a function not only of the number of letters in the sequence but of the probabilities of transition from each one to the next. Of special interest from the present point of view is the finding that, although there is a rise in the absolute number of letters correctly reported as the sequences become more like English words, nevertheless, the amount of information correctly handled in a given time remains roughly constant when Shannon's procedures are used to take account of the varying probabilities. This is important because it seems to show that the mathematical theory is applicable, at least in some circumstances, to the human 'communication channels'.

The task set in this experiment by Miller, Bruner, and Postman is, of course, remote in many ways from those with which this book has been mainly concerned. However, some of the demands set by the simpler task may well be relevant also to the successful handling of the more complex. The very brief time intervals

involved in tachistoscopic exposure and in the subsequent reporting of what is seen must not cause us to overlook the fact that
any perceptual task of this kind is also an immediate memory
task; and we have seen how failures of short-term memory appear
to figure as causes of error in a variety of much more complicated
task situations. It is interesting, then, that the results of an investigation which is more obviously – and avowedly – a study of
memory are to some extent in line with the findings of Miller
and his associates. In the conditions of Miller's task it is impossible
to tell, when error arises, whether it does so because the subject
has not 'seen' the letters or because he has not 'remembered' them
long enough to report them. But the subjects of Aborn and
Rubenstein (1952) were given a period of three minutes in which
to study the messages of nonsense syllables which they were then
to reproduce. Thus it is reasonable to regard most of their errors
(though, of course, not necessarily all) as failures of immediate
memory rather than as failures at some prior stage of 'input'. The
sets of nonsense syllables that formed the ensemble from which
signals could be drawn in this experiment were amenable to
various kinds of organization: that is, rules could be introduced
whereby a syllable of one kind must always be followed by a
syllable of a second kind. These rules then functioned like the
rules of syntax in a language and, by affecting the transition
probabilities, controlled the average amount of information per
syllable in any message. Working with subjects who had reached
a specified level of proficiency in the knowledge of the rules,
Aborn and Rubenstein found that, as the average amount of
information per syllable went down, the number of syllables
correctly reproduced went up, so that the total amount of information successfully handled was roughly constant. (This was true
at any rate until the average information per syllable dropped
below a certain level. After this point, increase in number of
syllables recalled was not enough to balance the reduction in
information value.)

So here, in a situation which is coming to resemble a little
more closely the ones with which we are directly concerned, the

notion of 'capacity' in the strict communication theory sense appears to have some relevance.

It must at once be added that the evidence at present available is not wholly consistent in this respect: in a number of studies of immediate memory, 'capacity' has been found to depend on the 'number of items' rather than on the total amount of information which the items carry; and much remains to be achieved by way of the reconciliation of conflicting findings. However, it seems clear that there are definite limits to the capacity of the human nervous system (a) to take in information in a given brief time interval;[1] (b) to go on taking it in at the same steady level of efficiency over longer time intervals; (c) to retain it briefly in short-term store; (d) to retain it briefly while at the same time manipulating it in various ways in order to produce the solution to a problem.

It is not at all clear at present how capacity at any one of these levels relates to capacity at the others: what, for instance, is the relation between the amount of information which can be simply retained for a given short interval and the amount which can be retained and also operated on in some specified manner during the same time interval. It is not certain that the addition of manipulations will lead to an appreciably greater loss than would be sustained through the mere fact of having to hold the information in mind. It cannot be assumed that more information can be simply transmitted than can be transmitted and transformed. Indeed, certain kinds of transformation are known to increase the amount of information that can be dealt with. Miller (1956) reports that, if a series of binary digits is presented and the subject is trained to translate these into familiar decimal digits and translate back again when asked for recall, he can reproduce a much

[1] This question is complicated by all the evidence of 'subliminal perception': evidence which shows that a subject may 'take in' information without knowing he has done so. Cherry (1957) says: 'Experiments suggest that the organism has a definite capacity for information which is a minute fraction of the content of the physical signals that reach the eyes, ears and epidermis....' We can judge what has been taken in only by observing some response. But the subception experiments point the danger of concluding that, because certain expected classes of response fail to occur, the stimuli in question have in no way 'impinged' – that is, that no information has been conveyed.

longer binary series than would otherwise be possible. Miller believes that 'recoding' of this kind is 'an extremely powerful weapon for increasing the amount of information that we can deal with'; and that we use it constantly in our daily behaviour.

We have, then, a variety of different tasks – ranging from straightforward perception and report through 'vigilance' and immediate memory situations to the whole range of problem-solving – all of which depend in some measure on the subject's capacity for handling information. But how do we assess this capacity? Shannon has been able to provide a 'capacity theorem' which enables one to calculate for any given telecommunication channel a theoretical upper limit. This limit may not be realized in practice, but any attempt to exceed it is bound to be a waste of time. It would be of the greatest value to have similar theorems applicable to the information capacities of nervous systems. But we do not have them. In their absence, we must base our estimates of capacity on measures of the actual functioning of the system in question, and attempts to do this show, of course, that the level of this functioning varies. If we want to estimate capacity in the sense of 'limit which cannot be exceeded', the best we can do, then, is to observe the actual functioning on a number of occasions and take the highest level of success which we find. But we may still not have reached the upper limit.

Of course, when one is dealing with telecommunication channels there is an absolute upper limit in a sense that has no strict counterpart in reference to a living nervous system. Nervous systems grow. Thus the absolute limit today may be exceeded tomorrow. Again, the point of peak efficiency passes and old age sets in. One has therefore the problem of distinguishing day-to-day irregular fluctuations from real growth and decay.[1] It is in this connection that some means of estimating capacity independently of the assessment of information successfully transmitted would be of such very great value.

The argument so far has been that the notion of the nervous system's limited capacity (in the strict communication theory

[1] See discussion on pages 54–60.

sense of the term) may have some relevance to the understanding of executive errors, though the measurement of amount of information – and the estimation of channel capacity – present the psychologist with difficulties not encountered by telecommunication engineers.

However, there are one or two points to be made by way of qualification. First, the notion applies more readily to some of the executive errors than to others. It is easy to see how errors which, like loss of hold, or incomplete elimination, involve failures of short-term memory may arise because the limit of capacity for handling information has been reached, but it is perhaps less obvious how one should deal in terms of communication theory concepts with an error like reversal of pairs in a series extrapolation task. Again, even when one is dealing with errors like loss of hold, there is a further reservation to be expressed concerning any suggestion that the error in question must always arise because of straightforward overloading.

The human being has feelings, purposes, hopes, and fears; and his attention and his memory do not function independently of these. It is now very well established that what we perceive is influenced by our interests, desires, and expectations, and Freud, of course, considered such phenomena as lapses of memory and slips of the tongue to be controlled by the functioning of the unconscious mind. We are not justified, then, in assuming, even where 'loss of information' seems to be a highly relevant notion, that this loss always arises simply because some quantitative limit has been reached.

Let us postulate the existence of a developmental sequence with respect to the solving of a certain type of problem such that there are four phases, $A \longrightarrow B \longrightarrow C \longrightarrow D$. A, B, and C may be taken to represent different types of error, while D is the error-free solution. There is no suggestion that every subject will pass through each of the 'stages': all that is postulated is a general trend in the direction of the arrows so that movement in the contrary direction will be relatively rare. Let us further suppose that two groups of subjects, *p* and *q*, are given a problem of this type to solve on two separate occasions (i) and (ii); and that the subjects of group *p* are on average less 'advanced' than those of group *q* – that is, they tend to start at a point nearer the beginning of the sequence. However, it is postulated that in both groups there is a certain amount of scatter so that some subjects in a group are more advanced than others.

Now, given this situation, we must expect to find:

(i) very few fresh instances of A on the second occasion in either group – that is, few people making this error on the second occasion who did not do so on the first one;

(ii) fewer instances of A in group *q* than in group *p*, on either occasion separately or on both combined;

(iii) some movements towards B from A and some away from B towards C or D, the former being more common in group *p* than in group *q*;

(iv) some movements towards C and some away from C to the correct solution, the latter being more common in group *q* than in group *p*.

Now suppose that one calculates indices of magnitude of error and of magnitude and direction of change for the two groups in respect of A, B, and C. The postulates then imply:

1. *for error A:* (a) IME higher in group *p* than in group *q*
             (b) IMC higher in group *q* than in group *p*
             (c) IDC of high negative value in both groups[1]

2. *for error B:* (a) IDC lower than for error A in group *p*
             (b) IDC lower than for error A in group *q*
             (c) IDC of higher negative value in group *q* than in group *p*

3. *for error C:* (a) IDC of higher negative or lower positive value in group *q* than in group *p*

---

[1] There is no reason to expect them to differ as regards *direction* where the earliest point of the sequence is concerned.

A Study of Children's Thinking

The predictions for B and C are more restricted than for A, because the balance of movements in the middle of the sequence must depend to a large extent on the relative positions of the two groups at the start, and the postulates merely say that one is more advanced than the other without giving any indication of the size of the gap. Also, a great deal must depend on the length of the interval between the two successive testings.

A general principle underlying the predictions of the IDC is that the nearer an error lies to the start of the sequence,[1] the nearer the IDC will lie to the negative maximum. Towards the end of the sequence, positive values may be expected to occur. However, the possibility of direct transition from points earlier in the sequence to the final error-free solution reduces the likelihood of obtaining positive values for the later errors.

The question which we now have to consider is whether the evidence obtained in the course of this study is compatible with the existence of any overall developmental trend in the occurrence of different types of error. For this purpose, group indices have been calculated for each of the three categories, arbitrary, structural, and executive, as was done previously for the individual errors. The group indices were arrived at, not by averaging the separate error indices, but by adding the raw figures and then

TABLE 27    GROUP INDICES

| Category of Error | Group | IME | IMC | IDC | Frequency |
|---|---|---|---|---|---|
| Arbitrary | Y | ·43 | ·63 | − ·69 | 102 |
|  | O | ·24 | ·78 | − ·67 | 34 |
| Structural | Y | ·34 | ·78 | − ·44 | 174 |
|  | O | ·29 | ·58 | − ·60 | 119 |
| Executive | Y | ·42 | ·80 | ·08 | 92 |
|  | O | ·40 | ·74 | − ·02 | 95 |

[1] 'Start of the sequence' must be interpreted here to mean effective start for any given group – that is, the point below which no one falls.

216

calculating indices on the basis of the totals. This was in order that the average so obtained should be weighted by the actual frequencies in the various columns. The resulting figures are given in *Table 27*.[1]

We shall now consider how the predictions made on the basis of a postulated developmental sequence agree with these findings if we take the arbitrary errors to correspond to stage A – that is, to the start of the sequence – the structural to stage B, and the executive to stage C; and if, further, we read Group Y for *p* and Group O for *q*.

We then find that:

1. (a) IME for arbitrary errors is higher in Group Y than in Group O;
   (b) IMC for arbitrary errors is higher in Group O than in Group Y;
   (c) IDC for arbitrary errors is of high negative value in both groups.
2. (a) IDC is lower for structural than for arbitrary errors in Group Y;
   (b) IDC is lower for structural than for arbitrary errors in Group O;
   (c) IDC for structural errors is of higher negative value in Group O than in Group Y.
3. (a) IDC for executive errors is of low negative value in Group O and of low positive value in Group Y.

Thus, all of the results are in the predicted direction, though some of the differences are small.[2] For instance, in Group O the IDC

[1] The results for the formal deductive reasoning problems were presented in Chapter 8 in a manner slightly different from that used in earlier chapters (see page 169). However, for calculation of the group indices the errors in these problems were analysed in a way which corresponds as closely as possible to the procedure used for the other problems.

[2] We are grateful to Dr. D. N. Lawley of the Department of Statistics, University of Edinburgh, for advising us that it would not be appropriate to apply tests of significance to the present results. This study was planned rather to provide hypotheses than to test them. Verification will have to be obtained by differently devised experiments with greater numbers.

for the structural errors is only slightly lower than that for the arbitrary ones – see prediction 2 (b).

This prediction was made on the basis of the general principle that the IDC will tend to drop from its highest negative peak as one moves away from the start of the sequence – a principle formulated on the basis of the reasoning that diminutions in the frequency of the earlier errors will manifest themselves as increases in the frequency of the later ones. However, if, for any group of subjects, it should happen to be the case that most of those who made the errors of type A on the first occasion had passed *beyond* B to C or D on the second occasion, then there would be few movements from A to B to reduce the value of the IDC for B.

If one derives predictions from postulates and then finds that the predictions are satisfied, one does not thereby prove that one's postulates represent the true state of affairs. For this to be established beyond doubt, it would have to be shown that no other set of postulates would enable equally successful predictions to be made. However, the stages in the sequence which we have postulated in this case have about them an element of logical connection, deriving from the very definitions of the errors. Arbitrary errors involve neglect of the given. If the given is wholly neglected, structural errors, which consist in failure to understand the given, cannot arise. The failure may, of course, be present, but it will not be able to manifest itself in observable error. Again, executive errors can usually be recorded only when the manipulations in the course of which they arise are correct in principle (see page 147 for illustration of this).

One may perhaps pause to ask at this point, whether, if the sequence has this logical coherence, there was any need to produce *Table 27* at all. The answer is that one must never base any psychological conclusion on arguments of logical dependence alone, since there is always the risk that these arguments may have overlooked some point that is of psychological importance.

However, there is also the further point that the agreement of *Table 27* with the predictions suggests that the actual sorting of errors into the three categories was reasonably successful – that those classified as 'arbitrary' did, on the whole, properly belong together, and so on.

It now remains to relate these findings to the arguments advanced in the first three chapters of this book – arguments which may be summarized as follows.

It is desirable to undertake close study of the ways in which children tackle problems of kinds commonly used in intelligence tests. These problems are already known to have 'high status' as predictors of academic success in secondary school. So if we can find out more about how they work, we may be able to learn to construct better tests in future, on a basis of insight rather than trial and error. The best way to proceed seems to be by trying to discover what are the sources of a problem's discriminating power – that is, of what nature are the difficulties which children encounter when they fail to solve it. Hence we must study errors in thinking and the best way to do this at present is probably to ask the children to 'think aloud'. The results of such a study ought to make a useful general contribution to knowledge of the development of thinking, as well as help to improve techniques of assessment. But the findings of a clinical study conducted with small numbers of subjects are chiefly useful, in either of these connections, as a source of hypotheses. They must be verified by subsequent statistical inquiries.

The present study is wholly clinical. So if it is to be judged in terms of the aims which guided it, the main question is whether it has provided useful hypotheses. At the same time, the value for test construction of some of the detailed observations may be immediate and not dependent on subsequent verification. In particular, it has been shown clearly that some of the problems investigated were faulty. Their weaknesses were unsuspected when they were selected for study and would have been difficult for an adult to foresee – or to appreciate from any analysis of solutions chosen. When the right solution was reached for the wrong reasons, it was often evident that this spurious success could have been avoided by a more informed use of distractors or by some seemingly minor change in the statement of the problem.

The addition of detailed knowledge of this kind to the sum of available information about how to construct test items is perhaps in itself enough to justify the inquiry. Still, the main criterion of success is the provision of useful suggestions of a more general kind.

In this connection, the most prominent features of the results are the establishment of three categories of error, the arbitrary, the structural, and the executive; the identification of certain characteristics common to diverse examples of structural error and suggestive of a widespread conceptual difficulty;[1] and the evidence for what appears to be a developmental trend in the occurrence of the three categories. All of these offer starting-points for further research in the attempt to discover what most importantly determines a problem's status as an index of intelligence. For example, the conceptual difficulty which appeared to underlie a number of different structural errors may have special prognostic significance at the age where it was common. In order to find out whether this is so, problems in which it can be shown to manifest itself will have to be compared for predictive success with others where the structural difficulties are of different kinds.

In a similar way, the comparative prognostic significance of the three main categories of error may be studied. It should be possible to devise tests which, with subjects of a given age, specially invite one or other kind. A first attempt at this was the construction of Problem A2 so as to invite, from ten-year-old children, relatively more structural and fewer executive errors than Problem A1. If group tests can be produced with this kind of control, it will then be possible to test their respective prognostic powers.

This involves asking the question: at a given age, what are the

---

[1] This was the tendency to hold apart and distinct the components of a problem, with associated failure to recognize in how many different statements of relationship the same term may figure.

best types of problem to use? But the evidence of a developmental sequence in the occurrence of the three categories of error suggests another question, namely: for a given problem, what is the best age at which to use it? It might well be true of some problems that they would sort children more importantly if given at an age when structural errors were frequently made in the solving of them than if given later when executive errors were the most common type – or, of course, the reverse might prove to be the case. In either event, the value of the problem would vary from one age to the other. (Shifts of this kind would reduce to simple increases in facility if the group of children getting the correct solution on the first occasion were wholly contained within the group getting the correct solution on the second. But otherwise they would not.)

These suggestions will not be easily or quickly put to thorough test. But as they – or others likewise derived from a close study of children's behaviour – are further studied, a better appreciation may gradually be gained of what things are the most important signs of how a child's thinking has progressed and is likely to continue to progress. The penicillin in the mouldy bread may be identified. And with this we may come to know better, not only how to predict development prophetically, but how to guide it with a more enlightened understanding.

# APPENDIX I

# *A Further Study of Overlap Error in Three-term Series Problems*

JOHN DUTHIE[1]

THE RESULTS reported here are the first findings which have come from research still in progress. This research attempts to derive hypotheses by the 'thinking-aloud' procedure, and to test them by the usual group methods – this being the first attempt in the present series of investigations to go beyond the stage of deriving hypotheses. However, although the present investigation has now reached the stage of verification by group testing, the results of this are not yet available. All that can be reported here are some further findings of the 'thinking-aloud' method as applied to the study of overlap error in the three-term series problems. These findings bear particularly on the question of whether overlap error is to be classed as structural or executive.

The overlap form of the three-term series problem[2] was first used in the two versions described in the main text. For ease of reference these are reprinted below:

### PROBLEM BI

We want to find out the ages of two girls called Jean and May. We know that a third girl, Betty, is 15, and that she is

---

[1] The author is indebted to Mr. R. B. Bett for his constructive criticism and advice on the presentation and interpretation of many of the findings reported in this appendix.
[2] Hereafter called an overlap problem.

3 years older than one of the two girls and 5 years older than the other. If we had one more piece of information we could calculate the ages of Jean and May. What is that piece of information?

Tom, Dick, and Harry are 3 boys. Dick, who is 5′ 4″ tall, is 6 inches taller than one of the other boys and 2 inches taller than the remaining one. Harry is taller than Tom.
Therefore: [Here followed five choices of answer.]

These are both problems of type (5) (see page 85).

Now if the aim is to discover whether a given type of error is or is not structural, then it would seem clear that the structure of relationships in which one is interested must be presented in the simplest possible manner, with no added complexities to obscure the issue. Then if all attempts to present the bare bones of the problem fail to prevent the occurrence of the error, this will support the view that it is structural. However, it must be added that if the error *does* disappear in these circumstances, it does not follow with equal certainty that it is executive. Here, as so often in research, one result may be decisive while another leaves the problem still open. A structural error was defined (see page 43) as one in which the subject fails '. . . to understand some principle that is necessary for solution'. Now suppose that the subject is given a simplified overlap problem followed by the more complex B2 (see page 86), that he has grasped the structure of the simplified problem-form, and that he has executed this problem without error; it may still be the case that when he comes to the more complex problem-form of B2 he may then 'fail to appreciate the structure of the problem', and his error may therefore be structural rather than executive.

The first attempt to simplify the original problems yielded a problem-form of which the following is an example:

We want to find out the ages of two girls called Jean and May. We know that a third girl, Betty, is 15, and that she is three years older than May and five years older than Jean. How old are Jean and May?

This problem, which we call B4, again conforms to type (5) (see page 85).

If the reader will compare B4 with Problems B1 and B2 he will notice that three major changes were made. The 'piece of information' requirement was omitted since it seemed to call for a different form of reasoning from that primarily involved in the overlap situation; the multiple-choice form was omitted (for reasons given in the main text); and the form of the problem was altered by specifying at once the terms involved in each of the relationships with the link (thus, we state '. . . and that she is three years older than May', rather than '. . . and that she is three years older than one of the two girls', etc.).

Within this problem-form, systematic manipulation of the relevant variables was carried out. The two variables which seemed at that time chiefly relevant were the relative size of the first and second intervals, and the nature and direction of the relationships between the terms. These relationships were varied, as before, by using ages and heights; they were now further varied by stating the relationships in both possible ways (e.g. 'older than' and 'younger than'). Combination of these criteria generated eight versions of the problem:

TABLE I

| | | Kind of relationship employed | | | |
| --- | --- | --- | --- | --- | --- |
| | | Ages | | Heights | |
| | | Older | Younger | Taller | Smaller |
| Relative size of first interval | Small | B4 | B8 | B11 | B7 |
| | Large | B6 | B10 | B9 | B5 |

Each of the relationships (e.g. 'older than' or 'younger than', etc.) remained constant within each question, that is, 'older than' *and* 'younger than' were never used in the same problem. The sex of the names used in the problems was not considered crucial and hence was not varied exhaustively. Common pre-names were used and the sex of these was alternated throughout the series. Thus the names in B4 were female, in B5 male, in B6 female, and so on.

As a further example of the problems generated by this procedure, we quote B7:

> We want to find out the heights of two boys called George and Jack. We know that a third boy, Tom, is 4 feet 8 inches, and that Jack is 2 inches smaller than Tom and that George is 3 inches smaller than Tom. How tall are George and Jack?

These problems, together with B1 and B2, were given individually to twelve children whose ages ranged from 8 years 2 months to 11 years 6 months. We call these children Group A. Since not all problems were given to all children, and since the sample was very small, no comparative counts of errors could be made; but we were able to examine the types and general trend of errors as they occurred throughout our sample.

### Results: Group A

Overlap error was not eliminated by the simplification – indeed it occurred more frequently than any other type of error. Only one child, however, persisted in making the error in spite of attempts which were made to help the children to overcome the difficulties. In this case, after overlap error had been made in the initial attempt, the experimenter covered one part of the question, and the child calculated the value of the dependent term correctly (in the part 'We know that a third girl, Betty, is 15, and that she is three years older than May'); this part was then covered and the other relationship '. . . and five years older than Jean' revealed, whereupon the child calculated Jean's age correctly. Finally the experimenter asked the child to do the whole question again, and she at once fell back into overlap error. She was quite unable to deal correctly with both relationships when they were presented within the context of a single question. In this case, then, overlap error would seem to be structural rather than executive in nature.

However, it occurred more commonly on the original than on the newer simplified problem-forms. Ann, for example, attempted the problems in the order B8, B9, B2, B11, and B10, and made no overlap error until she reached B2. The structure of B9 is (apart from the decrease in complexity) identical with that of B2 – both concern heights, both use the 'taller than' relationship, and in both the longer interval comes first. This happened also in the case of David. Here overlap error on B2 was preceded by correct solution of B7, B8, and B9 in that order. The tendency to overlap error on the more complex form of the problem was thus particularly strong in both these cases. And since B9 and B2 do not differ in their formal structure, the error in B2 *in these cases* may have been of an executive kind.[1] (In other cases where B2 was administered, it was part of an all-correct series.)

The trend of errors throughout the sample was puzzling. Overlap errors were made by the children who were approaching ten, or who were ten, but not by the eight- and nine-year-olds nor by the eleven-year-olds. But unlike the findings reported in Chapter 5 (where, it will be recalled, overlap error was usually preceded by some more primitive error) it was here found that with one exception the younger children achieved correct answers. This sample was so small and so unrepresentative that it was decided to replicate the experiment using large numbers of children at each age level and using a group form of the test. These children formed Group B.

*Group B*

One of the modifications of the test items suggested by the results of the study discussed above (Group A) was a simplification of the arithmetic involved in the solution. Two (and perhaps three) of

[1] But need not have been: see discussion on page 224.

the errors in this pilot study had been due to arithmetical difficulty, so it was decided to use no number higher than ten. As an example of the problem-form used we quote B12:

> We want to find out the ages of Jean and May. We know that Betty is 10, and that she is one year older than May and three years older than Jean.
> So Jean is . . . . . . years old.
> So May is . . . . . . years old.

A further modification thus included the dropping of 'two' [girls] and [we know that a] 'third' [girl]. This was done because of the possibility which had by then been discovered in the unquantified three-term series problems that the children might achieve a correct solution of the problem by thinking in terms of four girls rather than of three. It was thought desirable to specify in advance as little of the mode of solution as possible so that the thought processes in as 'pure' an overlap situation as possible could be studied.

In order to cut the length of the group test, it was decided to omit the 'heights' problems,[1] but otherwise to leave all four variations[2] as given in *Table I*. These four problems are called B12, B13, B14, and B15.

Spacer problems[3] of a related kind were interpolated with the overlap problems, and the eight items thus obtained were permuted in cyclical fashion to give eight forms of the test. The test

---

[1] Another reason was that our youngest group had not yet learned to deal in feet and inches.

[2] We did not at this stage equate the number of times that the link was mentioned in different types of problem. In the problem quoted on this page, for example, the link is mentioned only once (after the preliminary statement), and then only pronominally. In the problems in which the direction was reversed ('younger' instead of 'older'), however, the link was repeated. E.g.:

> We want to find out the ages of two boys called Bill and Harry. We know that a third boy, Jim, is 7, and that Bill is three years younger than Jim, and that Harry is two years younger than Jim.
> So Bill is. . . . . . years old.
> So Harry is. . . . . . years old.

In later forms of the problem, however, we equated the number of times the link was mentioned (see page 231).

[3] The spacers were of course intended to reduce interference (or facilitation) effects among the overlap items proper.

booklets were then distributed randomly among the 360 children of Group B at each of four age levels 7, 8, 9, and 10.

In spite of the larger numbers used in this cross-sectional study, however, no clear pattern of errors as a function of age emerged.

Two courses of action were therefore decided upon. First, a random sample comprising 63 of these children was selected and studied individually by the 'thinking-aloud' method; and second, an independent longitudinal group study using 890 children was instituted, the same children being tested on three occasions at intervals of one year. The results of the longitudinal study are not yet available; the results of the individual testing are given below.

*Results (individual testing): Group B*
In the individual interviews the child was presented with the problems – usually several weeks after the original group test – and asked to solve them again, but this time while thinking aloud. The complete interview was tape-recorded and later transcribed.

The first thing that was noticed was that many of the younger children passed the test and that many of the older children failed it. We are frankly puzzled by the successes of the younger children. It may be that their successes were spurious, based on a failure fully to understand what was involved in the problem situation,[1] but the thinking-aloud procedure gave no direct evidence for this. There were indeed one or two hints of failure to comprehend the situation in related problems given as spacers, and one or two indications that spurious success might be achieved by separating the premisses, but these were few.

A good example of failure in older children is that of Jessie, a nine-year-old who was in the 'A' stream of a four-stream school. Jessie had made a classical overlap error in the following problem:

B14: We know that Peter is 8 and that he is three years older than Ian and one year older than David.

[1] Much of the present research is, of course, directed towards achieving a problem-form which avoids this kind of ambiguity.

The experimenter then asked: '(Who will be one year older than David?)[1] Ian. (Ian, I see. It's definitely Ian, is it?) [Pause.] (It couldn't be Peter, could it?) No. (Why couldn't it be Peter?) Because it says that . . . see . . . that ". . . and that he is three years older than Ian and one year older than David". (So could it be Peter?) No.'

It is fairly certain, then, that this older (and intelligent) child was experiencing a real structural difficulty with overlapping relationships.

Among the oldest group (ten-year-olds) there were many overlap errors of an apparently structural kind. Here is an example from the 'A' stream:

> Problem B15: We want to find out the ages of Bill and Harry. We know that Jim is 7 and that Bill is three years younger than Jim, and that Harry is two years younger than Jim. How old are Bill and Harry?

*Janice:* 'Well, Jim is seven and Bill is three years younger than Jim; well, that means he is four. (Good.) And that Harry is two years younger than Jim. [Pause.] That means he's two. (Mmm. How do you know that?) Well, you take the two from the four years that Jim is. (How old is Jim?) He is four. (How do you know that?) You take the three from the seven . . . (How old is Jim?) Seven. (Just do it once more for me will you please? Start again, "We know that Jim is 7 and that Bill is three years younger than Jim", so how old is Bill?) Four. (Uh-huh, and then Harry is two years younger than Jim, so . . .) That is two. (Uh-huh). You take the two from the four. (Now you said that Jim was seven, and then that he was four. Now which is he?) Jim is seven. (Uh-huh.) And Bill is three years younger. Bill is four. (And Harry's two years younger than Jim, so how old is Harry?) Two.[1]

On the other hand, many of the errors among the older children were ambiguous, and were corrected by a very simple rephrasing of the question. Isabel, for example, made the classical overlap error by subtracting from the value of one of the dependent terms instead of from the link. When asked how she obtained her answer she made a clear statement to this effect. However, when the interviewer re-read the question for her fluently and with proper emphasis she was at once able to see that she should have returned to the link rather than to one of the dependent variables in order to calculate the value of the other dependent variable. Once she had achieved this insight she was quite certain that she had been wrong before, and that this was the correct way in which to tackle the problem.

In the course of work with these subjects, we became aware of the importance of the fact that in some of our problems the link was mentioned only once.[2] So we now devised a third simplified form, in which the link was always repeated. It still conforms, however, to type (5). We illustrate this form by B16:

Betty is 10. Betty is three years older than May. Betty is five years older than Jean. How old are May and Jean?

(The other versions of this form are known as B17–B19 inclusive.)

Here, if overlap error still occurs, it is less likely to be due to an executive error such as loss of hold of the link. The fact that it did still occur is further evidence that the overlap error is of a structural kind. The problem was evolved during the clinical study which we have been discussing, and was given to the latter part of that group.

Donald tackled the problem which we have just quoted. Donald is aged eight:

[1] This child's error may seem at the beginning of the protocol to be executive, but by the end of the quotation it becomes clear that it is structural.

[2] Hitherto the link in problems involving an 'older than' relationship was mentioned only once; but in problems involving a 'younger than' relationship it was mentioned twice (see page 228, footnote 2).

'Ten and three is thirteen, so May is thirteen. (What else?) Thirteen plus five is eighteen. So Jean is eighteen. (Yes. Now let me hear you doing the first part again.) Betty is ten. Betty is three years older than May, so May is thirteen. Betty is ten. Betty is five years older than Jean, so Jean is eighteen.'

Here then we have a very clear example of the conventional overlap error in spite of the fact that the child in his last statement has mentioned the link twice and has given it the same value on each occasion. The other error in this protocol is, of course, asymmetry, and the interviewer spent the rest of this particular session trying unsuccessfully to help the child to achieve insight into asymmetrical structure. Donald's answer to his next problem, quoted below, will be given at length, since it gives us unusual insight into the mental processes involved in his solution. Here is the problem:

B17: Bill is 7. Dick is two years younger than Bill. Jim is three years younger than Bill. How old are Dick and Jim?

When Donald had made the classical overlap error the experimenter wrote out the question again in a slightly different form:

Bill is 7. Jim is three years younger than Bill.
Bill is 7. Dick is two years younger than Bill.

The experimenter then asked: '(How old is Jim?) Jim is three years younger than Bill so Jim is four. Dick is two years younger than Bill. So Dick is five. (Now let's go back to this one [i.e. the original question].) Bill is seven. Dick is two years younger than Bill, so Dick is five. And Jim is three years younger than Bill, so Jim is two. (How many boys were there here? [indicating original form of the question].) Five. (Do it again and see [indicating special form of the question].) Bill is seven. Jim is three years younger than Bill so Jim is four. Bill is seven. Dick is two years younger than Bill so Dick is two. [The experimenter managed to correct this by hiding one part of the question at a time.] (How many boys are there then?) Three. [The subject then made overlap error again on the original question.]'

Later the same day the experimenter sent for Donald again and asked him to attempt the original form of the question once more. On this occasion he again made overlap error. On being asked why Jim was two he replied: 'I've got Dick's age. You take away three years from Dick's age which is two. (How do you know to take three years from Dick's age?) Because he is nearest youngest to him. (Why do you take it from the nearest youngest?) You can't take it from the biggest because you'll get the wrong answer. (How is that?) Because you'll get four and that wouldn't be right, so you take it away from the other age. (Yes, but why?) Because it's the wrong answer and I done it before and I got it right then. (Could four be the right answer?) Yes, if there was only two boys. But there's three boys. (Which two boys do you mean?) Bill and Jim. (Why do you think it's wrong with three boys?) [No reply.] Bill is five so Jim is two. (You say Bill is five. It says Bill is seven here. Have you got two Bills with different ages?) Yes.[1] (If both Bills were the same age – if they were both seven – what would be the ages of Dick and Jim then?) Dick would be five and Jim would be four. (If both Bills were the same boy, what would happen then?) Dick would be five and Jim would be two.'

There are many interesting aspects to this protocol, among them the explicit statement that Jim could be four if there were only one pair of terms. But the most interesting insight of all is that the correct solution can be achieved (at the end) only if there are *two* Bills of the same age. As soon as the two Bills become one, the overlap error appears again. This supports very strongly the hypothesis that the difficulty is in returning to the link.[2]

While overlap error on a simplified problem of this type is almost certainly significant for our purposes, a correct solution on the other hand is ambiguous. Just as in the earlier problem-form we suggested that the younger children might be achieving spurious success by separating the two premisses, so *a fortiori* in the case of these simplified problems. In these problems it is even easier to achieve a solution without conceiving that the relation-

---

[1] Here of course the child may just be agreeing with the experimenter.
[2] See discussion on pages 99 ff.

ships overlap (or that one is returning to the link) since the link is mentioned twice and the two sets of relationships can thus be dealt with separately.

To prevent this happening we attempted to construct problem-forms in which the subject, to achieve solution, would be forced to consider the overlapping of the relationships. These problems, of types (2) and (4), we have called 'partially quantified'. Here, as an example, is B20:[1]

> Betty is 3 years older than May. Betty is 2 years older than Jean. What is the difference between the ages of Jean and May?

As we explained in the main text this problem is called partially quantified because Betty (the link) is given no absolute age.

The trouble with this problem is that the difficulty of dealing with the partially quantified form has in practice occasionally overshadowed the overlap difficulty. Children who can deal adequately with a full quantified asymmetrical relation – e.g. 'Betty is ten. Betty is three years older than Jean' – are not necessarily able to deal with a partially quantified one – e.g. 'Betty is three years older than Jean'. They may be unable to say that if Betty is three years older than Jean then Jean is three years younger than Betty, although they are able to give Jean's age when Betty's is given.

The fact that these difficulties (and they are not uncommon) occur when dealing with a *single* asymmetrical relationship indicates that the difficulty is specific to the partially quantified situation and has nothing to do with overlap difficulty *per se*. For this reason it is probably safer at this stage (and it may always be necessary) to use the partially quantified form along with the simplified fully quantified form. The two problem-forms may together contribute the information which either alone is unable to provide.

It soon became obvious, however, that there were loopholes in this (partially quantified) form too. First of all, children tended to

[1] The usual variations of B20 are known as B21, B22, and B23.

solve it by attributing an absolute age to the link and then solving it as if it were a fully quantified problem. The children who did this fell into two groups – those who treated the adoption of an absolute age for the link explicitly as a *conditional* procedure, and those who believed that they were able legitimately to discover the value of the link from the information which is given. An example of the former kind of solution follows:

Isabel, who was presented with the following problem:

Jill is 3 years older than Sally. Jill is 1 year older than Rose.

showed that she was aware of the status of the value she attributed to the link: 'If Jill was ten, Rose would be nine and Sally would be six. (Mmm. How do you know?) Because if Jill was really ten – if she was ten or not – it would be right, because Sally would be the youngest and Rose would be the second oldest. [And later in the same protocol:] (Well, could you work it out again for me and see if you can do it?) With a different . . . (No. We'll still say Jill is ten.)'

An example of the latter kind of solution was given by Charles, who was presented with the same problem as Isabel. He began by saying that Jill was three: 'Oh, Jill's three. (How do you know Jill's three?) It tells you there. (Read out that bit.) "Jill's three years older than . . . S . . . than Sally." [Note his distress.] (Does that mean Jill's three?) No.'

This answer, which might superficially seem to be merely a misreading, is so common that it seems to spring from an anticipation of a fully quantified situation, rather like the anticipation of a non-overlapping structure suggested in the main text. Joanna, in her attempt to solve a partially quantified problem whose premises are stated in the opposite direction from those of the problem we have just discussed, made the same kind of error:

Tom is 4 years younger than Dick. Paul is 3 years younger than Dick. What is the difference between the ages of Tom and Paul?

'Well, Tom is four years younger than Dick and Paul is three years younger than Dick. (What is the difference between Tom and Paul?) [Pause.] One year. (How do you know that?) 'Cos you know that Tom is four and Paul is three and take three away from four. (How do you know that Tom is four?) It says that Tom is four years younger than Dick. (Does that mean Tom is four?) No.'

Thus, by converting the relatives to absolutes, she obtained the correct answer without tackling any form of overlap problem – either fully quantified or partially quantified.

Jessie made exactly the same error only she failed to see her mistake when a direct question was put to her. She said:

'Tom is four and Paul is three and Tom is one year older than Paul. (Now are you sure that Tom is four? Do you think Tom is four?) Yes. (How do you know that Tom is four?) [Pause.] Because it says that Tom is four years younger than Dick.'

Since the child went on working on this assumption it seems that, at least in this case, the error was the result of very much more than a mere misreading.

From the evidence given in the protocols it seems possible that there might be a developmental sequence of the following kind in the ability to solve partially quantified problems. The lowest level would be complete inability to deal with the situation; the next the 'discovery' of an absolute age in the information given; the next the adoption of a conditional value for the link; and finally solution without any absolute quantification at all (that is, at the partially quantified level).

While it would be of interest to collect such information by group test it is difficult at the moment to see how this could be done. The problems, as they stand, may be solved correctly at any of the levels we have suggested (except the first) and thus from the final solution alone we have no way of discovering the level at which the child was working.

Less obvious – but more serious perhaps – is the fact that in this form of the problem children use the word 'difference' as a signal to subtract, without really understanding why they should subtract. Thus, in the questions as they stand, they are able in this way to achieve the correct answer without comprehension. Here, as an illustration, is an excerpt from John's protocol:

Jill is 3 years older than Sally. Jill is 1 year older than Rose. What is the difference between the ages of Sally and Rose?

'Two. (Good. Now tell me how you worked it out.) If it's "difference" you always have to take away. (Oh, I see, this word here, "difference", is that why you took away?) Yes.'

The fact that John did the same thing in a non-overlap situation (and thus obtained the wrong answer) reinforces our interpretation of his statement:

Ruth is 3 years older than June. June is 2 years older than Kate. What is the difference between the ages of Ruth and Kate?

'(Now let me see if you can do it.) [Pause.] One. (How do you know it's one?) Two from three leaves one. (Why did you subtract?) To find the difference. To find the difference you have to subtract.'

Euphemia made the same error in a non-overlapping three-term series, and explained it as follows: 'Because the difference means take away and I have taken away.'

The problem-form was therefore modified again (generating versions B24 – B27 inclusive) and rephrased as follows:

B24: Jill is 3 years older than Sally. Jill is 1 year older than Rose.
Who is older, Sally or Rose? Write your answer here ......
How many years are there between Sally and Rose? Write your answer here ......

This form, it will be noticed, avoids the difficulty inherent in the previous form by omitting the word 'difference', but there is a little evidence which suggests that this form is still not perfect.

In his attempt to solve a non-overlapping three-term series problem, Thomas subtracted and therefore obtained the wrong answer. He went on: 'Please sir, I was thinking, adding it but it wouldn't come out right. (Why wouldn't it come out right if you added it?) Because it says how many years are there *between* Ian and Jim, and if you added them that would be putting them together, instead of splitting them up. [The experimenter asked why "between" meant splitting them up, but Thomas was unable to answer this.]'

This was, however, the only example of such an attempt that we came across, and it may be that since it is uncommon we shall be able to leave the problem in its present form. It is certainly difficult to conceive of how the problem-form may be modified further in this respect.

A much more common error, however, was to reply to the question 'Who is older, Sally or Rose?' with 'Jill' – the name of the link term.

It is much easier to see how to rephrase the question in order to overcome this difficulty. Some such question-form as the following might be suitable:

So . . . . . is oldest.
So . . . . . is next.
So . . . . . is next.

Any such form would, of course, have to be submitted to clinical tests before we could use it in a group test.

When we are satisfied with the problem-form, it is hoped to run a control group experiment using partially quantified and fully quantified overlap forms matched with partially quantified and fully quantified non-overlap forms, to test whether the overlapping form is more difficult to deal with than the non-overlapping form. We were unable to get any direct information on this during our clinical studies because of the high interference[1] between the two types of problem (overlap and non-overlap). Any attempt to investigate the two at once in an individual child was for this reason bound to be inconclusive.

---

[1] Because the two kinds of problem are very similar in general appearance, children who have just finished one kind tend to tackle the other kind in exactly the same way, often with some such comment as 'It's the same as the last one'.

This appendix so far has described historically, and in some detail, the search for unambiguous problem-forms to be used in group testing. During this search some findings were obtained which did not seem directly relevant to our historical description. These will now be summarized.

We have, first of all, some further evidence which tends to support the view that overlap error is structural. The first evidence of this kind is the persistence with which some children made the overlap error in spite of efforts by the interviewer to correct them. This is illustrated by Graham in the following problem:

> We want to find out the ages of Ann and Susan. We know that Joan is 9 and that Susan is two years younger than Joan and that Ann is three years younger than Joan. How old are Ann and Susan?

'[Pause.] Susan is seven. And Ann is – three. (How do you know that Susan is seven?) [Pause.] "We know that Joan is 9 and that Susan is two . . .", so I took two from nine and that leaves seven. (Ah, good, yes. How did you find out Ann's age?) Then I took . . . then I took another three from seven and that leaves four. (Mmm, I see. So Ann is four, is she?) Yes. (I see. It says Ann is three years younger than Joan; how old is Joan?) [Pause.] Nine. (Nine. So if Ann's three years younger than Joan, how old will Ann be?) Six. (Six. And if Susan is two years younger than Joan how old will Susan be?) Four. [That is, overlap error again but with terms reversed, since we started with the other term first – an example of how, even if the child's attention is drawn to the fact that he should subtract from the link, he will continue to make overlap error.] (Uh-huh. How do you know?) [Long pause.] (Why do you take two from six?) Because it's much easier. (Easier than what?) Taking six from two. [!] (But why from six? Why didn't you take two from nine? Susan is two years younger than Joan, isn't she? And Joan is what?) [Pause.] Is nine. (Mmm. So Joan is nine and Susan is two years younger than Joan . . .) She is seven. (Seven. Mmm, that's fine.) [Although Graham did not solve the overlap problem as a whole, the experimenter felt that to continue would disturb rapport.]'

Much of the rest of the evidence is interesting both intrinsically and with regard to the light that it throws on the nature of the overlap error.

It will be recalled that in the partially quantified problems the children were asked to find the difference between the two dependent terms. It will also be recalled that, in order to solve this type of problem, many children converted it into a fully quantified problem. When this happened the children were often asked by the investigator whether a change in the value of the link would lead to a change in their answer – that is, to a change in the difference between the two dependent variables. Many children believed that the difference would in fact change with a change in the value of the link term. Here, for example, is an excerpt from the protocol of Francis:

'Well, if Jill is ten then if Ann . . . Rose is one year younger, she must be nine; and if em . . . and Jill is three years older than Sally, Sally must be seven, and the difference between Rose and Sally is em . . . two years. (Lovely. Now if Jill is eight would there still be two years between them?) No. (Why not?) Because then . . . Rose would be seven . . . and Sally would be five, and then the difference would be . . . two years! (It's the same again, isn't it?) Yes. (Now if Jill is nine the difference would still be two years?) Yes. (Why is it always two years? That's a puzzle, isn't it?) It's because . . . [Long pause.] (Have you any ideas?) [Pause.] (Why is it always two years?) [Long pause.] I don't think I do know why it is always two years.'

Some of the children made several attempts, calculating the difference with varying values for the link term, before they were convinced that the difference would remain constant. This is evidence that these children had not fully grasped the structure of a three-term series, either overlap or non-overlap. It is difficult to conceive of a way in which a group test could be constructed to discover this disability, but an individual test item of this kind seems quite feasible. A useful index would be the number of times that the children had to do such examples before they believed that the difference between the variables is constant; another index would be their ability to explain this constancy. An alternative (or addition) to this last question would be 'Will it be possible to tell without knowing Jim's age?' (that is, the age of the link).

One particularly puzzling aspect of the children's solutions to these problems is their ability to order or seriate all three terms in a partially quantified problem (without having given a value to the link), followed by their failure to find the difference between the two dependent terms. Mary's protocol illustrates this point:

Jill is 3 years older than Sally. Jill is 1 year older than Rose. Who is older, Sally or Rose?

'Rose. (Yes, how do you know it's Rose?) 'Cos Jill is only one year older than Rose, and she is three years older than Sally. [Note that this is a very sophisticated explanation of her response, and yet she is unable to complete the rest of the problem.] (Now do this part for me, will you?) How many years are there between Sally and Rose? [Long pause.] (Have you any idea how to do that?) No. [The experimenter then repeated the question for her in order to encourage her to solve it, and obtained the following answer:] Four years.'

Thus although Mary was able to seriate the terms and to explain her seriation at a fairly high level, she was unable to continue. The fact that children also exhibit this behaviour when they are dealing with the non-overlap form of the three-term series suggests that it is the partially quantified rather than the overlap difficulty which is causing the trouble.

From the clinical evidence which we have so far presented, then, it seems that overlap error is usually structural in nature. When it is structural, the overlap error seems to be produced in at least two different ways. Of these, the first is the more frequent. In this mode of solution, the child discovers the value of the second dependent term by subtracting not from the link but from the first dependent term. This has already been illustrated by an excerpt from Jessie's protocol (see pages 229–230).

The second major process by which children arrive at overlap error is that in which the value of the link is changed when the child comes to deal with the second premiss. The protocol of Janice, quoted on page 230, gave us an example of this.

It is, however, important to notice that this discussion refers only to the problem-form where the link is mentioned once in the 'older than' version and twice in the 'younger than' version. It seems from the results that, where the link is *not* repeated, all or most of the children subtract from the dependent term; and where the link *is* repeated the majority (but not all) of the children subtract from the link, but change its value. (Since the change in frequency of mention of the link is accompanied by a change in the direction of the statement of the asymmetrical relation, however, we cannot be sure that this result is final. We have not used the new form – in which the link is always repeated – sufficiently often to give any further evidence at this stage.)

The results so far can be summed up roughly by the following table.

TABLE II    FREQUENCY OF OCCURRENCE OF PROCESSES WHICH LEAD
TO OVERLAP ERROR ACCORDING TO PROBLEM-FORM*

|  | Subtract from dependent variable | Change value of link |
|---|---|---|
| Link not repeated | $7x$ | — |
| Link repeated | $x$ | $4x$ |

* The results are given as multiples of $x$, to emphasize the fact that (as we have already said) we cannot rely on figures derived from a design in which not all problems were given to all subjects.

It can be seen that the new form in which the link is repeated does not guarantee uniform method of solution.

We named the overlap problem as we did[1] because initially

[1] See discussion page 90.

we saw in it the formal requirement that one relationship be included within the other. We now call this requirement *inclusion*.

The correct solution to the overlap problem may be represented thus:

### FIGURE 1

(a)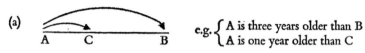

e.g. { A is three years older than B
{ A is one year older than C

and from this diagram the formal requirement of inclusion can be seen quite easily. In the same way, the 'classical' overlap error may be represented thus:

### FIGURE 2 [1]

(b)

e.g. { A is three years older than B
{ B is one year older than C

Here, obviously, there is no inclusion of one relationship within the other.

However, instead of the classical overlap error illustrated above, two other solutions of the overlap problem were frequently produced. In the first of these, the child calculates the first interval correctly and then *adds* to the value of the first dependent variable to achieve the value of the second. This procedure[2] can be represented in the following diagram:

### FIGURE 3

(c)

Thirteen of the sixty-three subjects in the clinical sample from Group B made this error and these represented all age-groups.

Mary gave a particularly clear example of this method of solution:

---

[1] This diagram fits equally well the case where the link changes **value.**
[2] Type *a* of the four types represented on page 106.

We want to find out the ages of Ian and David. We know that Peter is 8, and that he is three years older than Ian and one year older than David. How old are Ian and David?

'Ian's five. (Good.) And David's six. (Now how did you know that?) I took three years off that boy's age and took one year on that boy. (I see. You added one and five to get the six?) Yes.'

In the second of the alternative solutions, the child makes an asymmetry error on one of the relationships only:

FIGURE 4

(d)

This solution was given by five children of various ages.

Here is Ann's answer:

We want to find out the ages of Jean and May. We know that Betty is 10, and that she is one year older than May and three years older than Jean. How old are Jean and May?

'If May is one year older than Betty, she's eleven. And if she's ... Betty's three years older than Jean, Jean must be seven. (Now read it over to yourself again.) We know that Betty is ten ... [Subject looks surprised.] (What is it?) That she is one year older than May. May's nine. (What age would Jean be then? Would Jean still be the same age?) No. (What age will she be?) [Pause.] Six. (Why will she be six?) Because May is three years older than her.'

The possible significance of solution (c) has already been discussed (see page 99). There it was suggested that '... the fundamental error on both occasions [i.e. in full overlap error and in solution (c)] is the same, and consists in failure to return to the link term of the series[1] when the second calculation of interval has to be made'.

In other words, solution (c) was used as evidence only to show

---

[1] We must now add: 'at its original value, or failure to return to the link at all', in view of the evidence on the methods by which children arrive at overlap error.

that failure to return to the link is 'the fundamental error'. It was not used as evidence *against* inclusion as an overlap difficulty. This is satisfactory so long as we consider (as we did in the main text) that the inclusion which occurs in solution (c) is accidental. There is, however, another possibility – that the inclusion in solution (c) was conceived by the child as such.[1] If this were the case, then solution (c) would be evidence (of a clinical sort) against the original hypothesis that inclusion is one of the difficulties involved in overlap error.

Solution (d), however, to some extent suggests the opposite interpretation: that the difficulty did not lie in the returning to the link which formally this solution demands, but in inclusion, which is formally absent from this solution. At the level of the children's thinking, however, we cannot be sure that they were in fact returning to the link. In Ann's protocol (quoted above), for example, she rather treated the relationships as a non-overlapping three-term series: May-Betty: Betty-Jean. In none of these protocols is there clear evidence of a return to the link. And the evidence on inclusion is here only the evidence of omission as against the more positive evidence provided by solution (c) on this point.[2]

It could, however, be the case that both return to the link and inclusion are experienced by the children as difficulties and that in solution (c) the one is omitted and in solution (d) the other. The fact that solution (b) requires neither would thus account for its greater frequency.

What we have, then, is a hypothesis that the overlap difficulty consists in failure to deal adequately with either or both of these formal requirements: inclusion, and the need to return to the link.

[1] We cannot, of course, be sure of this from the information given in the protocols alone. By using as a problem a form similar to solution (c), however, we can test to see whether in fact this is happening (see page 246).

[2] Whatever the significance of solution (d) is, however, it is of great interest to note that, of the five children who made this error, four slipped into classical overlap error as soon as the asymmetry error was corrected. This strongly suggests that the error of single asymmetry was (like solution (c) and like classical overlap error) forced upon the child by an inability to deal with the overlap situation. We are therefore almost certainly correct in classifying it as a form of overlap error.

The alternative solutions to the overlap problem spontaneously produced by children in the 'thinking-aloud' situation (see *Figures 3* and *4*) suggest problem-forms which might be used to check the relative importance of these formal requirements for the solution of the overlap problem. We might, for example, in a group test, present children with a form similar to that in *Figure 3* (inclusion only) together with a form similar to that in *Figure 4* (return to the link only) and compare the results in these two forms with performance in the classical overlap problem (see *Figure 1*).

The evidence from the present investigation confirms the findings on asymmetry error reported in the main text. In many cases the error seemed particularly persistent, confirming that it is structural. It was also observed that asymmetry error seems to be much more frequent in problems using the 'older than' relationship than in those using the 'younger than' relationship.[1] It seems that, for some children at least, 'older than' acts as a signal to add, irrespective of the requirements of the problem, and 'younger than' as a signal to subtract. In these problems, as they stand, this leads to asymmetry error in the former case but not in the latter: had the problems been phrased differently the reverse might have been the case.[2]

Our attention was first drawn to this phenomenon by Graham's protocol:

---

[1] In fact, only one clear example of asymmetry error in a 'younger than' problem occurred and that was by no means persistent. Two other cases occurred but in these it seemed that the asymmetry error was a means of avoiding the overlap situation. Thirty cases occurred in' older than' type problems. (Again it must be emphasized that these figures illustrate a *trend* only, since not all problems were given to all subjects.)

[2] For example: 'Dick is ten. Dick is three years older than Jim. How old is Jim?' leads the child to add and he obtains thirteen for his answer. Had the problem been phrased: 'Jim is seven. Dick is three years older than Jim. How old is Dick?', we assume on the basis of this hypothesis that no asymmetry error would occur. (Since this version of the problem was never in fact used, we have no *evidence* for this.) In the same way: 'Dick is ten. Jim is three years younger than Dick. How old is Jim?' seldom led to asymmetry error since automatic subtraction led to the correct answer. Presumably, if we had phrased the question thus: 'Jim is seven. Jim is three years younger than Dick. How old is Dick?', asymmetry error would have occurred.

We want to find out the ages of Ian and David. We know that Peter is 8, and that he is three years older than Ian and one year older than David. How old are Ian and David?

'Ian is eleven and David is twelve. (Good. Yes. How did you get that? Tell me how you worked it out.) I just added on three and that made Ian eleven, and then I added on one and that made David twelve. (How did you know to add on three?) It says Ian is ... We know that Peter is 8 and that Ian is three years older than Ian (sic) and I added on the three and that made Ian eleven. [This explanation of asymmetry occurred fairly frequently. What the child seems to be saying is this: "It can't be Peter who is three years older than Ian, since Peter is eight and Ian is eleven (i.e. the child's answer), so the *he* must refer to Ian." The child is thinking in terms of "Ian is three years older than Peter" but reads *he* is three years older than *Ian*, and so says "Ian is three years older than Ian". This may be a *post hoc* attempt to justify his answer rather than the reasoning which originally led to the answer, but it shows how far a child will go in order to preserve his asymmetry interpretation.] (Good, and how did you know that David was twelve?) I added on ... I added on another one. (How did you know to add on another one?) David is one year older than Ian, so I added on the one. (Than Ian, I see.) [i.e. a conventional overlap error combined with asymmetry.] (Now listen to this. We know that Peter is eight and that he is three years older than Ian. Now if Peter is eight and he is three years older than Ian, how old is Ian going to be?) [Pause.] Peter is eleven. [From now on the child seems to be fighting against the temptation to make Ian eleven, his original asymmetry error. He knows that Peter is older than Ian (see below); he must add; therefore Peter is eleven, since it can't be Ian.] (No, Peter is *eight*, isn't he? It says Peter is eight and that he is three years older than Ian, so how old is Ian going to be?) [Pause.] Eight. [Graham still feels that he can't subtract since he's dealing with an 'older than' relationship; Ian is not eleven; Peter is not eleven; therefore Peter is eight *and* Ian is eight.] (Why will he be eight?) [Pause.] (How old is Peter?) Eight. (Eight, and Peter is three years older than Ian, isn't he? So how old will Ian be?) [Pause.] Eleven. [He seems now to have exhausted all the other possibilities, and since he feels that he must not subtract, he returns to the classical asymmetry error.] (How do you know he'll be eleven? [Pause.] If I said that Ian was three years younger than Peter, how old would Ian be?) [Pause.] Five [i.e. 'younger than' has led to subtraction and the correct answer]. Five, good, but it says that Peter is older than Ian so who is the oldest?) Peter. (Peter. Peter is older. Now he's *three* years older than Ian, so how old is Ian?) Five [i.e. when the experimenter built up from an unquantified situation, Graham was able to achieve the correct answer. It should be noted, however, that later in the same protocol Graham returned to asymmetry error once more.]

Again, it should be fairly easy to test this hypothesis; but it would seem that, initially, at least, this and any other specific study of asymmetry error should be carried out with two-term, rather than with three-term, series.

Although the present investigation did not suggest any modifications to the other analytical categories used in the main body of the book, it confirmed in all cases the findings reported there.

## SUMMARY

In this appendix we have attempted to trace the development, from a clinical to an experimental level, of an investigation into the thinking processes of children who were attempting overlap forms of the three-term series type of problem. The findings so far suggest strongly that the difficulties experienced by the children are in most cases structural rather than executive in nature.

At the clinical level, the fully quantified version of the problem was taken through a series of modifications in an attempt to achieve a simple statement of the essential logical relationships and to avoid the risk that the right solution might be erroneously reached. None of these simplifications eliminated structural error. It now seems, however, that if we are to be fairly sure about the mental processes involved, we must use a partially quantified and a fully quantified version of the overlap problem together.

During the clinical study it was discovered that the overlap error could occur in two different ways – by subtraction from the first dependent term, and by subtraction from the link, this having been given a different value. These differences seem to depend, to some extent, on the form of the problem.

Additional evidence was also obtained on the nature of asymmetry error.

At the experimental level we outlined two designs which would test our clinically derived hypotheses concerning the nature of overlap error. The first of these is designed to test the hypothesis that the overlap situation is structurally more difficult than the non-overlap situation. In this investigation overlap and non-overlap problems (both fully and partially quantified) will be given to matched groups of children. If the result of this inquiry should be positive we shall then proceed to the second stage in which we shall test the hypotheses concerning the nature of the structural difficulties. Children who make overlap error will be presented with two further problems. Each of these problems will test one of the mental processes which, from clinical investigation, we think may constitute overlap difficulty – namely, inclusion and return to the link.

We have also carried out a longitudinal study over three successive years to discover the patterns of development of overlap ability in a representative sample of individual children, and the results of this will be available in the near future.

# APPENDIX II

## *Statement of Problems*

### MATCHING PROBLEMS

#### PROBLEM A1

Five boys, Jack, Dick, James, Bob, and Tom, go to five different schools in the same town. The schools are called North School, South School, East School, West School, and Central School.

Jack does not go to North, South, or Central School.
Dick goes to West School.
Bob does not go to North or Central School.
Tom has never been inside Central School.

1. What school does Jack go to?
2. What school does Bob go to?
3. What school does James go to?
4. What school does Tom go to?

#### PROBLEM A2

Here are three boys:

Jack      Dick      Jimmy

And here are three schools:

Red School    White School    Blue School

Each of the three boys goes to one of the three schools.

Dick does not go to Red School.
Jimmy does not go to White School.
Dick does not go to White School.

What school does Jack go to? ————
What school does Dick go to? ————
What school does Jimmy go to?————

### THREE-TERM SERIES PROBLEMS

#### PROBLEM B1

We want to find out the ages of two girls called Jean and May. We know that a third girl, Betty, is 15, and that she is 3 years older than one of the two girls and 5 years older than the other. If we had one more piece of information we could calculate the ages of Jean and May. What is that piece of information?

#### PROBLEM B2

Tom, Dick, and Harry are 3 boys. Dick, who is 5′ 4″ tall, is 6 inches taller than one of the other boys and 2 inches taller than the remaining one. Harry is taller than Tom.
Therefore:

(1) Tom is 5′ 2″ tall.
(2) Harry is 4′ 10″ tall.
(3) Harry is 5′ 0″ tall.
(4) Tom is 4′ 10″ tall.
(5) Harry is 5′ 2″ tall.

#### PROBLEM B3

*Structure I.1*

Tom is taller than Dick.
Dick is taller than John.
Which of these three boys is the tallest?

*Structures of Problem B3*

I. A>B; B>C ⎤    1.    2.
II. A>B; C<B ⎥ Tallest? Shortest?
III. B<A; C<B ⎥
IV. B<A; B>C ⎦

## SERIES EXTRAPOLATION

### PROBLEM C1

..., Q, N, K, ...

### PROBLEM C2

XC, VE, TG, ..., ...

### PROBLEM C3

KL, JK, IJ, ..., ...

## RELATED SERIES PROBLEMS

### PROBLEM D1

If all fast-moving animals were smaller than slower-moving ones, which of the following would be the largest?

(cat/snail/horse/squirrel/elephant)

### PROBLEM D2

If all rough cloth were thicker than smoother cloth, which of the following would be the thickest?

(silk/blanket/sacking/nylon/velvet)

### PROBLEM D3

If all light-coloured foodstuffs were sweeter than darker-coloured ones, which of the following would be the sweetest?

(honey/treacle/jam/brown sugar/milk)

### PROBLEM D4

If all small articles weighed less than larger ones, which of the following would be the heaviest?

(an alarm clock/an iron/a cushion/a teacup/a nail)

## FORMAL DEDUCTIVE REASONING

### PROBLEM E1

If all people who were born in July were lazy, and Bob was lazy, then:
(1) We would know that Bob had been born in July.
(2) Bob's teacher would tell him to try harder.
(3) We would not know that Bob had been born in July.
(4) Bob would not want to tell anyone when his birthday was.
(5) Bob might learn to work harder.

### PROBLEM E2

If all boys with red hair played football well and Tommy did not have red hair, then:
(1) Tommy would not play football well.
(2) Tommy might still play football well.
(3) Tommy would have no hope of playing in the school team.
(4) Tommy would probably play other games.
(5) Tommy would wish his hair was red.

### PROBLEM E3

No animals that can only move slowly can climb trees.
A hedgehog is a prickly animal.
All prickly animals can only move slowly.
Therefore:
(1) All animals that can only move slowly are prickly.
(2) A hedgehog has no need to climb trees because it can curl into a prickly ball.
(3) All animals that can move quickly can climb trees.
(4) A hedgehog can move quite fast sometimes.
(5) No hedgehogs can climb trees.

# REFERENCES

ABORN, M. & RUBENSTEIN, H. (1952). Information theory and immediate recall. *J. exp. Psychol.*, **44**, 260-6.

ADRIAN, E. D. (1954). Science and human nature. *Advanc. Sci.*, **11**, 121-8.

AMERICAN PSYCHOLOGICAL ASSOCIATION, COMMITTEE ON PSYCHOLOGICAL TESTS (1954). Technical recommendations for psychological tests and diagnostic techniques. *Psychol. Bull.*, Suppl., **51**, 201-38.

ANDERSON, C. C. (1958). Function fluctuation. *Brit. J. Psychol.* Monogr. Suppl. No. 30.

BAKER, L. E. (1937). The influence of subliminal stimuli upon verbal behaviour. *J. exp. Psychol.*, **20**, 84-100.

BARTLETT, F. C. (1958). *Thinking: an experimental and social study.* London: George Allen & Unwin.

BINET, A. (1911). Qu'est-ce qu'une émotion? Qu'est-ce qu'un acte intellectuel? *Année psychol.*, **17**, 1-47.

BINET, A. & SIMON, TH. (1905). Méthodes nouvelles pour le diagnostic du niveau intellectuel des anormaux. *Année psychol.*, **11**, 191-244.

BINET, A. & SIMON, TH. (1914). *Mentally defective children.* London: Edward Arnold. (Translated by W. B. Drummond.)

BROADBENT, D. E. (1958). *Perception and communication.* London: Pergamon.

BRUNER, J. S., GOODNOW, J. J. & AUSTIN, G. A. (1956). *A study of thinking.* London: Chapman & Hall.

BURT, C. (1919). The development of reasoning in school children. *J. exp. Ped.*, **5**, 68-77 and 121-7.

CHERRY, C. (1957). *On human communication.* London: Chapman & Hall.

CLARK, C. A. (1959). Developments and applications in the area of construct validity. *Rev. educ. Res.*, **29**, 84-105.

CLARKE, A. D. B., CLARKE, ANN M. & BROWN, R. I. (1959). Regression to the mean: a confused concept. *Brit. J. Psychol.*, **51**, 105-17.

COFER, C. N. (1957). Reasoning as an associative process. III: The role of verbal responses in problem solving. *J. gen. Psychol.*, **57**, 55-68.

FERGUSON, G. A. (1954). On learning and human ability. *Canad. J. Psychol.*, **8**, 95-112.

FISKE, D. W. (1961). The matching problem with multiple judges and objects. *Psychol. Bull.*, **58**, 80–6.

GAGNÉ, R. M. & SMITH, E. C. (1962). A study of the effects of verbalization on problem-solving. *J. exp. Psychol.*, **63**, 12–18.

GALTON, F. (1869). *Hereditary genius: an inquiry into its laws and consequences.* London: Macmillan; Collins Fontana, 1962.

GALTON, F. (1890). Remarks on an article by Cattell. *Mind*, **15**, 380–1.

GOLDSTEIN, K. & SCHEERER, M. (1941). Abstract and concrete behaviour: an experimental study with special tests. *Psychol. Monogr.*, **53**, No. 2.

HAFNER, A. J. (1957). The influence of verbalization in problem-solving. *Psychol. Rep.*, **3**, 360.

HALDANE, J. B. S. (1955). A logical basis for genetics? *Brit. J. Phil. Sci.*, **6**, 245–8.

HEBB, D. O. (1949). *The organization of behaviour.* London: Chapman & Hall.

HEIM, A. W. (1954). *The appraisal of intelligence.* London: Methuen.

HENLE, M. (1960). On error in deductive reasoning. *Psychol. Rep.*, **7**, 80.

HENLE, M. & MICHAEL, M. (1956). The influence of attitudes on syllogistic reasoning. *J. soc. Psychol.*, **44**, 115–27.

HUNTER, I. M. L. (1957). The solving of three-term series problems. *Brit. J. Psychol.*, **48**, 286–98.

INHELDER, B. & PIAGET, J. (1958). *The growth of logical thinking from childhood to adolescence.* London: Routledge & Kegan Paul.

JANIS, I. L. & FRICK, F. (1943). The relationship between attitudes towards conclusions and errors in judging logical validity of syllogisms. *J. exp. Psychol.* **33**, 73–7.

LEFFORD, A. (1946). The influence of emotional subject-matter on logical reasoning. *J. gen. Psychol.*, **34**, 127–51.

LOEVINGER, J. (1957). Objective tests as instruments of psychological theory. *Psychol. Rep.*, **3**, 635–94.

LUCHINS, A. S. (1951). The Einstellung-effect as a test of rigidity. *J. cons. Psychol.*, **15**, 89–94.

LURIA, A. R. (1961). *The role of speech in the regulation of normal and abnormal behaviour.* London: Pergamon.

LURIA, A. R. & VINOGRADOVA, O. S. (1959). An objective investigation of the dynamics of semantic systems. *Brit. J. Psychol.*, **50**, 89–105.

MILLER, G. A. (1956). The magical number seven, plus or minus two. *Psychol. Rev.*, **63**, 81–97.

MILLER, G. A., BRUNER, J. S. & POSTMAN, L. (1954). Familiarity of letter sequences and tachistoscopic identification. *J. gen. Psychol.*, **50**, 129–39.

MORF, A. (1957). Les relations entre la logique et le langage lors du passage du raisonnement concret au raisonnement formel. In *Logique, langage et théorie de l'information* by L. Apostel, B. Mandelbrot, and A. Morf. Paris: Presses Universitaires de France.

MORGAN, J. J. B. & MORTON, J. T. (1944). The distortion of syllogistic reasoning produced by personal convictions. *J. soc. Psychol.*, **20**, 39–59.

PEIRCE, C. S. (1931). *Collected papers.* Ed. by C. Hartshorne and P. Weiss. Cambridge, Mass: Harvard University Press.

PIAGET, J. (1921). Une forme verbale de la comparaison chez l'enfant. *Arch. Psychol.*, **18**, 141–72.

PIAGET, J. (1928). *Judgment and reasoning in the child.* London: Kegan Paul.

PIAGET, J. (1950). *The psychology of intelligence.* London: Routledge & Kegan Paul.

PIAGET, J. (1953). *Logic and psychology.* Manchester: Manchester University Press.

POPPER, K. (1957). *The poverty of historicism.* London: Routledge & Kegan Paul.

QUINE, W. van O. (1952). *Methods of logic.* London: Routledge & Kegan Paul.

REY, A. (1956). Mise en correspondance de données perçues sur le plan représentatif. In *Le problème des stades en psychologie de l'enfant* by P. Osterrieth *et al.* Paris: Presses Universitaires de France.

RYLE, G. (1949). *The concept of mind.* London: Hutchinson's University Library.

SHANNON, C. E. & WEAVER, W. (1949). *The mathematical theory of communication.* Urbana: University of Illinois Press.

SPEARMAN, C. (1910). Correlation calculated from faulty data. *Brit. J. Psychol.*, **3**, 271–95.

THOULESS, R. H. (1936). Test unreliability and function fluctuation. *Brit. J. Psychol.*, **26**, 325–43.

WELFORD, A. T. (1958). *Ageing and human skill.* London: Oxford University Press.

# Index

formal deductive reasoning
  formal analysis, 161
  problems E1 to E3, 163 ff.
formal schemata, 195 ff.
Freud, S., 214
functions of mind, 57

Gagné, R. M. & Smith, E. C., 31 n.
Galton, F., 3, 13
general factor, 12
Goldstein, K. & Scheerer, M., 206 ff.
groups, composition of
  Group A, 226
  Group B, 229
  Group O, 37 f.
  Groups S1 and S2, 75
  Group Y, 62 f.
guessing, 47 f., 110

Hafner, A. J., 31 n.
Haldane, J. B. S., 4
Hebb, D. O., 8
Heim, Alice, 16 ff.
Henle, M., 204
  & Michael, M., 162 n.
heredity, and intelligence, 3 ff.
Hunter, I. M. L., 83, 84, 85, 115, 123, 128, 129 n.
hypotheses, 31 ff., 196, 219, 223, 249

implication, 200
index
  of direction of change (IDC), 61, 62, 69, 97 f., 113, 140 f., 146, 156, 158, 170 ff., 178, 180 ff., 215 ff.
  of magnitude of change (IMC), 61, 62, 69, 97 f., 113, 141, 146, 156, 158, 170 ff., 178, 180 ff., 215 ff.
  of magnitude of error (IME), 60 f., 62, 69, 97 f., 113, 141, 146, 156, 158, 170 ff., 178, 180 ff., 215 ff.
information, capacity of nervous system

and error, 45 f., 101, 209 ff.
and recoding, 213
information theory, *see* communication theory
Inhelder, B. & Piaget, J., 194, 200
intelligence
  A and B, 8
  development of, 3 ff.
  distinguished from attainment, 3, 5 ff.
  generality of, 10 ff.
  innate and developed, 8
  prophetic view of, 3
  quotients, change with age in cultural subgroups, 19 f.
intelligence tests
  construction of, 11 ff.
  history of, 13 ff.
  justification of item choice in, 11 ff., 111
internal consistency, validation by, 12
interpolation, substituted for extrapolation, *see* error
introspection, 24
intuition, and item choice, 12
irrelevance, *see* error

Janis, I. L. & Frick, F., 162 n.
judgements of membership, *see* error

Lefford, A., 162 n.
link term
  attempt to calculate value of, *see* error
  repetition of, 231
  return to, 99, 105 f., 231, 233 f., 241 ff.
Loevinger, J., 11 n.
loss of hold, *see* error
loyalty to the given, 66 ff., 82, 183, 202
  *see also* rigour, deductive